World-Systems Evolution and Global Futures

Series Editors

Christopher Chase-Dunn, University of California, Riverside, CA, USA

Barry K. Gills, Political and Economic Studies, University of Helsinki, Helsinki, Finland

Leonid E. Grinin, National Research University Higher School of Economics, Moscow, Russia

Andrey V. Korotayev, National Research University Higher School of Economics, Moscow, Russia

This series seeks to promote understanding of large-scale and long-term processes of social change, in particular the many facets and implications of globalization. It critically explores the factors that affect the historical formation and current evolution of social systems, on both the regional and global level. Processes and factors that are examined include economies, technologies, geopolitics, institutions, conflicts, demographic trends, climate change, global culture, social movements, global inequalities, etc. Building on world-systems analysis, the series addresses topics such as globalization from historical and comparative perspectives, trends in global inequalities, core-periphery relations and the rise and fall of hegemonic core states, transnational institutions, and the long-term energy transition. This ambitious interdisciplinary and international series presents cutting-edge research by social scientists who study whole human systems and is relevant for all readers interested in systems approaches to the emerging world society, especially historians, political scientists, economists, sociologists, geographers and anthropologists.

This book series is indexed in Scopus.

All titles in this series are peer-reviewed.

Nestor Rodriguez

Capitalism and Migration

The Rise of Hegemony in the World-System

Nestor Rodriguez [iD]
The University of Texas at Austin
Austin, TX, USA

ISSN 2522-0985   ISSN 2522-0993   (electronic)
World-Systems Evolution and Global Futures
ISBN 978-3-031-22066-1   ISBN 978-3-031-22067-8   (eBook)
https://doi.org/10.1007/978-3-031-22067-8

© The Editor(s) (if applicable) and The Author(s), under exclusive license to Springer Nature Switzerland AG 2023

This work is subject to copyright. All rights are solely and exclusively licensed by the Publisher, whether the whole or part of the material is concerned, specifically the rights of translation, reprinting, reuse of illustrations, recitation, broadcasting, reproduction on microfilms or in any other physical way, and transmission or information storage and retrieval, electronic adaptation, computer software, or by similar or dissimilar methodology now known or hereafter developed.

The use of general descriptive names, registered names, trademarks, service marks, etc. in this publication does not imply, even in the absence of a specific statement, that such names are exempt from the relevant protective laws and regulations and therefore free for general use.

The publisher, the authors, and the editors are safe to assume that the advice and information in this book are believed to be true and accurate at the date of publication. Neither the publisher nor the authors or the editors give a warranty, expressed or implied, with respect to the material contained herein or for any errors or omissions that may have been made. The publisher remains neutral with regard to jurisdictional claims in published maps and institutional affiliations.

This Springer imprint is published by the registered company Springer Nature Switzerland AG
The registered company address is: Gewerbestrasse 11, 6330 Cham, Switzerland

In memory of,
Lucinda Rodriguez
Susanne Jonas

Preface

This book began as my doctoral dissertation at The University of Texas at Austin. It was a time in the late 1970s and early 1980s when political economy (Marxist political economy) was still popular among many graduate students in the social sciences as they tried to understand inequality in society and among societies as a consequence of capitalist exploitation. It seemed to me that focusing on class structure was a good place to begin a sociological understanding of migration, a process that my mind increasingly conceptualized as a major social force. For this understanding, I would have to study the structure of capitalism and the role that migration played in its development.

My introduction to the concept of capitalist exploitation came not from graduate school but from growing up in a working-class family with parents who were first-generation urban dwellers after migrating from peasant lives in sharecropping farms in the dispossessed agricultural region of southern Texas. The United States took over the region from Mexico after a war that ended in 1848. And the Mexican American migration to the cities was a consequence of the takeover a hundred years later when a new generation of Mexican American young people born in rural poverty chose to look for a better life in urban labor markets. The political nature of the transition was not lost on my father who with only a first-grade education explained to me as a boy how the accumulation of wealth was based on the exploitation of the dispossessed and powerless.

Two readings especially affect my attraction to world-systems theory as an analytical framework and as a method. One reading was 'Hegel' *The Phenomenology of Spirit* where he states, "The truth is the whole." I found that Immanuel Wallerstein's theory of the capitalist world-system met Hegel's dictum for understanding the development of capitalism. World-systems theory is a holistic theory for the reasons that it covers all of capitalism historically, spatially, and in terms of the interconnections of core, peripheral, and semiperipheral regions of the world-economy. But for a dissertation project, the use of a world-systems perspective to understand the role of migration in capitalist development had to be made manageable, as one could not study migration for all of capitalist development in a single project.

I chose to make my dissertation project manageable by selecting periods of hegemony in world-systems theory as the unit of analysis. Periods of hegemony are historical intervals when a single core country rises as the dominant power in the word-system in terms of economic and political power and control. According to Wallerstein, three periods of hegemony have occurred in the history of the world-system: Dutch hegemony in 1625–75, British hegemony in 1815–1873, and US hegemony in 1945–1970. The three hegemonic countries expanded or strengthened capitalism in the world in their eras, affecting development (and the development of underdevelopment) in regions such as Africa, Asia, and Latin America, often through colonialism. My work in the dissertation research was to analyze the role that migration patterns of capital and labor played in this development in the three periods of hegemony. While I initially focused mainly on labor migration, I later realized that to better understand labor migration it was necessary to also understand capital migration, as the latter often opens the path for the former.

A second reading that influenced my research approach was Emile Durkheim's instructions regarding historical research. According to Wallerstein and the eminent historian Fernand Braudel, capitalism emerged in Europe in the long sixteenth century (1450–1640 CE). I should have been satisfied with this dating, but a reading of Durkheim's *The Elementary Forms of the Religious Life* took me in a different path. According to Durkheim, "[e]verytime we undertake to explain something human … it is necessary to go back to its most primitive and simple form to try to account for the characterization by which it was marked at that time, and then to show how it developed and became complicated little by little, and how it became that which it is at the moment in question." This method motivated me to explore for evidence of capitalism even earlier than the long sixteenth century.

But what to observe for evidence of capitalism? What is the evidence supposed to look like? Capitalism is more than just free trade, which has been on-going since the dawn of hominids when they traded items in the intersections where they met. Capitalism is also more than the accumulation of wealth, which was a routine process of imperial powers that raided and sacked villages, towns, and cities in their paths of pillage even before the Middle Ages. In accordance with Wallerstein and other social scientists, I took the presence of a *ceaseless process* of capital accumulation (e.g., accumulation for the sake of accumulation) to be an indication of capitalism. A second indication I adopted was the presence of class struggle. At its most basic level, capital is based on the relation between capital and labor, and especially in historical eras, this relationship was often tumultuous as emerging capitalist entrepreneurs sought to wrestle control of labor processes from craftworkers and their trade guilds.

My examination of labor history looking for cases of conflict between employers and wage workers finally took me to the setting of Florence, Italy, in the 1300s. Florentine merchant-bankers had set out as tax collectors for popes in the 1200s in Catholic Europe and in the process gained dominance of the region's wool trade, since often taxes were paid by bishops in wool. Through their roles as tax collectors, the Florentine merchant-bankers developed widespread networks and circuits of capital accumulation through trade and financial loans to royalty in Catholic Europe and surrounding regions of the Mediterranean.

The Florentine dominance of the wool trade brought so much wool to Florence that Florentine merchant-bankers worked to increase production in Florence by restructuring woolen production from the putting-out system of artisan production to a capitalist system of social production under employer supervision. The restructuring in the late 1200s and early 1300s involved a class struggle in which the merchant-bankers organized into a guild to acquire political power in Florence to throw woolen artisans out of their guilds and subjugate them to the will of the emerging capitalist entrepreneurial class. The Catholic hierarchy, which often received financial loans from merchant-bankers, supported the rise of the capitalist entrepreneurs and their struggle to dominate and control the labor force in woolen production in Florence.

This historical finding of capitalism in the wool and woolen industries in Europe in the thirteenth and fourteenth centuries contrasts with the proposition that capitalism emerged two to four hundred years later in the long sixteenth century. And the central roles that Catholic merchant-bankers and the Catholic Church played in this emergence certainly is a major counter-fact to Max Weber's prominent theory of the special connection between Protestantism and the spirit of capitalism.

The analyses for the periods of Dutch, British, and US hegemony supported my view of the important role migration has had for capitalist development in core countries and in peripheral and semiperipheral areas of the word-system. Simply put, capitalism cannot exist as we know it today without migration in societies and between societies. Yet not all migration related to capitalist development and expansion has served the needs of capital. In colonial eras of the world-system, migration included the movement of native peoples away from centers of European colonization, and in the present era, migration includes return migrants who leave centers of intense capitalist production in large cities in core countries for more traditional forms of life back home.

Much has been said of China as a rising superpower in the world-economy. In the conclusion of the book, I take up the question of whether China will become the next hegemon. I give this possibility a low rating. The pattern that emerged in the Dutch, British, and US periods of hegemony was that hegemony involves a merging of economic and political/military power to implement policies of expansion and control in world regions. While China certainly has become a world economic power with the second strongest economy in the world, it has not demonstrated major militarily ambitions across world regions, as the Dutch, British, and United States did in their periods of hegemony. It is likely that hegemony in the world-system by a single country is no longer possible in today's much more complicated world.

A part of the book was written during the last years of the Trump presidency. It was a time in which the US government produced social constructions of undocumented and asylum-seeking migrants arriving in the country as dangerous people. And the government took harsh measures to restrict the migration. The measures included an immigration ban for certain countries, the construction of a border wall, the separation of small children from their migrant parents at the border, and the continuation of deporting hundreds of thousands of immigrants from the country. These policies taken against migrants increased my dedication to the book project. Mindful of Stephen Hawking's statement that the greatest enemy of knowledge is not ignorance but the illusion of knowledge, I wanted to contribute to the research literature that shows how migration from the periphery and semiperiphery of the world-system to core countries is due in considerable measure to the workings of a world social system that core powers played a big role in producing.

I gratefully acknowledge the dissertation committee that oversaw my doctoral research. The committee members were Professors Joe R. Feagin, Gilbert Cardenas, Walter Firey, José E. Limón, and Gideon Sjoberg. Feagin played a special role with his confidence that I could successfully undertake an historical-theoretical project that would span hundreds of years of capitalist development. His power-conflict theories inspired many graduate students to investigate sources of inequality and oppression. I also owe gratitude to Juanita Rodriguez-Marroquin for typing drafts of the 499-page dissertation on a typewriter, to Charles Mundell for sharing historical insights in the early part of my research, to my students for helping check the book's bibliography several times, and to Anne Chandler for being a constant companion, patiently listening to my finding of historical capitalism and migration in the drafting of the book manuscript. Finally, I owe gratitude to the reviewers of the book manuscript for making insightful, key suggestions and recommendations to improve its presentation.

Austin, USA   Nestor Rodriguez

Contents

1. **Migration and Hegemony in the World-System** 1
   1.1 Medieval Migrations 7
   1.2 Development of the Capitalist World-Economy 10
   1.3 Capital and Labor Migration and Capitalist Expansion 13
   1.4 Hegemony and Migration 19
   1.5 Analytical Perspectives 24
   References 28

2. **Capital Migration and Florentine Dominance in the European Medieval Wool Industry** 33
   2.1 Business Migration, Papal Revenue Collection, and Capital Accumulation 35
   2.2 Three Major European Areas of Woolen Production 39
   2.3 Capitalist Production and Class Structure in the Woolen Industry 41
      2.3.1 Emergence of Merchant-Capitalists 42
      2.3.2 Expropriation of Artisan Production 44
      2.3.3 Development of Propertyless Wage Workforces 47
      2.3.4 Women in Woolen Work 51
   2.4 Fleeing Harsh Economic Conditions 52
   2.5 Migration and the Development of Medieval Capitalist Production 54
   2.6 Conclusion 58
   References 59

3. **Migration and Dutch Capitalist Development** 63
   3.1 Dutch Hegemony 64
      3.1.1 Industrial Development 64
      3.1.2 Commercial Expansion 66
   3.2 Migration in the Northern Netherlands 68
      3.2.1 Capital Migration in the Northern Netherlands 68
      3.2.2 Labor Migration in the Northern Netherlands 70

xi

	3.3	Migration in the Periphery	76
		3.3.1 East Indies	77
		3.3.2 Atlantic Peripheral Zone	77
		3.3.3 Colonizing Northeastern Brazil	78
		3.3.4 Settlement in New Netherlands	81
		3.3.5 Migration to the Caribbean	81
	3.4	Indigenous Migration in the Periphery	84
	3.5	Class Struggle	86
	3.6	Technological Development	91
	3.7	The Economic Cycle	95
	3.8	The State	98
	3.9	Conclusion—Interrelation of Migration	99
	References		100
4	**British Hegemony and Migration**		**105**
	4.1	British Hegemony, 1815–1873	107
		4.1.1 "Workshop of the World"	108
	4.2	Capital Migration	110
	4.3	Labor Migration and Industrial Development	114
		4.3.1 British Labor Migration	115
		4.3.2 Irish Migration to Britain	122
		4.3.3 Indentured-Labor Migration	125
	4.4	Class Struggle and Migration	126
	4.5	Technological Development	128
	4.6	Economic Cycles	131
	4.7	The State	134
	4.8	Conclusion	136
	References		137
5	**Monopoly Capital, US Hegemony, and Migration**		**141**
	5.1	Nineteenth-Century Prelude	143
	5.2	Monopoly Development and US Hegemony	145
		5.2.1 Restructuring in the United States	147
	5.3	Circulation of US Capital to the Periphery	148
	5.4	US Capital Expansion into Mexican Agriculture	149
	5.5	Labor Migration and US Hegemony	151
		5.5.1 Internal Migration	152
		5.5.2 Racial Minority Migration	155
		5.5.3 Mexican Bracero and Immigrant Labor	159
		5.5.4 Jamaican Temporary Workers	165
	5.6	Analysis	166
	5.7	Class Relations	166
	5.8	Technological Development	170
	5.9	The Economic Cycle	172

	5.10	The State	174
	5.11	Conclusion	177
	References		179
6	**Migration and Hegemonic Development**		**187**
	6.1	Discussion of Findings	190
		6.1.1 Class Relations	190
		6.1.2 Technological Development	191
		6.1.3 The Economic Cycle	192
		6.1.4 The State	195
	6.2	Labor Migration and Work Segmentation	197
	6.3	After US Hegemony	200
	6.4	Future Migration in the World-System	204
	References		206

Migration and Hegemony in the World-System

Migration has characterized human populations since the beginning of humankind. It has been the source of human spread across the globe since almost two million years ago when *Homo erectus,* considered the first human species to have migrated out of Africa, reached the region that today is eastern China (Qiu 2016). Through millennia, human migration led to the development of cultures, religions, trade, and empires across the earth. In the last eight hundred years, human migration has again brought about another global spread, the spread of a world-system to pursue economic gain, or more precisely to pursue capital accumulation. This world-system—capitalism—operates with the social forces of fluidity, incessant change, and migration at its core.

The thesis of this book is that the migration of capital and labor has been a critical resource for the development of capitalism as a world-system across different historical eras. I use the framework of periods of hegemony in world-systems theory to analyze the association between migration and capitalist development. Periods of hegemony were historical eras when a single country rose to political and economic dominance in the capitalist world-economy.[1] During these eras, hegemonic countries experienced heightened economic development internally and in peripheral world regions under their control or influence. The migration of capital and labor, including forced labor migration, was often integral for hegemonic development.

World-systems theory recognizes three periods of hegemony in the development of the modern world-system: Dutch hegemony during 1625–1675, British hegemony during 1815–1873, and US hegemony during 1945–1970 (Wallerstein 1979a). These periods of hegemony were situated in and helped define different historical eras of capitalism. Dutch hegemony occurred during the era of mercantile capitalism in Europe, which lasted from the sixteenth to the eighteenth century.

---

[1] The terms "world-system" and "world-economy" are used interchangeably in the book.

© The Author(s), under exclusive license to Springer Nature Switzerland AG 2023
N. Rodriguez, *Capitalism and Migration*, World-Systems Evolution and Global Futures,
https://doi.org/10.1007/978-3-031-22067-8_1

In mercantilism, state policies promoted economic nationalism and placed major concern on trade and trade balances (Wallerstein 1980). Much of the work in mercantilism to support trade concerned extracting goods produced by nature such as mining, fishing, and agriculture. Migration in core states of the world-system during European mercantilism included movements of workers within and between rural and urban areas. The migration also included groups of hundreds and at times thousands of people who left Europe to settle in peripheral world areas undergoing colonization by their home countries. The more than 10.5 million African people abducted and forcibly transferred in the Atlantic slave trade from the sixteenth to the eighteenth century constituted one of the largest labor transfers affected by European mercantilism (Curtin 1969).

British hegemony occurred in the era of industrial capitalism in which state policies favored industrialization and global expansion, including colonialism, to reach new markets of raw materials and consumers of factory products. Work in the age of industrialism was increasingly concentrated in large manufacturing and construction industries, while other works remained in extractive and service industries. Rural to urban migration became a source of labor power for industrializing cities in core states of the world-system. This included the migration of peasants to manufacturing cities in Britain, Germany, and other core states in Europe (Moch 2003). It is in the age of industrial capitalism that the migration out of Europe reached sustained levels of millions of migrants (Hobsbawn 1979). The migrants included peasants displaced by commercial farming and artisans displaced by the factory system (Moch 2003). These migrants were joined by other Europeans seeking to establish new livelihoods, such as in farming and ranching, in the United States, Latin America, and in other world regions (Hansen 1961). In the periphery and semiperhiphery of the world-system, migrations continued traditional patterns, but also shifted in reaction to policies of colonial and other foreign powers. Agriculture, mining, railroad construction, etc., in the periphery and semiperiphery required mobile labor forces to accomplish economic projects designed by capitalist interests in European core states.

US hegemony occurred in the present era of monopoly capitalism where state policies support the concentration and centralization of monopoly capital in the form of large corporations, many of which enjoy a global reach (Barnet and Miller 1974). Service jobs dominate the labor market of monopoly capitalism. Manufacturing industries brought a growing number of jobs after the Great Depression, but the industries entered a long-term decline four decades later as many factory jobs were relocated to low-wage, peripheral, and semiperipheral countries (Harris 2020). Inter- and intra-urban migration characterized the movements of capital and labor in core states as monopoly capitalism reshaped the built environments of business administration and industrial work in the central cities and suburbs of metropolitan areas. Abroad, in less-developed regions of the world-system, peasant populations relocated to look for work in large cities, and in an increasing number of cases since the late twentieth century, the migration of displaced and marginalized rural and urban working populations was directed toward the job markets (and sanctuaries) of core states.

Arrighi (2010) adds an earlier dominant economic power to historical capitalism, i.e., the Italian city-state of Genoa, which gained capitalist dominance in interregional trade and finance in areas of southern Europe, the Mediterranean, and the Levant in the fifteenth and sixteenth centuries. In this book, I add to Arrighi's focus on medieval Italian capitalist dominance by presenting the case of Florence, from where business investors rose to gain considerable control of the wool trade and finance in some regions of western Europe in the thirteenth and fourteenth centuries. This control depended heavily on the migration of Florentine merchant-bankers across European regions.

In the four analytical chapters that follow, I trace the association between capital and labor migration and capitalist development in the city-state of Florence and in the three hegemonic countries of the United Provinces, Britain, and the United States. I also analyze migration linkages between these states and peripheral regions under their control or influence during the countries' rise to hegemony. The intention is not to present all migration patterns that materialized in the dominant country and between the country and peripheral area, since such a presentation would require an encyclopedic series. Rather, the plan of the book is to focus on two levels of migration patterns associated with hegemony, i.e., patterns that occurred within the dominant country and were central to its hegemonic rise, as well as patterns that illustrated relations that evolved between the dominant country and peripheral regions. In the world-system perspective, it is the holism of multi-level interrelationships that has the greatest power of analysis.

Let me immediately set forth the definition of capitalism I use in this book. By capitalism, I am not referring to free trade in open markets, what is sometimes referred to as the free-market system. People freely traded items for thousands of years before the development of capitalism.[2] What I mean by capitalism is a social system characterized by a ceaseless drive to accumulated capital from profits for the sake of accumulation (Cleaver 1979). In the phase of industrial capitalism, relations among economic classes, especially the relations between those who own or control the means of production and those who work for the owners and managers, whether for wages or under conditions of forced work, characterize the system of capitalism. Capital accumulation is the driving force of capitalist work and capitalism in general, and capitalist actors become involved with political and other non-economic matters to gain advantages for their economic pursuits.

The capitalist class is heterogeneous with different capitalist groups striving to derive capital accumulation in different regions and industries. New investment groups often propel the spatial expansion or depth of the capitalist world-economy and usually do so in arrangements with political structures (Arrighi 2010). Especially in the early eras of the capitalist world-economy, capitalism constituted the top layer of a three-layer structure in which market economies constituted the

---

[2] Archeological research has found merchants used standardized weights from Europe to Mesopotamia 3000 years ago, indicating the first known common Eurasian market in the ancient era (Curry 2021).

middle layer of production and exchange in local or regional populations and conditions of mainly self-sufficiency characterized the very broad bottom layer (Braudel 1981). In contrast to market economies, which evolved naturally from the tendencies of local and regional production and exchange, capitalism developed from deliberate political-economic strategies implemented in the pursuit of capital accumulation. For Braudel (1982: 230), the layer of capitalism represented "the zone of the anti-market, where the great predators roam and the law of the jungle operates."

In the history of the modern world-economy, capital migration has often brought about labor migration as free or coerced movements of labor. Arrangements between capital and labor have varied considerably across the history of the world-system. But labor power always integrates with capital through the commodity form as one commodity among others (Cleaver 1979). Yet, it is a different commodity from other commodities (e.g., raw materials and machinery) used in production because it has the critical role of producing the goods and services through which capital derives profit.[3] Without labor, there is no production and no capitalism; just as without consumers, there are no sales and no markets.[4]

Labor migration patterns do not have to cross international borders to affect the expansion of the capitalist world-system. While some labor migration patterns are obviously global as workers migrate from one world region to another, other migration patterns have a national grounding and yet contribute to economic production that reverberates throughout the worldwide framework of capitalism.[5] The most obvious case of this latter development today is occurring in China, where more than 200 million rural people have migrated to Chinese cities and many to work in factories that produce or assemble clothing and electronic devices exported worldwide (China Labour Bulletin 2020). According to Sassen (2006), it is an endogeneity trap to attempt to portray the development of global institutions and globalization as new conditions independent and separate from the national realm. In the view of Sassen (2006), new global formations have linkages with, and are affected by, past national conditions. Moreover, international migration is a more recent process given that nation-state borders are relatively new in world history.

It is important to note the capitalist significance of the world-economy that emerged centuries ago, and within which specific states gained regional or worldwide dominance. At a minimum, three socioeconomic conditions characterize the capitalist world-economy: (1) a division of labor with different modes of labor

---

[3] To be sure, labor as human activity is not an inanimate commodity similar to other commodities. According to Polanyi (2001), labor is a "fictitious" commodity with the potential to resist the economic dislocations of the market in capitalist economies. Marx's *Capital* (1967) remains a classic study of worker resistance in capitalist production.
[4] Even "lights-out" manufacturing still requires a minimal human presence for inspection, maintenance, and repair (Brann et al. 1996).
[5] Not all migrant workers set out from the home country with labor intentions. Many migrant men, women, and children end up as a labor supply abroad after fleeing from dangerous and life-threatening conditions in their communities of origin (e.g., see Jonas and Rodriguez 2014).

control, regulated by owners and managers, (2) circuits of capital accumulation based on trade with world markets, whose operations transcend national or regional boundaries, and (3) the development of class structures of owners/managers and workers whose relational dynamics affect relations in the larger society (Wallerstein 1974). Moreover, regional differentiation of economic development and prosperity distinguishes three zones in the capitalist world-system, that is, the core, periphery, and semiperiphery (Wallerstein 1974). Core states have the most developed economies and the greatest prosperity, and peripheral areas have the least developed and prosperous economies in the world-system, with semiperipheral areas falling in-between with functions that are more useful politically than economically in dealing with the large economic gaps between core and peripheral states (Wallerstein 1979a).

This regional characterization held true for most of the existence of the modern world-economy, but by the late twentieth century, and certainly by the early twenty-first century, the movements of capital and labor had produced significant variations in this global tri-designation. Some urban areas in peripheral countries have developed advanced technological centers with considerable prosperity, so much so that business districts and wealthy neighborhoods in these areas, such as in Asia, Latin America, and the Middle East, resemble business and elite districts in core cities, such as New York, Tokyo, or Berlin. At the same time, some urban and rural districts inhabited by racial minorities and poor whites in core countries have become zones of "advanced marginality" characterized by large-scale joblessness, poverty, and crime and resemble poor urban areas in peripheral countries (Wacquant 2008).[6]

Other world-systems existed before the capitalist world-economy in the form of world empires or established economic systems of commerce across large geographical domains ("world economies," as described by Abu-Lughod 1989), but, according to Wallerstein (1974), they lacked a capitalistic purpose, or failed to maintain one, to expand production and trade in order to enlarge the circulation and accumulation of capital. Understanding the capitalistic significance of the capitalist world-system is important because the very nature of capitalist production affects the dynamics of labor migration. At the surface, it may appear that it is simply the presence of work that attracts workers to migrate, but, as we shall see in the analysis of the book, more importantly it is the particular labor demanded by capitalist enterprises that stimulate the labor flow.

Furthermore, while labor migration conjures images of individual men and women workers migrating to job markets, in many cases labor migration also involves the movement of families and communities, if not all at once, then through

---

[6] Wacquant (2008) uses cases studies in the South Side of Chicago and an immigrant district in the area of Paris to illustrate his concept of advanced marginality. He analyzes advanced marginality as resulting from policies (or the lack of policies) by state decision-makers to create spatial containers as forms of ethnoracial enclosures and control in the post-Fordist era where Black people and other poor populations are being institutionally disengaged and reassigned to reserved labor status or permanent exclusion.

step migration.[7] Family units, including same-sex unions, enable the essential production and social reproduction of migrant labor. For individual workers, this involves having nourishment, rest, and other resources to renew their capacity to work, and for the working class, as a whole it requires the reproduction of new generations of workers and cultural institutions that sustain the working population. Individual migrants and other sojourners can sustain themselves away from their families for long periods of time, but ultimately re-connection to the family, or the formation of new families abroad, is the optimal condition for the fulfillment of social reproduction. Family units provide social and psychological nourishment and the means to biosocially reproduce new generations of workers (Burawoy 1976).

Social reproduction also has a subjective component for many migrant workers. Especially in long-term migration, labor migrants can create a demand for cultural products and activities they enjoyed back home, such as traditional foods and festivals. This in turn can motivate migrants with entrepreneurial ambitions to establish ethnic businesses (restaurants, music shops, etc.) to meet the demand. Over time, some immigrant settlements develop into ethnic enclaves providing familiar cultural resources to the immigrants, as well as places of employment for some of the immigrant residents (Portes and Manning 1986; Bankston III 2014; see also Waldinger 1993).

In the next section, I briefly describe the restriction of migration among peasant populations in the Middle Ages and the transition from the manorial system of labor servitude to tenant farming by free peasants. This is the prelude to capitalist agriculture and the beginning of the European world-system. The latter part of the medieval era saw a rise of migratory labor in areas where the manorial agricultural system lessened control of obligatory serf labor. Undoubtedly, the conversion of some manorial lands to tenant farming and the opening of new lands for production with wage labor increased opportunities for migrant labor (Slicher Van Bath 1963). However, this should not be considered to have been a drastic change, since there were major fluctuations in population sizes of free and unfree peasant workers due to calamities such as famine, epidemics, and conflicts (Wrigley 1969; Postan 1972). Labor mobility to new farmlands or to find wage work could increase relative to earlier times when smaller proportions of workers migrated, but the absolute number of migrants could be smaller than in previous times when populations were larger, such as in pre-epidemic years.

---

[7] There is no hard-and-fast rule for when the family joins the migration or not. The New Economics of Labor Migration Theory (Stark and Bloom 1985) postulates that the rationality of sending the income earners abroad and keeping non-workers at home where consumption costs are lower drives the dynamics of family migration, but plenty of exceptions and intervening conditions exist for this to be an iron law of family migration (e.g., see Hagan 1994; Jonas and Rodriguez 2014).

1.1 Medieval Migrations

In the Middle Ages, the social relations of feudalism (c. fifth-twelfth centuries) restricted migration among the peasantry (serfs and other workers), who composed the labor forces of the manorial system and were the largest populations in the European societies.[8] Feudalistic laws maintained obligatory, and in some cases hereditary, attachment in the service of the lord of the manor, and thus, manorial workers were not free to move at will (Heer 1962; Postan 1972; Hohenberg and Lees 1985). European estates varied considerably, however, in the degree and manner of bondage because of ancient and local customs.[9] According to Hohenberg and Lees (1985), having the freedom to migrate was not always a positive sign, since migrants were often persons who had lost their domiciles and were searching for a means of survival, or were fleeing deadly conflict or persecution (see also Clark 1979). Yet, some occupations required freedom of movement and had the protection of royal edicts to secure movement across lands. These occupations included journeymen who followed construction projects, soldiers, clerics, peddlers, traveling merchants, etc. More wanderers than migrants, since they rarely ceased their movement long enough to establish a new residence, traveling merchants were especially valued and protected by royalties on their lands because the merchants increased trade and revenues from market-tolls (Pirenne 1925). Rulers of kingdoms sometimes decreed the punishment of death for highway robbers to protect traveling merchants and other travelers (Diamond 2004), and the Catholic Church administered the punishment of excommunication for highway crimes as well. Traveling merchants also secured their movements by traveling in caravans (Pirenne 1925).

Feudal serfs were obligated to remain on manorial lands, but some ran away to towns to look for better work opportunities and attempt to survive without being captured and returned to the manors from which they fled. Towns and cities were a main attraction of people traveling freely or clandestinely. As Pirenne (1925) describes, by the beginning of the eleventh century there was a clear movement into cities and towns from surrounding rural land. The migrants to urban centers included workers with professions such as "bakers, brewers, butchers, smiths, and

---

[8] As explained by Ganshof (1961: xv–xvi), "feudalism" has been given many different meanings. One broad meaning includes personal dependence on a higher ruling authority, a high-status military class, subdivision of rights of property and rights over land (fief), and distribution of political authority in a hierarchy of persons with power usually associated with a state. This characterization covered western Europe in the tenth-twelfth centuries. A narrower and legal definition included institutions concerned with regulating the obedience and service (including military service) of free men (vassals) to other free men (lords) and the obligations of the lords to the vassals, which usually included the granting of heritable land (fief). The two definitions are related, since the fief was a key element in the granting of graded rights.

[9] Manors consisted of lands (demesnes) cultivated by the lord of the manor and lands (tenant farms) cultivated by tenant peasants. The amount and method of rent payment, and of the required labor service on the demesne, varied and in some cases was connected partly to tribal customs of the populations who settled the lands after migrating from other regions of Europe.

so on," that moved from nearby lands or other towns (Pirenne 1925:109). As urban commerce increased, poor workers who lived near starvation arrived in the towns to attempt to survive on the very low wages paid by merchants. When diseases or food shortages occurred in the urban centers due to harvest failures in the surrounding countryside, the impoverished migrants were often the first casualties given their weakened condition (Hohenberg and Lees 1985).

Poor migrants were usually regarded as outsiders and foreigners in the urban centers and were relegated to the lowest social stratum, which performed the dirty and menial work that town citizens shunned. The migrants were accepted nonetheless as a necessary resource in times of labor scarcity due to population decline (Hohenberg and Lees 1985; Clark 1979). Urban populations in the Middle Ages lived only one or two bad harvests away from a major population decline due to food shortages because they depended mostly on local food production, with few or no alternative food supplies to survive crop failures.[10]

Several major changes transpired from the twelfth to the fifteenth century that brought a transition of the manorial system of labor servitude to tenant farming and peasant wage labor. The changes brought increased opportunities for migration, if for no other reason than rural workers gained greater freedom. The changes included the deterioration of the ability of landlords to enforce the servitude of serfs; the reduced need for servile labor as the lands reserved for cultivation by the lords were reorganized or increasingly rented out; the need to reduce or abolish labor servitude to keep serfs from fleeing to look for wage work; the increased use of money wages to attract workers into new lands for production; and the rising cost of customary foods and drinks that had to be provided to serfs when they worked on the lands of the lords (Slicher Van Bath 1963; Postan 1972). A crisis of poor harvests and famine, rising food prices, the Black Death, and subsequent population decline also marked the years of the transition to tenant farming and peasant wage labor, especially in the first half of the fourteenth century (Wrigley 1969).

Historians have debated whether it was the reemergence of new commerce or the inefficiency of the manorial system of coerced labor that brought about the transition to tenant farming with free peasants. Maurice Dobb's (1963) *Studies in the Development of Capitalism* remains instructive of the different perspectives in the debate. The reemergence of commerce after 1100 CE is seen as spurring the change to tenant farming, but as Dobb (1963) explains the areas that converted often were new agricultural areas or areas that were distant from major commercial arteries. Moreover, the transition was not a uniform process across Europe. In some European areas such as in the Baltic region, commercial expansion did not bring

---

[10] Examining the impact of a bad harvest in the late seventeenth century on Breteuil, a community in northern France with a dense population, Wrigley (1969: 68) states, "The 'cushion' against harvest failure was slight and the results were devastating." The "burial surplus" in Breteuil after the bad harvest was about 24% of the total population. Starvation was not the main cause of death however but the inability to resist diseases with malnourished bodies or contamination from infections spread by poor, starving people moving about the land (Wrigley 1969).

1.1 Medieval Migrations

about a transition to tenant or wage labor, but to an increase of servile obligation, sometimes to extreme degrees that reduced the peasantry to wretchedness (Coulton 1919; Bennett 1937; Dobb 1963). For Dobb (1963: 42), the conflictive and highly exploitative internal relations of feudalism were the "decisive influence" for the transition. Toward the end of feudalism, the illegal migration of peasants away from their obligatory servitude also added to the crisis of the manorial system in European areas, contributing to the transition of the system.

In contrast to Dobb (1963), Wallerstein (1992) gives four cumulated collapses to explain the "crisis of feudalism," which eventually led to the new economic arrangement of the capitalist world-economy. The four collapses were the collapse of the seigniors, the collapse of the states, the collapses of the Catholic Church, and the collapse of the Mongols. These simultaneous collapses of social structures of power and authority enabled the transition to a new economic system, with new social strata, and the new system would advance without the threat of an invasion from the East, since the Black Death had severely weakened the Mongols and their control in Asia (Abu-Lughod 1989; Wallerstein 1992). Nonetheless, feudal serfdom did not completely disappear in the crisis of feudalism; it remained in eastern Europe into the nineteenth century, but now used by landowners not to cultivate agricultural products to sell in local villages but to produce cash crops for the capitalist world-economy (Wallerstein 1974).

The transition to tenant farming and peasant wage labor did not necessarily bring an improved quality of life for the peasantry, since survival and the quality of life were dependent on having access to land to grow food. In the Middle Ages, having access to crop lands, even in servitude, increased the resources for a better quality of life more than having personal freedom (Postan 1972). Moreover, "rent gouging" in tenant farming impoverished peasants so severely that it led to their depopulation in some cases (Herlihy 1965: 239). We can assume that the crisis and very high land rents restrained the migration of workers compared with what could have occurred in a more favorable environment for free peasants. It is important to keep in mind, however, that for the Middle Ages, we generally are talking about small rural populations. For example, the population in the surrounding countryside of Pistoia near Florence, Italy, declined from more than 30,000 in the mid-thirteenth century to 24,000 before the Black Death and to under 10,000 by 1404 (Herlihy 1965, 1967).

The dissolution of the European manorial economies in the Middle Ages and the transition to capitalistic economic conditions constitutes a large field of historical study with elaborate analyses and debates (e.g., Marx 1967; Wallerstein 1974, 1992; Braudel 1981; Abu-Lughod 1989; Sanderson 1999). These studies indicate that there was nothing predetermined about the transformation from medieval society to social structures of capitalist production (see, Hobsbawn 1976; Wallerstein 1992).[11] The capitalistic structure that emerged in Europe followed a

---

[11] Indeed, historians have characterized the transformation that occurred to the capitalist system as having been *"unlikely"* (Wallerstein 1992: 600; italics in the original).

political struggle in which a new social and economic actor, the capitalist class (in whatever form of metamorphosis it appeared), wrestled control of the social relations of production, and thereby of the production process itself (as Chap. 2 will illustrate regarding the medieval capitalist formation in Florence). In the following section, the discussion addresses different views about the beginning of the capitalist world-system and the expansion of the system to world regions.

1.2 Development of the Capitalist World-Economy

When did the capitalist world-economy begin? Unlike the beginning of the universe whose origin can be traced back to a single point in time of the Big Bang, the beginning of the capitalist world-economy had many components, e.g., interregional trading, monetary investment, waged labor forces, etc., that were in operation prior to their consolidation into a recognizable capitalist world-system.[12] For Wallerstein (1974), the world-system came together in Europe in the long sixteenth century of 1450–1640. A world-system not in the sense that it covered the whole globe, but in the sense that it represented the world that European people knew in their time. According to Wallerstein (1974), the regions that made up the capitalist world-economy at the beginning generally were the regions of northwestern, central, and eastern Europe (except Russia), the Christian Mediterranean, the Baltic region, some parts of the Americas under Spanish or Portuguese control, and a few coastal areas of Africa.

Some scholars, e.g., Abu-Lughod (1989) and Frank and Gills (1993), have questioned the specifics of Wallerstein's dating for the emergence of the capitalist world-economy. In her book, *Before European Hegemony: The World System A.D. 1250–1350*, Abu-Lughod (1989) argues that something capitalistic was already happening in parts of Europe in the thirteenth century. Flanders and parts of Italy were definitely manifesting capitalistic activities, so much so that for the eminent historian Fernand Braudel (1982), Italy had reached capitalist status in the thirteenth century. For Abu-Lughod (1989: 12), Europe was an "upstart peripheral" in a commercial network ("world-system") that stretched from Europe to the Middle East to India and to China, and that in 1250–1350 experienced a balance between the eastern and the western sides of this economic constellation. Abu-Lughod (1989: 8–14) refers to the commercial region from Europe to China as an "international trade economy" and a "world-system," but she does not call it a capitalistic formation. She does, however, cite Fernand Braudel's argument that by the thirteenth-century Italy had acquired the features of a capitalist world-economy.

---

[12] The coalescence did not require that earlier modes of peasant and artisan production expire. Indeed, they continued, but they no longer held the momentum of economic growth compared with capitalistic enterprises. Even in the present time, Mexican peasant seasonal migration to the United States for work has shown how surviving peasant work in a developing country helps provide semi-proletarians for US wage work (e.g., see Greene 2017).

1.2 Development of the Capitalist World-Economy

Frank and Gills' (1993) challenge to Wallerstein's modern world-system theory is to question Wallerstein's argument that the capitalist world-system emerged in the long sixteenth century as a uniquely new development. In *The World System: Five hundred years or five thousand?*, Frank and Gillis (1993: 17) take a very long reach (5000 years) of history to argue that human civilizations have maintained a unity that Eurocentric study has obscured: "We suggest that there is a common river and unity in history in a single world system and that it is multicultural in origin and expression, which has been systematically distorted by Eurocentrism." In *ReORIENT: Global Economy and the Asian Age*, Frank (1998) presents an abundance of historical evidence to document the highly active trade and other economic exchanges in the Asian region, whose eventual economic decline set the stage for the rise of the West as a power in the world-economy beginning in the fifteenth century.

Wallerstein's (1992) response to the claims that European regions had capitalistic features and operated in a world-economy centuries before the long sixteenth century was to argue that the trade involved precious commodities and not bulk goods of capitalist production. His response to Frank's argument was to call the extensive production, profit-seeking activity, wage work, etc., in the Asian region described by Frank (1998) a condition of "protocapitalism." According to Wallerstein (1993: 293), this economic development did not reach the condition of a capitalist system pursuing the "*ceaseless* accumulation of capital" (italics in the original), but consisted of economic activity between "world empires" trading in luxury goods more than in bulk goods produced through capitalist economic arrangements.

Arrighi (2010) traces the development of capitalism as a world-system back to the beginning of systemic cycles of capital accumulation, for which he gives the thirteenth and fourteenth centuries as the starting era. This period saw the end of a trade expansion in select areas in Eurasia and Africa that was followed by a financial expansion. According to Arrighi (2010: 88–89), Italian city-states such as Genoa and Venice were the leaders of the financial expansion in the European world-economy, after having been among the "main beneficiaries" of the transcontinental trade expansion (see also, Abu-Lughod 1989). For Arrighi, systemic cycles of accumulation became the transformative source of the world-system's development after launching the beginning of capitalism as a world-system.

Notwithstanding the historical criticism of temporal specificity or whether some levels of capitalistic activity existed previously in the Asian region, clearly the long sixteenth century saw the presence of a new world-system centered in western Europe, one characterized by the pursuit of economic exchange for profit to accumulate capital at ever greater levels of business and geography. A world-system in which the migration of *both capital and labor* became crucial for the spatial expansion of capital accumulation.

In comparison with earlier economic systems, the capitalist world-system brought dynamic strategies to expand economic growth for profit, which included expanding social relations of production to distant world regions. This was a "modern" business culture that contrasted sharply with previous economic systems, such as feudalism, in which "[c]onservation of the old modes of production in unaltered form" was the dominant economic principle (Marx and Engels 1976: 487). Capitalist investors altered economic social arrangements continually to fit market advantages. Furthermore, capitalist commercial investors and financiers joined other social actors, such as governments and religions, in advancing at a global level. Mokyr (2017: 120–121) has described how the ideas and achievements of "materially oriented" small elite groups "eventually reached larger and larger segments of the population," creating a culture of economic growth.

In their global pursuits, capitalist investors developed a new perception of distant spaces as they expanded commercial networks across world regions. Superstitions and myths were important elements of folklore in medieval Europe, and cartographers drew images of sea serpents and monstrous people on maps and globes to warn of possible dangers in unknown ocean regions and faraway lands (Brotton 2014; Costantino 2014). But the expansion of the capitalist world-system in the long sixteenth century and afterward indicated that capitalist investors viewed distant world regions as opportunities for commercial expansion, including through the use of force when native populations resisted, or when European rivals fought each other to dominate trade in foreign lands. The drive of capital to continually expand capital accumulation to new markets to obtain raw materials or to sell industrial products pushed the economic reach farther and farther out into distant lands. Given the need to reach new markets, capitalism could not be a local or national system—it had to be a world-system, the totality of which represented a global matrix for capitalistic commercial expansion. It did not take long for European investors to reach for new, faraway, global markets through sea routes once Iberian explorers began exploring for a seagoing passage to the East, including sea exploration for a westward passage (Fernández-Armesto 2008). As early as the 1200s, for example, Italian financiers settled in Portugal (Lisbon), and later in Spain, to financially participate in the exploratory voyages taken by Iberian mariners to reach India by sea (Smith 1993).[13]

In the long sixteenth century, Iberian and other European economic interests deepened their links to Africa, Asia, and the Americas to obtain labor power through imperialism and colonialism and through the slave trade. In Europe, employers in capitalistic industries controlled labor forces through established normative structures (governmental, religious, etc.), including through coercive practices, but in the periphery of the world-system, European colonizers and their descendants often used brute force and coercion aided by religious indoctrination to detach native populations from their traditional ways of life and reshape them into colonized labor forces to work in local and remote places.

Peripheralization involved extending social relations of exploitation to populations and cultures in remote regions. The periphery thus *was developed* as a sector

---

[13] Italian merchant-bankers were much involved in the Mediterranean trade of the time. In his book, *European Expansion in the Later Middle Ages*, Chaunu (1979) characterizes these medieval financiers as, "the originators of all the techniques of commercial capitalism" (quoted in Smith 1993: 25).

of capital accumulation through capitalist expansion and often through political domination as well. Peripheralization occurred at a high social cost to native peoples as they often experienced colonial dispossession, displacement, violence, and oppression[14] and as they experienced the long-term consequence that Frank (1969) has called, "the development of underdevelopment." Over time, European trading companies, some with quasi-governmental powers, and other capitalist investment groups incorporated many world areas into the evolving global system of capital accumulation. The following section discusses the role of capital and labor migration for capitalist expansion.

1.3 Capital and Labor Migration and Capitalist Expansion

Capital migration has been a major source of capitalist expansion whether as attempts to counteract economic restrictions in home markets, locate raw materials and labor abroad, invest in high-profit regions, or expand consumer markets. Taking different forms such as the relocation of employers and managers, or the transfer of production equipment, capital migration has often affected the movement of labor through the arrangement or rearrangement of markets and production since its early beginning. In the Dutch, British, and US periods of hegemony, capital migration brought about or redirected labor flows as it restructured or created new production sites in the hegemonic countries. In the early beginnings of capitalist production, this involved the takeover and commercialization of peasant farming and handicraft production through use of labor forces that included migrant labor. By the late twentieth century, capital migration in the United States included the movement of industries to southern states with low-wage structures and a growing presence of Latin American and Asian immigrant labor (Kandel and Parrado 2005).

For much of the history of the world-system, capital migration to peripheral regions produced colonial structures that reorganized production in the regions for the benefit of capitalist interests in European core states. This development changed native labor arrangements or introduced new labor systems that depended partly or completely on migrant labor and the relocation of populations. Coercion and brute force were often the means to establish new labor flows (Galeano 1997). In the sixteenth and seventeenth centuries, for example, Spanish and Portuguese capital migration originated the massive slave trade from Africa to the West Indies for the production of raw sugar (Curtin 1969). In Latin America,

---

[14] The social cost, however, was not evenly distributed among the subjugated native populations. In Latin America, at least in the initial stages of the conquest, native populations that assisted the Spanish overthrow of regional empires in Mesoamerica and the Andes generally fared better than the populations who resisted (e.g., see Matthew and Oudijk 2007). Moreover, native leaders (such as Mexican *caciques*) who operated the systems of tribute and compulsory labor used by the Spanish colonizers had higher social and economic status than the native people they regulated (Gibson 1964).

Spanish, Portuguese, and other European colonizers also created coercive labor arrangements of native workers for mining and other economic production for the benefit of colonizers and European coffers (Gibson 1964; Himmerich y Valencia 1991; Andrien 2001). Moreover, native elites maintained oppressive labor systems of migrant labor in many Latin American countries even after the countries gained independence in the early nineteenth century. In many other regions of the world-economy, e.g., Asia, Africa, and the Middle East, European colonialism and its use of migrant labor lasted into the twentieth century. By this time, the United States also had over a century of undertaking economic and political control of foreign lands in the periphery of the world-system.

The influence of capital migration on labor migration, including forced labor transfers, in peripheral and semiperipheral regions has varied by European power. For example, the Dutch and British governments commissioned quasi-governmental companies of merchants and investors, such as the Dutch West India Company and the British East India Company, to undertake colonial expansion abroad without specifying how labor was to be organized in colonized areas. The Spanish Crown, by contrast, authorized specific numbers of slaves that slavers could transport to sell in the Americas, and from which the Crown gained revenue per slave. Moreover, the Spanish government provided colonial policies to regulate the use of indigenous labor and prohibit labor abuses, but which Spanish colonial overseers ignored (Poole 1963).

The question may be raised as to whether migration is an organic part of capitalism, that is, is migration necessary for capitalism to expand across world regions? The answer from Wallerstein's "world-system" perspective is yes. According to Wallerstein (1976), the capitalist world-system had a single origin—northwestern Europe during the long sixteenth century—from which it expanded to other world regions through trade, colonialism, and other modes of interregional interaction. The world development of capitalism thus did not occur through simultaneous, parallel invention in different world regions, but through global diffusion. Moreover, the migration of capital in its various forms involved coercion when capitalism was forced upon native populations (sometimes at the cost of many lives) through colonialism or through imposed trade such as through the Opium Wars that Western powers waged with China in the nineteenth century.[15]

A few general observations can be made regarding the needs of capital that bring about labor migration. In some cases, migrant labor is necessary because capital has set up production in remote areas that do not have local labor supplies, such as in mining or in remote oil fields where workers have to travel and spend time in the worksites. To give an historical example, during the period of Dutch hegemony in the seventeenth century, thousands of workers migrated to large land reclamation projects to convert Dutch coastal areas under water into profitable

---

[15] In the Opium Wars in the nineteenth century, the British and French governments forced the Qing dynasty to open Chinese ports to trade with the West, including the European importation in China of opium from India (Platt 2018).

1.3 Capital and Labor Migration and Capitalist Expansion

agricultural lands (De Vries 1974). Capitalist expansion has historically paved the way for labor migrant streams, and this source of labor supply continues in the twenty-first century.

But having just enough workers is not what capital seeks. Employers need an over-supply of labor, a "surplus-population," of workers to control wages with redundant labor (Marx 1967). An over-supply of labor also means having workers ready in almost standby status to replace workers who depart to other jobs (or who are deported by immigration authorities). An over-supply also minimizes the time and effort needed to find new workers during a business expansion, which is an important advantage for capitalistic enterprises to maintain a smooth pace of production and distribution to markets.[16]

From the perspective of the social relations between capital and labor, employers seek to control or dominate the production process and working conditions (intensity of work, length of the workday, etc.) in order to maximize the benefit of labor power as a commodity. The capitalist struggle to control and dominate labor and working conditions was especially harsh in early phases of industrial capitalism when capital was wrestling control of production processes from the medieval guild system.[17] Capital's ability to dominate the social relations of production was based considerably on the segmentation of workforces through the employment of non-skilled workers. Early capitalist employers sought the labor power of young women (girls), children age 6–13, orphans, and less-skilled workers—i.e., workers who were less able than organized craftworkers to resist the inferior and harsh factory working conditions of the time (Marx 1967).[18] These young and unorganized workers formed a mobile and malleable labor force made available as a "reserve army of labor" partly through capital's displacement of old agricultural modes of production and artisan guilds in the towns.

Included in the reserve army of labor were weakened former agricultural workers who had been forcibly and often illegally driven from their lands and villages by the emerging capitalist class and hurled as migrants into lives of "mere slaves" for capitalist farmers and manufacturers (Marx 1967: 692). Also included in the

---

[16] The desire to produce and maintain a surplus-population of workers likely motivated the measures of capitalist employers who restricted the out-migration of labor in various historical times. A change in labor migration from the age of empires to the age of nation-states is that employers in the age of empires did not have to wait for labor to migrate to them. In large projects, including public construction projects, employers could have slave workers delivered to them from imperial conquests to do the construction work. Slave workers were also used in the southern United States during slavery for construction of public buildings.

[17] The struggles of capital were not necessarily a function of greed, but of the need to accumulate capital for investment to gain advantages in competition, such as through the expansion of workforces and the introduction of new technology in production.

[18] Using historical case studies, Burawoy (1984) demonstrates that the domination of capitalist production varied by "factory regime," i.e., by different institutional social spheres that affect struggles in worksites. According to Burawoy (1984), Marx's depiction of Lancashire textile factories ruled by market despotism in the 1800s as the prototype of capital's harsh domination was only one type of several factory regimes in textile production of industrial capitalism in the 1800s.

surplus-population of workers were workers displaced from industries by technological advancements that lessened the proportional role of labor in production (Marx 1967). The relative surplus-population existed in constant poverty, and some segments in extreme poverty and starvation, and fluctuated in size as it was attracted and then repelled by the swings of economic cycles. It took as one of its forms a floating surplus-population, which Marx (1967) analyzed to be a critical resource for capitalist employers to maintain control and dominance in the social relations of production. Thus, migratory populations produced by capital's expropriations in agricultural lands and by technological development in urban industries provided more than a labor supply to be employed in times of expansion—it provided a vulnerable and mobile industrial reserve army, "a mass of human material always ready for exploitation" (Marx 1967: 632).

The eighteenth- and nineteenth-century conditions of capitalist production described by Marx have changed in important ways in the formal labor markets in core countries of the capitalist world-economy. In these labor markets, workers have gained rights and other protections through union contracts and state regulations of the minimum wage, length of the workday, laws against child labor, etc. But the same is not always true for working conditions in peripheral countries of the world-system, the so-called developing countries, where child labor and even slave labor remain present, and where the majority of workers struggle to survive with the meager wages they receive. In Mexico, for example, in mid-2020 the average wage reached 408.02 Mexican pesos (US$18.89) *per day*, while in the United States, the average wage was $29.47 *per hour* (Trading Economics 2020). For an 8-h workday, the Mexican average daily wage was only 8.0% of the US average daily wage. With this large difference in wages, it should not be surprising that US employers have found a reserve army of exploitable labor in the Mexican working class as millions of Mexican men and women have migrated to work in the United States (Garip 2017). Millions of these workers haves migrated without visas, enhancing their vulnerability as an industrial reserve army for US employers. Yet, to be sure, the unauthorized migrants who migrate to economies in core states represent a small percentage of the poor, working populations in peripheral and semiperipheral areas of the world-economy. A series of factors such as distance, lack of social capital to arrange travel, border enforcement, and the desire to remain in one's country act against larger unauthorized labor migration patterns.

Labor migration also helps capital meet the need for special labor qualities, especially when these are not readily available in the domestic labor market. For example, in US settings today of arduous, labor-intensive work, including construction, landscaping, and agricultural work, employers need disciplined, young workers who can withstand work spans of eight or more hours per day, for five or more days per week, week after week, month after month, including in times of very hot weather. The slave trade from Africa provided such a labor force for most of the first century of the United States in the Deep South, and by the twentieth century, the demand for arduous labor was met partly through the immigration of men and women from different world regions that included Europe, Asia, the Caribbean, and other Latin American areas (Portes and Rumbaut 2014). While some US workers are up to the task of physical, strenuous work, many other US workers lack the motivation for this work because they have access to a wide opportunity structure in the US economy, and many also have the option to train for jobs beyond manual work. Still, work opportunity structures may not be equally available to all US-born. US-born children and grandchildren of immigrants may face restricted opportunities for upward mobility in labor markets because of racial and gender discrimination (Feagin and Cobas 2014).

Migrant labor can also provide labor advantages to capital through the special work qualities some migrants bring. As Chaps. 2 and 3 will indicate, respectively, in the fourteen-century Florentine merchant-capitalists promoted the immigration of workers skilled in cloth production into their city. The same was true in seventeenth-century Holland when the municipal government of Amsterdam enacted policies to provide housing and other inducements to skilled foreign textile workers from the southern Netherlands and other countries to revitalize the textile industries of the city after a Spanish invasion (Barbour 1950). In a twentieth-century example, sizeable numbers of skilled Mexican mechanical workers migrated to the Houston area in the 1980s after being displaced by industrial restructuring in the Monterrey metropolitan area in northern Mexico (Hernández-León 2008). Unemployed machinists and other mechanical workers from Monterrey found employment in industrial firms that made the Houston metropolitan area a major business center in the oil world-economy. In the late nineteenth and early twentieth centuries, a similar movement to Monterrey of skilled workers occurred when German brewmasters moved to the city to build and operate industrial breweries.

In other industries, to name a few more US examples, non-capitalistic enterprises such as public hospitals, school districts, and places of worship have for decades recruited foreign temporary workers (e.g., nurses, bilingual teachers, and clergy) from peripheral areas such as the Philippines and Latin American countries to meet their required professional staffing (Bartlett 2014; Hohn et al. 2016; Kandel and Wasem 2016). As such, these non-profit-making enterprises employ foreign-born labor for which peripheral and semiperipheral countries paid the cost of upbringing, schooling, and training.

While industries or community institutions may formally recruit foreign employees for their needs, millions of workers have also migrated without government authorization across world regions to supply labor demands in core countries and other economies. Many of these migrant workers travel across international borders without visas to work in personal-service jobs created by the growth and concentration of professional and other highly skilled workers in major urban centers. According to Sassen-Koob (1984), the concentration of lawyers, certified public accountants, investment bankers, computer engineers, etc., has created a new labor demand in metropolitan areas for a wide range of personal services, e.g., house cleaning, yard work, dog walking, etc., that professional and highly skilled workers do not have time to do, or would rather pay someone else to do. Often men and women immigrant workers without visas take these jobs, and, thus, while they may not work directly for capitalistic enterprises, they support the professional and highly skilled sector (the upper-middle class in general) that does. Again, this supports stable production in the social and economic spheres of capital.

International migration enables employers to reach surplus worker populations far from the vicinity of their capitalistic enterprises. Through contacts with hometown and kinship migrant networks, employers gain access to a ready supply of workers abroad (Flores-Yeffal 2013). By the late twentieth century, with the conveniences of instant communication and rapid travel, migrant workers could arrive at job sites in core countries in just a few days from towns and villages in remote hinterlands in the periphery of the world-economy (e.g., see Jonas and Rodriguez 2014: Chap 5).

We can summarize the employment levels of peripheral and semiperipheral migrant labor in core countries of the world-system as follows. At the primary level, migrant workers from less-developed world regions are employed as producers of goods and services through which capitalistic enterprises and employers derive profits. At the secondary level, the migrant labor takes jobs in a host of industries, but mainly in the service sector, to support primary-level workforces and workplaces. The secondary-level work includes working in restaurants, cleaning office buildings and other workplaces, and working in service jobs as domestics and yard workers in upper-class and upper-middle class households. While in the primary level the main function of migrant workers is to produce commodities for the realization of profits and capital accumulation, in the secondary level the defining feature of migrant labor is supporting the social reproduction of the national labor force, as well as the social reproduction of immigrant communities that provide labor for the secondary level.[19]

In the tertiary level, migrant labor is at its most tenuous and uncertain condition trying to survive mainly on brief opportunities that appear for work such as in day-labor pools in street corners, and for many irregular migrant workers, trying to survive threats of arrest and removal by immigration authorities. The work and legal disadvantages of many migrant workers in the tertiary level place many of the workers in a reserved labor status making them willing to accept jobs with poor working conditions and low pay—jobs that domestic workers shun.

It should be recognized that off-shore production has given many employers, especially employers in large manufacturing firms, the option of not depending on migrant labor in the home country. Through off-shore production, large manufacturing firms can take their manufacturing work directly to foreign countries (e.g., China, Mexico, and Vietnam) with low wages to meet their labor needs. Free-trade agreements, regional trading markets, and other international trading arrangements give firms in core states access to foreign labor, without having to be concerned with immigrant labor policies in the home country (Peters 2017).

---

[19] Some secondary-level migrant workers also work in capitalistic enterprises, such as in restaurant chains, but the outstanding characteristic of the work is supporting the social reproduction of workforces.

1.4 Hegemony and Migration

Wallerstein (1980: 38) defines hegemonic status in the world-system as a condition where a core state achieves "productive efficiency" beyond that found in other core states and thus becomes the "primary beneficiary" of open markets. The hegemonic state must have a dominant military force to prevail against attempts by other states to impose economic barriers. For Wallerstein, the first hegemonic period of a core state in the world-economy occurred soon after the takeoff of capitalism in the long sixteenth century when the Dutch rose to unequaled economic development during 1625–1675. Dutch military power defeated European commercial rivals in the East Indies, in the western coast of Africa, and in the Pernambuco region of Brazil during the Dutch rise to economic dominance.

Arrighi (2010) has elaborated on, and expanded, the concept of economic rise to dominance in the world-system through his concept of systemic cycles of capital accumulation. According to Arrighi, reoccurring alternations between the expansion of material commodities and phases of financial expansion frame systemic cycles of accumulation, and a cycle may introduce a break from the mechanisms of previous cyclical patterns. Moreover, Arrighi distinguishes between dominance and hegemony. In Arrighi's (2010: 28–29) conceptualization, dominance by a state refers to having control or command by virtue of superior power "pure and simple," and hegemony includes "the power of a state to exercise functions of [moral] leadership and governance over a system of sovereign states."

A dominant state has hegemonic power, according to Arrighi, when it leads a system of states in a direction perceived to be in the general interest of the system. Arrighi (2010: 118) articulates four systemic cycles of accumulation, with the first cycle being the Genoese economic and financial restructuring that elevated Genoese merchant-bankers into "the most powerful capitalist class of sixteenth-century Europe." The three other systemic cycles of accumulation concern the hegemonic states identified by Wallerstein (i.e., the United Provinces, Britain, and the United States), but across time periods longer than a century.

In this section, I briefly list migration patterns that will be examined in Chaps. 2–5 in the context of hegemonic development in the world-system. I begin the brief review of migration patterns in the setting of Florence, Italy, in the thirteenth century. This time interval falls within the era of the thirteenth and early fourteenth centuries given by Arrighi (2010: 88) as the "zero-point in the development of capitalism as world system." Next, I briefly list selected historical patterns that developed in the Dutch, British, and US periods of hegemony in the world-economy from the seventeenth to the twentieth century.

Florentine Capitalist Development A capitalistic woolen industry emerged in Florence beginning in the 1200s complete with waged workers laboring in workshops owned by members of a woolen merchants' guild. This development resulted from an interregional arrangement of wool trade and finance in Catholic Europe developed by Italian merchant-bankers acting as tax collectors for the papacy. The Florentine dominance of the wool trade in regions of western Europe brought a windfall of wool to Florence in the twelve and thirteen centuries. To handle the enlarged wool supply, merchant-bankers reorganized the making of woolen products from the putting-out system to centralized workshops of waged work for the most labor-intensive tasks of woolen production. To enlarge the woolen textile industry, Florentine merchant-bankers promoted the in-migration of workers, especially workers experienced in cloth production, through their influence in the city government of Florence and through a major guild they controlled (Waley 1969). In collaboration with the guild, the city government gave support to immigrant families recruited for textile production in the city. Some migrant labor was also obtained through the forced importation of cloth workers captured in a conflict with the city of Lucca. Additionally, the city government relaxed citizenship requirements to attracted cloth workers from textile centers in Flanders. While the city government promoted the in-migration of cloth workers, it restricted the emigration of surrounding agricultural labor to prevent a shortage of food producers for the city (Whewell 1977).

Dutch Hegemony Class conflict and other restrictions truncated Florentine's economic rise by the mid-fourteenth century, but a hundred years later, economic conditions in areas of Europe began to coalesce into a geographically extensive capitalist economy in which the Dutch Republic (i.e., the United Provinces, formed after the Netherlands Revolution of 1566–1576), developed into the first hegemonic power (Wallerstein 1980). Dutch dominance in the new world-system during 1625–1675 demonstrated a dynamic relationship between migration and capitalist development. As Chap. 3 elaborates, several migrant patterns supplied labor power during Dutch industrialization in the seventeenth century. Rural to urban migration provided labor for industrialization particularly in the province of Holland in the urban industrial centers of Amsterdam and Leiden.

In addition, the invasion of the southern Netherlands (present-day Belgium) by Spanish forces in the 1560s caused investors, artisans, merchants, and workers to emigrate to the northern Netherlands, and the migration continued into the seventeenth century, providing capital, labor, and industries to the northern Netherlands (Wallerstein 1980). The importation of children from domestic sources and foreign orphanages also provided labor to emerging capitalistic industries of the United Provinces. In addition, rural to rural migration supplied labor for economic development projects in the Dutch countryside, e.g., land reclamation and peat production, and for urban industries that relocated to rural areas (Wagret 1968; De Vries 1974). While the majority of production during feudalism and the medieval era depended mostly on fixed, agricultural, labor forces, the emerging system of capitalism significantly depended on the mobility of capital and labor, and this was especially true in the expansive, takeoff phase of the capitalist world-economy.

The mobility of capital and labor to the periphery of the world-system (e.g., Africa and the East Indies and West Indies) often occurred within the processes of imperialism and colonialism, making political domination and social oppression a part of capitalist development in peripheral regions. Dutch expansion into the East Indies to trade in spices in the 1600s involved the migration of Dutch traders and administrators of the Dutch East India Company, accompanied by a military force (Wallerstein 1980). The Dutch East India Company established its headquarters in Batavia (Djakarta) to trade in the Malay Archipelago, and Chinese merchants and workers immigrated to participate in the new Dutch economic arrangement (Vlekke 1945).

It was in the Atlantic realm of the emerging world-system, however, where migration in the form of the forced transfer of African people as slaves became a major facet of economic expansion. In the East Indies, Dutch expansion involved the immigration of several hundred to a few thousand Dutch traders, administrators, and soldiers, but in the Atlantic zone, the Dutch importation of African slaves alone reached into the hundreds of thousands (Curtin 1969). While the Dutch never became the biggest slavers in the Atlantic area in the seventeenth century, they expanded the traded geographically more than their English and Portuguese rivals across Atlantic regions such as northern Brazil, Barbados, Curacao (Emmer 1972).

British Hegemony British capital never lagged far behind Dutch capitalist expansion, and it rose to dominance in the world-economy between the end of the Napoleonic Wars in 1815 and the Great Depression of 1873. In this era, British hegemony expanded the capitalist world-economy through sharp increases in capital investments, international loans, and commodity exports, and through colonization, e.g., in India and Egypt. Through its Industrial Revolution, Britain rose to be the dominant manufacturing country in the world, accounting for about a fourth of the world trade by the mid-1800s (Rostow 1978). Migration played major roles in the rise of British power in the world-economy. British foreign investments and colonialism affected labor mobility in British colonies. In Britain, rural migration, townward migration, and immigration from Ireland were particularly important for British industrialization in its era of hegemony (Redford 1968). Abroad, British, Irish, and other European emigration supported capitalist growth in regions in the Western Hemisphere and in other parts of the world. Composed of different occupational backgrounds, the emigrant streams supported capitalist economies and the general social reproduction of society, including unpaid housework, that served to renew economic institutions and labor forces.

From the late 1700s to the 1830s, cotton textile production led the Industrial Revolution, and it remained mainly a rural industry (Pollard 1978). Unemployed and displaced farmers and other agricultural workers and their families migrated to cotton textile-producing industrial villages, as did town workers recruited to do textile work in the countryside. Contracted child workers and wives and children in working families also migrated to work in mining and other rural industries besides textile production (Marx 1967).

The defeat of Napoleon at the Battle of Waterloo in 1815 caused British agricultural prices to drop causing a decline in cultivation and releasing agricultural labor to migrate to rural and urban areas. Migrant labor in Britain took a townward direction especially in the 1830s–1840s with the rise of the factory system in urban areas, and as the production of capital-goods (tools, machinery, etc.)

overtook textile production. During the 1840s to the 1860s, thousands of migrants settled each decade in the eight largest industrial and commercial northern towns of Britain (Deane 1979). Irish migration to Britain rose during 1820–1860 (Redford 1968). Famine, agricultural decline, evictions, steamship travel, etc.—all spurred the migration of hundreds of thousands of Irish to Britain, as well as to the United States and other countries where the Irish often took the most undesirable, laborious work.

Along with the Irish, British migration to the United States increased from tens of thousands in the first decades of British hegemony to over half a million by the last decade in 1861–1870 (Easterlin et al., 1980). The British migration, along with other European immigration, helped to meet the labor demands of US industrial development in the 1800s and provided human resources for the western expansion of the country into farming and ranching regions (Redford 1968; Greenleaf 1970). The British migration involved a host of occupational backgrounds, e.g., farmers, engineers, machinists, professionals, and business owners. But common laborers made up the largest occupation among the British migrants beginning in the 1840s (Redford 1968; Erickson 1972).

British capital migration and colonization across world regions also effected the forced transfer of labor forces outside Europe. Before the British period of hegemony, British slavers had accounted for about 2.0 million to 3.4 million of the estimated 12.5 million slaves transported to the Americas during the whole era of the Atlantic slave trade (Curtin 1969; Eltis and Richardson 2008). After the British parliament abolished the British slave trade in 1807 and freed the West Indies slaves in 1833, thousands of migrant workers from India and other world regions resupplied the West Indies workforces (Williams 1966).

US Hegemony The Industrial Revolution helped launch Britain's ascendance to global hegemony in the nineteenth century,[20] and war and monopoly capitalism helped elevate the United States to a similar status during 1945–1970 (Wallerstein 2006). By wrecking the industrial power of other developed countries, World War II enabled the United States to operate in the world-economy without equal competitors after the war ended. The period of US hegemony involved the maturation of monopoly capital, which had commenced in the United States and other capitalist countries in the late nineteenth century (Baran and Sweezy 1966; Foster 2016). Monopolistic mergers created powerful economic actors in domestic and world markets. Through mergers, a relatively small number of large firms accounted for a large majority of an industry's capital assets and for most workers in industrial labor forces. The mergers of corporations affected the spatial distribution of labor forces as workers migrated to the centers of capital concentration and centralization.

---

[20] The effect between industrialization and global hegemony was reciprocal. Industrialization made Britain the most powerful economic actor in the world, and British global dominance opened markets for British products, which promoted industrialization.

According to Manuel Castells (1976), the monopolistic stage of capitalism brought about urban processes of metropolitanization and suburbanization, which drew partly from migration. During the US period of hegemony, metropolitan growth in the United States gained about 21 million people through net migration, which averaged about 35% of the total metropolitan population increase across the decades from the 1940s to the 1960s (US Census Bureau 1974). Initially, farm areas were a major source of migrants to metropolitan areas, but by the 1960s international migration and migration between metropolitan areas became the major sources of metropolitan growth.

African Americans, Mexican Americans, and Puerto Ricans, the three largest US minority populations, were part of the domestic migration that accompanied urban growth associated with the concentration of capital. Out-migration from the South and rural–urban migration characterized African American migration during the period of US hegemony (Lemann 1992). Much of the out-migration of African Americans from the South headed to the industrial centers of Boston, Chicago, New York, and Los Angeles and to intermittent cities (Tilly 1979). Similar to Blacks, Mexican Americans underwent rapid urbanization in the first half of the 1900s, and by the 1950s, almost 80% of Mexican Americans lived in urban areas (Grebler et al. 1970). In contrast to African Americans, however, Mexican American migrated mainly to urban areas in the Southwest, with the exception of migrant streams to the Midwest (Cardenas 1978) and seasonal migrations to agricultural regions of the country.

Immigrating from a US colony, Puerto Ricans had a more complicated experience of migration than African Americans and Mexican Americans. Although smaller in number than African Americans and Mexican Americans, Puerto Ricans along with other workers from the British West Indies were a source of migrant workers for rural and urban industries during the economic and urban transition of US monopoly capital. Migrant workers from Puerto Rico took low-paying jobs that were hard to fill with US workers, especially in New York City. Jamaican peasant workers were imported to the United States through a temporary labor program for farm work on the East Coast (Betancur et al. 1993).

US immigration from foreign countries increased in 1946 after the war ended to hundreds of thousands of new immigrants annually, primarily from Europe (US INS 2002: Tables 1 and 2).[21] Alongside this immigration was the annual importation of Mexican temporary workers (*braceros*) mostly to work in corporate farms of agribusiness (Craig 1971). Lasting from 1942 to 1964, the bracero program arranged by the US and Mexican governments increased from tens of thousands to almost half a million Mexican workers imported annually by the mid-1950s. The program stimulated a parallel but unauthorized Mexican migration of millions of workers by the 1980s (Meissner 2004; Rodriguez and Hagan 2016).

---

[21] In 1965, the US Congress amended the Immigration and Nationality Act to abolish the national-origin quotas, which had favored immigrants from northern and western Europe, and instituted a system of family-related and employment preferences for visas for legal permanent residence.

1.5 Analytical Perspectives

Chapter 2 analyzes the medieval rise of capitalist relations in the wool trade and woolen industry of western Europe through interregional trade in which Florence emerged as a financial and commercial power. This development brought about woolen production with wage workers in the most labor-intensive tasks of Florence's woolen industry. Chapters 3–5 analyze the rise to dominance and major trends of capital and labor migration associated with the Dutch, British, and US eras of hegemony, respectively. The chapters analyze selected migration patterns from the perspectives of class relations between employers and workers, technological development in the workplace, economic cycles, and actions of the state concerning migration. The analysis uses these perspectives according to their relevance in the different periods of hegemony.

At the most basic level, capital is grounded on the social relation between employers and workers. Employers own the means of production, and they control the process of production where workers produce commodities that employers sell in the market. Since commodities sell for an exchange value greater than what the workers are paid to produce them, the social relation between employers and workers is an economic exploitation, i.e., a condition of unequal exchange, which is the source of profit and capital accumulation. In the social relations of production, employers look for ways to maintain or increase profit and maintain a stable process of production, while workers attempt to increase their wages and improve their working conditions. Across the history of capitalism, employers have used migrant labor to draw advantages in the processes of production and capital accumulation.

The advantages that employers can gain in the social relations of production from the use of migrant labor, including forced migrant labor, vary by a host of economic conditions such as stages of economic development and industrial sectors, as well as by the characteristics of workers. Across the history of the capitalist world-system, owners and managers of economic enterprises have used migrant workers for a host of functions that include the following: to do the most dirty and physically strenuous work that local labor forces shun; to work in lower-skill occupations created by the degradation (deskilling) of artisan work; to fill highly skilled jobs such as engineers and software designers with workers from international labor markets; to segment workforces by creating racial and ethnic divisions among workers; to facilitate labor recruitment through social networks of migrant workers, etc. (Redford 1968; Marx 1967; Piore 1979; Gordon et al. 1982; Mize 2016). While advantages gained by employers from migrant labor vary by economic era and work conditions, the principle for using migrant labor remains the same—to gain benefits for capital in the social relations of production.

From the perspective of labor, workers migrate to areas with better working conditions than the ones they leave behind. Some international workers are "circular migrants" migrating seasonally, for example, to supplement their peasant work at home with wage work abroad (Garip 2017; Greene 2017). Migrant workers may also migrate to establish their families in more favorable institutional environments abroad. In the stratification of the capitalist world-system among the core, periphery, and semiperiphery, migration enables men and women workers in the poorer regions to relocate to more prosperous areas of the world-system where labor struggles have produced better working conditions. In core countries, not all migrant workers settle into jobs in capitalistic enterprises, however. As mentioned above, some migrant workers from the periphery find jobs in in ethnic establishments (restaurants, herbal shops, music stores, etc.) that support the social reproduction of immigrant labor in core countries (Portes and Manning 1986; Light and Bonacich 1998; Xie and Gough 2011).

The use of migrant labor from domestic or foreign sources also varies by the level of technological development. Labor-intensive industries such as agriculture and construction may draw more use from labor migration than industries using higher levels of technology. By definition, labor-intensive industries depend heavily on manual labor to get the work done. In the labor-intensive technological settings of capitalist expansion into Caribbean sugar production during European colonialism, for example, the importation of African slaves became the preferred labor source of plantation owners (Dunn 1972). In Europe, migrant labor became associated with the degradation of handicraft production especially in the nineteenth century. The mechanization of production displaced craftworkers, enabling employers to hire cheaper and less contentious labor, including migrant labor (Marx 1967).

Some British craftworkers displaced from their trade by mechanized factories in the nineteenth century emigrated to colonies and countries abroad, i.e., to areas seeking skilled labor to develop new industries (Redford 1968; Easterlin et al. 1980). Other European craftworkers also left in the late nineteenth and early twentieth centuries to setup industries abroad, such as German brewmasters who built breweries in Mexico and Japan (Benbow 2017). Skilled labor migration remained a feature in the world-system, and in the late twentieth and early twenty-first centuries, high-tech migrant labor from developing countries such as India and China reinforced the workforces of computer and software corporations in core countries of the world-economy.

Different economic fluctuations that vary by source and duration characterize capitalistic economies. Some fluctuations are business cycles of a few to several years, while "long waves" are seen by some analysts as representing processes of long-term structural change in the world-system, such as in the incorporation of global regions into the world-economy. Long waves are seen as spanning several decades or even longer (Grinin et al. 2016). The ebb and flow of economic cycles affects migration in a variety of ways. Rising economic prosperity may stimulate domestic and international migration as workers may seek to transfer to areas of increasing prosperity that provide better opportunities than what they leave behind. Employers may also directly stimulate migration by actively recruiting migrant workers in times of economic growth to increase workforces or slow the rise of wages. From the perspective of an economic downturn, migrant workers may return to their home communities to wait for an economic upturn in core societies, or they may be expelled by the core state to prevent job competition with native workers during a recession.

Workers are usually not free, however, to freely migrate across nation-state borders. Especially since the late nineteenth and early twentieth centuries, states have regulated who can enter a country and increasingly restricted foreign-born workers' access to labor markets in core countries (FitzGerald and Cook-Martín 2014). Nonetheless, restriction does not necessarily mean absolute closure, and foreign labor has migrated to core areas through special labor measures (guest-worker programs) or through irregular ways. Moreover, the emergence of a for-profit "migration industry," especially since the nineteenth century, has helped migrants obtain financial, transportation, and legal support for their migration (Hernández-León 2012).

Not all migrant labor may seek the most prosperous economic sectors during economic upturns. Some migrant workers from peripheral countries, for example, may seek work in lower-paying service occupations that support the lifestyles of higher-income earners. Moreover, some migrant workers that arrive in core countries during economic upturns may return to their home countries during economic recessions in core countries (Constant and Massey 2002; Rendall et al. 2011; Greene 2017).

Since at least the Middle Ages, states have implemented policies to promote or deter the in-migration of specific groups or individuals, but it was not until the late nineteenth and early twentieth centuries that countries in the West enacted legislation to directly manage immigration (FitzGerald and Cook-Martin 2014). In the United States, for example, the first law that gave the federal government power to prohibit "undesirable immigrants," was enacted in 1875, and the first law to prohibit the immigration of a specific nationality (Chinese) was enacted in 1882 (Lee 2003). In Britain, concern over Jewish immigration partly motivated the initial legislation in 1905 to regulate the arrival of foreigners, which was followed by additional regulatory provisions enacted in 1914 and 1919 (Panayi 1994). While states were slow to develop immigration policies to regulate immigration, organized labor, and political groups opposed immigration in earlier years through social movements. By the late twentieth and early twenty-first centuries, immigration became a central policy concern of countries in the West after millions of migrants from peripheral and semiperipheral countries migrated to core states of the world-system, many without visas, to seek work, refuge, and stable social environments (Leal and Rodríguez 2016). Political reactions to immigration complicated the role of migrant labor in the world-economy after immigration and border restrictions sometimes, or often, kept migrant workers from employers who sought them.

A large number of studies have investigated domestic and transnational migration patterns of individuals, groups, and whole communities in different world regions. These studies have produced a wealth of knowledge regarding why people migrate, how they migrate, and the consequences of migration, including the effects of state policies, that differ by gender, sexuality, race/ethnicity, national origin, legal status, etc. My study in this book takes a different approach. I am

1.5 Analytical Perspectives

principally concerned with the role that migration has played as a social force in the development of the capitalist world-system. That is, how voluntary or forced migration has helped produce and reproduce the macro social structure we know today as the world-economy, which frames much of the everyday lives of millions of people on the earth.

A growing number of studies have also focused on migration from an historical-world perspective and includes such excellent works as Dirk Hoerder's *Cultures in Contact* (2002), Katharine M. Donato and Donna Gabaccia's *Gender and International Migration* (2015), and Patrick Manning's *Migration in World History* (2020). Within this perspective, my book differs from these studies in that I stay within the framework of world-systems theory. My goal is to demonstrate the association of migration with the world systemic dynamics of historical capitalist development.

It is impossible to analyze the totality of migration involved in the global expansion of capitalism in a single book. My plan in the chapters that follow is to highlight the significance of selected migration patterns for capitalist development that transpired during the heightened economic activity in the specified periods of hegemony. I use the eras of Dutch, British, and US hegemony as units of analysis to standardize the historical intervals of comparison. No single migration pattern in the analysis is considered *sine qua non* for capital accumulation in the expanding world-system. But together the patterns illustrate the fluidity of capital and labor that supported the rise of Florence to dominance in the wool trade of Catholic Europe and the Dutch, British, and US rise to hegemony in the world capitalist system.

Given the extensive historical and global development of the capitalist system, it is easy to lose sight of its effects on migration. Simply stated, there is no other present economic world order to compare it with to determine capital's particular effects on migration. Yet many of the conditions associated with international migration are grounded on the structural location of communities and populations in peripheral and semiperipheral regions of the world-system. In many cases, economic and political interests in core countries developed structures of unequal exchanges with these regions in the pursuit of profit. This structuration created lasting social inequalities that restrict life chances—and life itself—and propel populations into migrant streams.

The four chapters that follow take a chronological order. Chapter 2 focuses on the rise of capitalist woolen production in Florence in the 1200s and the role of capital and labor migration in this development. The chapter addresses what to some scholars will seem as an anomaly of depicting such an early historical era as the takeoff point for capitalism. Chapter 3 focuses on migration patterns associated with the Dutch period of hegemony. Dutch business interests expanded their commerce aggressively in Europe and forcefully in other world regions creating conflict as part of their global reach for profit. Chapter 4 examines migration patterns during the British era of hegemony that were related to the Industrial Revolution and world capitalist expansion. I consider this to be the classic era of hegemony, in which British interests aggressively coerced peripheral populations to comply with their will under an imperialistic banner that accumulated power and profits for Britain.

Chapter 5 examines domestic and international labor migration patterns in the United States during the US period of hegemony. In contrast to the two earlier eras of hegemony, these migration patterns involve a much larger economy and national population subdivided into racial and ethnic categories across segmented labor markets. It is also an era in which unauthorized migration into the United States became a major trend, enhancing debates on US immigration policies. Finally, Chap. 6 highlights and discusses findings from the analysis of the book. The chapter also discusses migration developments in the world-system in the post-US hegemony era.

References

Abu-Lughod, Janet. 1989. *Before European Hegemony: The World System A.D. 1250–1350*. Oxford: Oxford University Press.
Andrien, Kenneth. 2001. *Andean Worlds: Indigenous History, Culture, and Consciousness Under Spanish rule, 1532–1825*. Albuquerque: University of New Mexico Press.
Arrighi, Giovanni. 2010. *The Long Twentieth Century: Money, Power and the Origins of Our Times*. New York: Verso.
Bankston III, Carl L. 2014. *Immigrant Networks and Social Capital*. Cambridge: Polity Press.
Baran, Paul A., and Paul M. Sweezy. 1966. *Monopoly Capital: An Essay on the American Economic and Social Order*. New York: Monthly Review Press.
Barbour, V. 1950. *Capitalism in Amsterdam in the Seventeenth Century*. Baltimore: The Johns Hopkins Press.
Barnet, Richard J., and Ronald E. Muller. 1974. *Global reach: The Power of the Multinational Corporations*. New York: Simon and Schuster.
Bartlett, Lora. 2014. *Migrant Teachers: How American Schools Import Labor*. Cambridge, MA: Harvard University Press.
Benbow, Mark. 2017. German Immigrants in the United States Brewing Industry (1840–1895). Accessed November 30, 2022. http://www.immigrantentrepreneurship.org/entries/german-immigrants-in-the-united-states-brewing-industry/.
Bennett, H.S. 1937. *Life on the English Manor: A Study Of Peasant Conditions 1150–1400*. Cambridge: Cambridge University Press.
Betancur, John J., Teresa Cordova, and Maria De Los Angeles Torres. 1993. Economic restructuring and the process of incorporation of Latinos into the Chicago economy. *Latinos in a changing US economy: Comparative perspectives on growing inequality* 7: 109–132.
Brann, D.B., D.A. Thurman, and C.M. Mitchell. 1996. Human Interaction with Lights-Out Automation: A Field Study. In *Proceedings Third Annual Symposium on Human Interaction with Complex Systems, HIC'96*. Accessed July 23, 2018. https://ieeexplore.ieee.org/abstract/document/549525/
Braudel, Fernand. 1981. *Civilization and Capitalism 15th–18th Century, vol. 1: The Structures of Everyday Life*. New York: Harper & Row, Publishers.
Braudel, Fernand. 1982. *Civilization and Capitalism 15th–18th Century. vol. 2: The Wheels of Commerce*. New York: Harper & Row, Publishers.
Brotton, Jerry. 2014. *Great Maps*. New York: Dorling Kindersley Publishing.
Burawoy, M. 1976. The Functions and Reproduction of Migrant Labor: Comparative Material from Southern Africa and the United States. *American Journal of Sociology* 81 (March): 1050–1087.
Burawoy, Michael. 1984. Karl Marx and the Satanic Mills: Factory Politics Under Early Capitalism in England, and the United States, and Russia. *American Journal of Sociology* 90 (2): 247–282.
Cardenas, Gilbert. 1978. Los Desarraigados: Chicanos in the Midwestern Region of the United States. *Aztlan* 7 (2): 153–186.

References

Castells, Manuel. 1976. The Wild City. *Kapitalistate* 4–5 (Summer): 2–30.

Chaunu, Pierre. 1979. *European Expansion in the Later Middle Ages*. Amsterdam: North-Holland Publishing Company.

China Labour Bulletin. 2020. Migrant Workers and Their Children. Hong Kong, May 11. Accessed August 2, 2020. https://clb.org.hk/content/migrant-workers-and-their-children

Clark, Peter. 1979. Migration in England in the During the Late Seventeenth and Early Eighteenth Centuries. *Past & Present* 83 (May): 57–90.

Cleaver, Harry. 1979. *Reading Capital Politically*. Austin: University of Texas Press.

Constant, Amelie, and Douglas S. Massey. 2002. Return migration by German Guestworkers: Neoclassical Versus New Economic Theories. *International Migration* 40 (4): 5–38.

Constantino, Grace. 2014. Five "Real" Sea Monsters Brought to Live by Early Naturalists. *Smithsonian,* October 27. Accessed August 4, 2018. https://www.smithsonianmag.com/science-nature/five-real-sea-monsters-brought-life-early-naturalists-180953155/

Coulton, G.G. 1919. *Social Life in Britain from the Conquest to the Reformation*. Cambridge: Cambridge University Press.

Craig, Richard B. 1971. *The Bracero Program*. Austin: University of Texas Press.

Curry, Andrew. 2021. These Ancient Weights Helped Create Europe's First Free Market More Than 3000 Years Ago. *Science*. June 28. Accessed June 28, 2021. https://www.sciencemag.org/news/2021/06/these-ancient-weights-helped-create-europe-s-first-free-market-more-3000-years-ago?utm_campaign=news_daily_2021-06-30&et_rid=17775700&et_cid=3832437

Curtin, Philip D. 1969. *The Atlantic Slave Trade: A Census*. Madison: University of Wisconsin Press.

Deane, P. 1979. *The First Industrial Revolution*, 2nd ed. Cambridge: Cambridge University Press.

De Vries, 1974. *The Dutch Rural Economy in the Golden Age, 1500–1700*. New Haven: Yale University Press.

Diamond, A.S. 2004. *Primitive Law, Past and Present*. New York: Routledge.

Dobb, Maurice. 1963. *Studies in the Development of Capitalism*. New York: International Publishers.

Donato, Katherine M., and Donna Gabaccia. 2015. *Gender and International Migration*. New York: Russell Sage Foundation.

Dunn, Richard C. 1972. *Sugar and Slaves: The Rise of the Planter Class in the English West Indies, 1624–1713*. New York: W. W. Norton & Company Inc.

Easterlin, Richard A., David Ward, William S. Bernard, and Reed Ueda. 1980. *Immigration*. Cambridge: Harvard University Press.

Eltis, David, and David Richardson. 2008. *Extending the Frontiers: Essays on the New Trans-Atlantic Slave Trade Database*. New Heaven, CT: Yale University Press.

Emmer, Pieter C. 1972. The History of the Dutch Slave Trade: A Bibliographical Survey. *Journal of Economic History* 32: 728–747.

Erickson, Charlotte. 1972. *Invisible Immigrants: The Adaptation of English and Scottish Immigrants in 19th Century America*. Coral Gables, FL: University of Miami Press.

Feagin, Joe R., and J. Cobas. 2014. *Latinos Facing Racism: Discrimination, Resistance, And Endurance*. Boulder, CO: Paradigm Publishers.

Fernández-Armesto, Felipe. 2008. *Amerigo: The Man Who Gave His Name to America*. New York: Random House.

FitzGerald, David, and David Cook-Martín. 2014. *Culling the Masses: The Democratic Origins of Racist Immigration Policy in the Americas*. Cambridge: Harvard University Press.

Flores-Yeffal, Nadia Y. 2013. *Migration Trust-Networks: Social Cohesion in Mexican US-Bound Emigration*. College Station: Texas A&M University Press.

Foster, John Bellamy. 2016. Monopoly Capital at the Half-Century Mark. *Monthly Review* 68 (3): 1–25.

Frank, Andre Gunder, and Barry K. Gills. 1993. *The World System: Five Hundred Years or Five Thousand?* London: Routledge.

Frank, Andre Gunder. 1969. *Latin America: Underdevelopment or Revolution*. New York: Monthly Review Press.

Frank, Andre Gunder. 1998. *ReORIENT: Global Economy in the Asian Age*. Berkeley: University of California Press.
Galeano, Eudardo. 1997. *Open Veins of Latin America: Five Centuries of the Pillage of a Continent*. New York: Monthly Review Press.
Ganshof, F.L. 1961. *Feudalism*. New York: Harper & Row, Publishers.
Garip, Filiz. 2017. *On the Move: Changing Mechanisms of Mexico-U.S. Migration*. Princeton: Princeton University Press.
Gibson, Charles. 1964. *The Aztecs Under Spanish Rule: A History of the Indians of the Valley of Mexico, 1519–1810*. Stanford: Stanford University Press.
Gordon, David M., Richard Edwards, and Michael Reich. 1982. *Segmented Work, Divided Workers: The Historical Transformation of Labor in the United States*. Cambridge: Cambridge University Press.
Grebler, Leo, Joan W. Moore, and Ralph C. Guzman. 1970. *The Mexican-American People, The Nation's Second Largest Minority*. New York: The Free Press.
Greene, Joshua. 2017. From Mexico to Hawaii: Tracing the Migration History of one Family in Esperanza, Jalisco. In *Deportation and Return in a Border-Restricted World: Experiences In Mexico, El Salvador, Guatemala, and Honduras*, ed. Bryan Roberts, Cecilia Menjívar, and Néstor. Rodríguez, 47–66. Switzerland: Springer.
Greenleaf, Barbara Kaye. 1970. *American Fever: The Story of American immigration*. New York: Four Winds Press.
Grinin, Leonid, Andrey Korotayev, and Arno Tausch. 2016. *Economic Cycles, Crises, and the Global Periphery*. Switzerland: Springer.
Hagan, Jacqueline. 1994. *Deciding to be Legal: A Maya Community in Houston*. Philadelphia: Temple University Press.
Hansen, M. 1961. *The Atlantic Migration 1607–1860*. New York: Harper & Row.
Harris, Katelyn. 2020. Forty Years of Falling Manufacturing Employment. *Beyond the Numbers* 9 (16). Accessed February 21, 2022. https://www.bls.gov/opub/btn/volume-9/forty-years-of-falling-manufacturing-employment.htm
Heer, Friedrich. 1962. *The Medieval World*. New York: The New American Library Inc.
Herlihy, David. 1965. Population, Plague, and Social Change in Rural Pistoia, 1201–1430. *The Economic History Review* 18 (2): 225–244.
Herlihy, David. 1967. *Medieval and Renaissance Pistoia: The Social History of an Italian Town, 1200–1430*. New Haven, CT: Yale University Press.
Hernández-León, Rubén. 2008. *Metropolitan Migrants: The Migration of Urban Mexicans to the United States*. Berkeley: University of California Press.
Hernández-León, Rubén. 2012. L'industrie de la migration. Organiser la mobilité dans le système migratoire Mexique-États-Unis. *Hommes et Migrations* 1296: 34–44.
Himmerich y Valencia, Robert. 1991. *The Encomenderos of New Spain, 1521–1555*. Austin: University of Texas Press.
Hobsbawn, Eric. 1976. From Feudalism to Capitalism. In *The Transition from Feudalism to Capitalism*, ed. R. Hilton, 159–164. London: New Left Books.
Hobsbawn, E.J. 1979. *The Age of Capital: 1848–1875*. New York: New American Library.
Hoerder, Dirk. 2002. *Cultures in Contact: World Migrations in the Second Millennium*. Durham: Duke University Press.
Hohenberg, Paul M., and Lynn Hollen Lees. 1985. *The Making of Urban Europe, 1000–1950*. Cambridge: Harvard University Press.
Hohn, Marcia D., Justin P. Lowry, James C. Witte, and José Ramón. Fernández. 2016. *Immigrants in Health Care*. Fairfax, VA: Institute for Immigration Research, George Mason University.
Jonas, Susanne, and Nestor Rodríguez. 2014. *Guatemala-U.S. Migration: Transforming Regions*. Austin: University of Texas Press.
Kandel, William A., and Ruth Ellen Wasem. 2016. *U.S. Immigration Policy: Chart Book of Key Trends*. Congressional Research Service. Washington, D.C. Accessed August 4, 2018. https://fas.org/sgp/crs/homesec/R42988.pdf

References

Kandel, William, and Emilio A. Parrado. 2005. Restructuring of the US Meat Processing Industry and New Hispanic Migrant Destinations. *Population and Development Review* 31 (3): 447–471.

Leal, David L., and Nestor Rodríguez, eds. 2016. *Migration in an Era of Restriction and Recession: Sending and Receiving Nations in a Changing Global Environment.* Switzerland: Springer.

Lee, Erika. 2003. *At America's Gates: Chinese Immigration During the Exclusion Era, 1882–1943.* Chapel Hill: University of North Carolina Press.

Lemann, Nicholas. 1992. *The Promised Land: The Great Black Migration and How it Changed America.* New York: Vintage Books.

Light, Ivan, and Edna Bonacich. 1988. *Immigrant Entrepreneurs: Koreans in Los Angeles 1965–1982.* Berkeley: University of California Press.

Manning, Patrick. 2020. *Migration in World History.* New York: Routledge.

Marx, Karl. 1967. *Capital*, vol. I. New York: International Publishers.

Marx, Karl, and Frederick Engels. 1976. *Manifesto of the Communist Party. Collected Works* of *Marx & Engels,* vol. 6. New York: International Publishers.

Matthew, Laura E., and Michel R. Oudijk, eds. 2007. *Indian Conquistadores: Indigenous Allies in the Conquest of Mesoamerica.* Norman: University of Oklahoma Press.

Meissner, Doris. 2004. *U.S. Temporary Worker Programs: Lessons Learned.* Migration Policy Institute. Washington, D.C., March 1. Accessed August 5, 2018. https://www.migrationpolicy.org/article/us-temporary-worker-programs-lessons-learned

Mize, Ronald L. 2016. *The Invisible Workers of the U.S.-Mexico Bracero Program: Obreros Olvidados.* Lanham, MD: Lexington Books.

Moch, Leslie Page. 2003. *Moving Europeans: Migration in Western Europe Since 1650.* Bloomington: Indiana University Press.

Mokyr, Joel. 2017. *A Culture of Growth: The Origins of the Modern Economy.* Princeton: Princeton University Press.

Panayi, Panikos. 1994. *Immigration, Ethnicity, and Racism in Britain, 1815–1945.* Manchester: Manchester University Press.

Peters, Margaret E. 2017. *Trading Barriers: Immigration and the Remaking of Globalization.* Princeton: Princeton University Press.

Piore, Michael. 1979. *Birds of Passage: Migrant Labor and Industrial Societies.* Cambridge: Cambridge University Press.

Pirenne, Henri. 1925. *Medieval Cities.* Garden City, NY: Doubleday & Company Inc.

Platt, Stephen R. 2018. *Imperial Twilight: The Opium War and the End of China's Last Golden Age.* New York: Alfred A. Knopf.

Polanyi, Karl. 2001. *The Great Transformation: The Political and Economic Origins of Our Time. 2001.* Boston: Beacon Press.

Pollard, Sidney. 1978. Labour in Great Britain. In *The Cambridge Economic History of Europe,* vol. VII, *The Industrial Economies: Capital, Labor, and Enterprise (I),* ed. Peter Mathias and M. M. Postan, 97–179. Cambridge: Cambridge University Press.

Poole, Stafford. 1963. The Church and the Repartimientos in the Light of the Third Mexican Council, 1585. *The Americas* 20 (1): 3–35.

Portes, Alejandro, and Robert D. Manning. 1986. The Immigrant Enclave: Theory and Empirical Examples. In *Competitive ethnic relations,* ed. J. Nagel and S. Olzak, 47–68. New York: Academic Press.

Portes, Alejandro, and Rubén G. Rumbaut. 2014. *Immigrant America: A Portrait,* 4th ed. Oakland, CA: University of California Press.

Postan, M.M. 1972. *The Medieval Economy and Society.* New York: Penguin Books Ltd.

Qiu, Jane. 2016. How China is Rewriting the Book on Human Origins. *Nature* 535: 22–25.

Redford, Arthur. 1968. *Labor Migration in England, 1800–1850.* New York: Augustus M. Kelly Publishers.

Rendall, Michael S., Peter Brownell, and Sarah Kups. 2011. Declining Return Migration from the United States to Mexico in the Late-2000s Recession: A Research Note. *Demography* 48 (3): 1049–1058.

Rodriguez, Nestor, and Jacqueline Hagan. 2016. U.S. Policies to Restrict Immigration. In *Migration in an Era of Restriction and Recession: Sending and Receiving Nations in a Changing Global Environment*, ed. David L. Leal and Nestor Rodriguez, 27–38. Switzerland: Springer.

Rostow, W.W. 1978. *The World Economy: History & Prospect*. Austin: University of Texas Press.

Sanderson, Stephen K. 1999. *Social Transformation: A General Theory of Historical Development*. Lanham, MD: Rowman & Littlefield Publishers Inc.

Sassen, Saskia. 2006. *Territory, Authority, Rights: From Medieval to Global Assemblages*. Princeton: Princeton University Press.

Sassen-Koob, Saskia. 1984. The New Labor Demand in Global Cities. In *Cities in Transformation: Class, Capital, and the State*. ed. Michael Peter Smith, 139–171. Beverley Hills: Sage Publications.

Slicher Van Bath, B. H. 1963. *The Agrarian History of Western Europe*. New York: St. Martin's Press, Inc.

Smith, Roger C. 1993. *Vanguard of Empire: Ships of Exploration in the Age of Columbus*. Oxford: Oxford University Press.

Stark, Oded, and David E. Bloom. 1985. The New Economics of Labor Migration. *The American Economic Review* 75 (2): 173–178.

Tilly, Charles. 1979. From the Metropolitan Enigma: Race and Migration to the American City. In *Urban Scene: Myths and Realities*, ed. Joe R. Feagin, 188–207. New York: Random House.

Trading Economics. 2020. *Mexico Minimum Daily Wage*. Accessed October 3, 2020. https://tradingeconomics.com/mexico/minimum-wages

US Census Bureau. 1974. *Current Population Reports*, Series P-23, No. 49. *Population of the United States, Trends and Prospects: 1950–1990*. Washington, D.C.: Government Printing Office.

US Immigration and Naturalization Service (INS). 2002. *2000 Statistical Yearbook of the Immigration and Naturalization Service*. Washington, D.C.: Government Printing Office.

Vlekke, Bernard H. M. 1945. *The Story of the Dutch East Indies*. Cambridge: Harvard University Press.

Wacquant, Loïc. 2008. *Urban Outcasts: A Comparative Sociology of Advanced Marginality*. Cambridge: Polity Press.

Wagret, Paul. 1968. *Polderlands*. London: Methuen & Co.

Waldinger, Roger. 1993. The Ethnic Enclave Debate Revisited. *International Journal of Urban and Regional Research* 17 (3): 444–452.

Waley, Daniel. 1969. *The Italian city-republics*. New York: McGraw-Hill.

Wallerstein, Immanuel. 1974. *The Modern World System: Capitalist Agriculture and the Origins Of The European World-Economy in the Seventeenth Century*. New York: Academic Press.

Wallerstein, Immanuel. 1976. From Feudalism to Capitalism: Transition or Transitions? *Social Forces* 55 (2): 273–283.

Wallerstein, Immanuel. 1979. *The Capitalist World-Economy*. London: Cambridge University Press.

Wallerstein, Immanuel. 1980. *The Modern World-System II: Mercantilism and the Consolidation of the European World-Economy, 1600–1750*. New York: Academic Press Inc.

Wallerstein, Immanuel. 2006. The Curve of American Power. *New Left Review* 40: 77–94.

Wallerstein, Immanuel. 1992. The West, Capitalism, and the Modern World-System. *Review* 15 (4): 561–619.

Wallerstein, Immanuel. 1993. World System Versus World-Systems: A Critique. In *The World System: Five Hundred Years or Five Thousand?*, ed. Andre Gunder Frank and Barry K. Gills, 292–296. London: Routledge.

Whewell, C. S. 1977. Textile Industry. *Encyclopaedia Britannica*. 15th ed, vol. 18, 170–189.

Williams, Eric. 1966. *Capitalism & Sugar*. New York: Capricorn Book Editions.

Wrigley, E.A. 1969. *Population and History*. New York: McGraw Hill Book Company.

Xie, Yu, and Margaret Gough. 2011. Ethnic Enclaves and the Earnings of Immigrants. *Demography*, *48* (4): 1293–1315.

Capital Migration and Florentine Dominance in the European Medieval Wool Industry

This chapter analyzes the dominant rise of Florentine merchant-bankers in the wool commerce of Catholic Europe in the thirteenth and early fourteenth centuries. The rise to dominance in the wool trade enabled the simultaneous rise of Florentine merchant-bankers as major financiers for royalty and the papacy in Europe.[1] This Florentine capitalist development predated the emergence of the Genoese systemic cycle of capital accumulation described by Arrighi (2010) by two hundred years. The economic dominance of Florence in the wool trade and in finance in the thirteenth and early fourteenth centuries created some of the original interregional circuits of capital accumulation in Europe.

I refer to the Florentine superiority in the wool trade and high finance in Catholic Europe as dominance rather than as hegemony because the Florentine superior standing concerned only the business sphere and did not involve military dominance abroad, as would occur in the Dutch, British, and US periods of hegemony that followed. Moreover, the Florentines did not make imperial claims to lands outside their city-state. Capital migration abroad from Florence by merchant-bankers was at the base of the Florentine dominant economic development.

Regional trade and finance appeared in populations long before the rise of capitalism (Lopez 1967; Abu-Lughod 1989). What distinguished the Florentine dominant rise as particularly capitalistic, and as a source of proto-development of the world-system, were the drive to accumulate capital ceaselessly for the sake of accumulation and the systemic tendency to expand the circuits of accumulation in Europe and adjacent regions. The Florentine amassing of great quantities of wool through interregional trade and finance in the thirteenth and early fourteenth centuries led to a class struggle in Florence between capitalist entrepreneurs and

---

[1] Arrighi (2010) credits the Florentine financiers as the inventors of high finance "in its modern, capitalist form… during the late thirteenth and early fourteenth centuries." According to Arrighi, this development occurred during the trade expansion of the same time period.

© The Author(s), under exclusive license to Springer Nature Switzerland AG 2023
N. Rodriguez, *Capitalism and Migration*, World-Systems Evolution and Global Futures, https://doi.org/10.1007/978-3-031-22067-8_2

propertyless workers to restructure much of the woolen industry in the city-state into a capitalist mode of production.

While theories of the transition to capitalism look at processes that traversed in the slow pace of historical social change (e.g., see Wallerstein 1992; Sanderson 1999), as the discussion below will describe, the financial pressures of a pope, including a need to finance a conflict with a Holy Roman Emperor, initiated the chain of events that transformed much of the Florentine woolen industry into a capitalist class structure beginning in the 1200s. The chain of political and economic events that brought about full-blown capitalist woolen production in Florence occurred centuries before the fifteenth century, which world-system analysts depict as the beginning of the transition to capitalism in Europe. Moreover, the early emergence of Florentine capitalist production and finance predated the rise of Protestantism in the sixteenth century, which some analysts associate with the rise of capitalism.

Wallerstein's views of the significance of capitalistic ("proto-capitalist") conditions in the medieval era appear to have changed in his writing. In an early analysis of the medieval prelude to the capitalist world-system, Wallerstein refers to occurrences of these conditions in the Mediterranean region during 1150–1300 as "abortive" transformations (Wallerstein 1976: 276). In later analysis, however, he acknowledges that historical systems earlier than the capitalist world-economy had "proto-capitalist elements," "extensive commodity production," "investment of capital," "wage labor," and so forth, but according to Wallerstein the elements did not coalesce into a genuine capitalist system driven by the pursuit of ceaseless capital accumulation (Wallerstein 1992: 589). Wallerstein's characterization of the medieval pre-stage of capitalism resembles Marx's (1967: 715) depiction of medieval traces of capitalist production as occurring "as early as the fourteenth or fifteenth century, sporadically, in certain towns of the Mediterranean." But Marx (1967: 715) did not view these medieval traces as part of the "capitalist era," which he viewed as beginning in the sixteenth century, when the Middle Ages had mostly disappeared.

In contrast to the views of Wallerstein (1992) and Marx (1967), in this chapter I view the appearances of medieval or pre-stage conditions of capitalist production as *a decisive phase of class struggle* between employers and workers that enabled the transition to capitalist production when the former group prevailed. Much of the discussion of the transition to capitalism focuses on the rural transition from feudalism to capitalist agriculture (e.g., Dobb 1963; Marx 1967; Wallerstein 1974), but, as this chapter will describe, in the medieval, transregional woolen economy the transition to the social relations of capitalist production also occurred in urban areas. This was a decisive phase because in the cities and towns craftworker guilds directly, and at times militantly, confronted the transition to capitalist production, which represented the end of the power of craftworkers to control work. A key part of the struggle concerned the ability of employers to circumvent or in other ways successfully confront the power of the craft guilds in order to organize economic production with propertyless wage labor. Emerging capitalist entrepreneurs in Florence directly took on the dominant woolen craft guild to displace the craftworkers from control of woolen production. Undoubtedly experiences with prior conflicts, such as in wars with other city-states, motivated the emerging Florentine capitalist entrepreneurs to take drastic political action against the woolen craftworkers.

The focus in this chapter on a beginning of European capitalist development in the thirteenth century has a long historical reach: some 300 years before the beginning of the Protestant Reformation. Given Max Weber's popular thesis of the Protestant ethic and capitalist development, some historical analysts may raise issues with conceptualizing about capitalist development in this early time and setting dominated by Catholic traditional values. Weber (1958) characterized Protestant qualities, such as Calvinistic ethics, ascetic values, and dedication to work, as "the spirit of capitalism," and some scholars have viewed these Protestant characterizations as the foundation of modern capitalism.

Generations of university students have been taught in introductory sociology courses the notion that, according to Weber, Protestantism (Calvinism) enabled or even created capitalism. Weber's writings are canon in classical sociology, and thus, even some leading sociologists have deferred to his ideas of the influence of Protestant attitudes on capitalist development. Wallerstein (1992: 598), for example, takes Luciano Pellicani to task for arguing that capitalism begun in Italy (a Catholic country) without addressing "the Weber argument on the critical importance of the Protestant ethic." Yet, as Weber (1958: 64–65) explained, the capitalist form of an enterprise and its operating spirit have "some sort of adequate relationship to each other, but not one of necessary interdependence," and both could "very well occur separately." Weber's main argument was not that Protestant (Calvinistic) attitudes were the determinant of capitalism, but that Western enterprises of modern capitalism reached their "most suitable motive force" when they became imbued with the Protestant ethic (1958: 65). By comparison, according to Weber (1958), capitalist conditions in non-Protestant countries remained ethically inferior and backward.

Notwithstanding the Weberian thesis, in this chapter I will describe the material involvement of the Roman Catholic Church in the development of a capitalist class structure in Florence that occurred hundreds of years before the rise of Protestantism. Indeed, I will describe how papal tax revenues collected in Catholic lands in the 1200s became the original sources of capital accumulation that led to the development of capitalist production in Florence. From this perspective, thus, it was the financial need of the Catholic hierarchy, and not Protestantism, that brought about in a material manner the early rise of capitalism in Europe.

2.1 Business Migration, Papal Revenue Collection, and Capital Accumulation

Facing rising financial costs related to crusades to the Holy Land, an on-again–off-again war with the emperor Frederick II, and other financial obligations, Pope Gregory IX and his successors contracted Italian merchant-bankers in the thirteenth century as revenue agents to collect tithes and other revenues owed the papacy by members of royalty and clergy, and by lay persons (Lunt 1965). The Italian merchant-bankers were hired by the Pope from cities throughout Italy, but eventually merchant-bankers from Florence became among the most powerful revenue agents in the papal service. Their roles as *camsores papae*, that is, as papal revenue collectors, and as papal bankers placed them in an advantaged business position in the growing European wool trade. The Guelph-Ghibelline Wars between supporters of the papacy and supporters of the Hohenstaufen family of German emperors divided Italy at the time,[2] and Pope Gregory IX and his successors in the thirteenth century favored pro-Guelph merchant families, and especially those in Florence, to assist in the administration of revenue collections (Schevill 1963).

Many of the wealthy business families in medieval Italy had started out by participating in trading organizations.[3] In coastal cities, where trading was oriented toward sea travel, investors in a temporary association called a *commenda* or a *collegantia* would pursue a particular venture in the risky sea commerce and divide up the profits after completion of the venture (Ferguson 1962). In cities inland, the *campagnia* was the common trading organization, consisting of long-term partnerships of shared responsibility and risks. By the middle of the thirteenth century, some of the simple trade organizations had developed into major commercial firms. According to Sapori (1970), among the most financially powerful of these family firms were the Florentine families of the Bardi, the Frescobaldi, and the Peruzzi.[4] These family companies were involved in woolen commerce and moneylending and had branch offices in many places in the Christian and Moslem worlds. For example, the Bardi family company had branch offices in Italy in Ancona, Aquila, Bari, Barletta, Castello, di Castro, Genoa, Naples, Orvieto, Palermo, Pisa, and Venice. Outside Italy, the family business migration opened offices in Avignon, Barcelona, Bruges, Cyprus, Constantinople, Jerusalem, London, Majorca, Nice, Paris, Rhodes, Seville, and Tunis (Sapori 1970).

The expansion of Italian commerce outside Italy by business family members who migrated "in great numbers across the different countries of Europe" produced an administrative infrastructure that popes used for revenue collection and transportation (Sapori 1970: 80). Eventually, the revenue roles of the Italian

---

[2] In Florence the conflict was especially bitter, as city officials and merchants tended to side with the Guelph in support of the Papacy, and members of the nobility sided with the Ghibelline side in support of the German empire. The basic contention, however, was the issue of communal independence for Florence, according to Sapori (1970).

[3] While these early investment groups had a simple temporary organization, they used sophisticated risk transfer contracts and "sea loans" that took into account "moral hazards" for insurance purposes (Bell et al. 2007: 7).

[4] Lopez (1967) describes the wealthiest Florentine trading families as having no parallel in other countries. The Bardi and the Peruzzi, two of the richest merchant families in the woolen industry of Florence, had a capital worth of 875,000 and 100,000 florins, respectively (Lopez and Miskimin 1962; Lopez 1967). Lopez describes the significance of this wealth by stating that in 1348 Pope Clement VI bought Avignon for his capital from the queen of Naples for 80,000 florins and that the following year the king of France bought Montpellier (the most important town on the Mediterranean coast between Marseilles and Barcelona) for 133,000 florins (Lopez 1967).

merchant-bankers increased their powers as traders and financiers "in the entire area from Constantinople and Alexandria in the east to Bruges and London in the west" (De Roover 1965: 49–51).

Popes assigned the Italian tax agents to different areas of the Christian world and changed the assignments based on shifting political alliances of the Italian families in the Guelph-Ghibelline conflict or based on the personal preferences of the popes. In the 1270s, Pope Nicolas III assigned the Florentine business families of the Alfani and the Frescobaldi to collect the revenues from the Germanic areas, and assigned the Battosi and the Caccianimici of Lucca to collect the tax revenues in Portugal, Sardinia, and Corsica (Sapori 1970). The Ricciardi of Lucca were assigned to England. In 1281, Pope Martin IV changed assignments and gave the responsibility of England and Scotland to a group of six Florentine merchant families, which included the woolen merchants of the Spini and the Frescobaldi families (Sapori 1970). Undoubtedly, the Florentine merchant-bankers involved in the woolen industry lobbied the papacy to get the assignments in England, given its large supply of high-quality wool.

Italian business families drew several major business advantages serving as papal revenue agents. In addition to their commissions for services rendered and the gains from monetary exchanges from foreign to Italian currency, the Italian revenue collectors were given the protection of the Church in all their travels (Sapori 1970). This was an important benefit in the medieval days of regional hostilities and suspicion of outsiders. As agents of the pope, the Italians gained access to foreign governments, and acting as financiers they made large loans to governments and royal families (Sapori 1955; Hunt 1990). For example, during their assignment as tax collectors in England, the woolen merchant families of the Frescobaldi, the Bardi, and the Peruzzi made extensive loans to the English crown to finance military campaigns in Scotland and France (Gimpel 1976).[5] In many countries, the Italian revenue collectors also were appointed by crown officials to important government positions, such as ambassadors, directors of the mints, and treasurers (Sapori 1970). According to Sapori (1970: 79), on seeing that the ambassadors of foreign countries who visited him were all Florentines, Pope Boniface VIII exclaimed: "These Florentines are truly the fifth element of the universe!" In their foreign governmental posts, the Italian merchants had the advantages of accessing commercial and financial information, and the possibility of influencing foreign policies to benefit their trading activities.

The principal advantage, however, that the Italian woolen merchants derived from their positions as papal revenue agents was that they gained direct access to the largest suppliers of wool (Ferguson 1962; Bell et al. 2007). Moreover, the tax revenues they collected constituted a large pool of capital that they used in their international business dealings, given that the revenue payments were not

---

[5] Lending to royal members could lead to bad results for Italian banking families if royal debtors refused to pay back the loans. Loan defaults by royal members might not have caused Italian moneylenders to go bankrupt, but it could add to a list of deficits that caused some Italian business families to go broke (Bell et al. 2007).

immediately turned over to the financial offices of the popes. As described by Ferguson (1962), tax revenues collected in England were used by the Italian papal agents to buy and export English wool and unfinished cloth to Flanders and Italy, where the materials were made into a finished product and re-exported at a profit. The papal tax revenues were submitted by a simple transfer of funds or credits from the main offices in Italy to Rome or Avignon.

In the thirteenth and fourteenth centuries, England, with its bountiful supply of fine wool, was a major attraction for Italian woolen merchants.[6] Coming to England in the second half of the thirteenth century as papal revenue collectors, Italian wool merchants, including the Riccardi of Lucca and the Frescobaldi, Bardi, and Peruzzi of Florence, entered the English wool trade and dominated it for fifty years after 1280 (Hodgett 1972). With their powerful financial strength, and the help of an English royal ban against wool merchants from Flanders, the Italians displaced Flemish and other foreign merchants from prosperous positions in wool and cloth trading in England and in other places of Europe by buying wool supplies years in advance (Gimpel 1976; Ferguson 1962). The Italians contracted to buy wool twenty years in advance with the biggest producers in Britain, such as the Cistercian and Premonstratensian monasteries (Hodgett 1972; Bell et al. 2007). By 1294, the Italians were buying wool from 49 of the 74 Cistercian monasteries in England (Bell et al. 2007). After dominating the English wool trade, the Florentine merchant-bankers continued to export wool to manufacturing cities in Flanders. But by the end of the thirteenth century, Italians woolen merchants were sending increasing supplies of wool to the developing woolen industry in Florence (Schevill 1963).

Trade and finance were integrated in the Italian merchant-bankers' process of wealth accumulation, in which wealth acted as capital for business expansion. The unity of trade and finance can be illustrated by the business activities of the Italian tax collectors in England (see Ferguson 1962). Often when an English monastery was presented with a tax bill the abbot was unable to pay. The Italian tax collector, acting as a financier, then made a loan to the monastery which was later paid in wool (Britnell 2004).[7] When a monastery had enough wool to pay the taxes without a loan, the abbot simply sold the wool to the Italian agent to get money to pay the tax due. Tax payments with and without the use of loans, thus, consisted of the abbots handing over an amount of wool to the Italians and the latter making a credit transfer from their main offices in Italy to the pope in Rome or Avignon.

---

[6] "During the Middle Ages Britain grew the wool with the finest fibres, and this fetched the highest price since the supply did not meet the demand "(Ryder 1984: 24). According to Ryder (1984), an apparent uniqueness of one type of fine English wool was its longer length, which could be combed to make worsteds. Genetic and nutritional conditions affected wool quality, making the richer British pasture a probable reason for the higher quality English wool (Ryder 1984).

[7] Since the loans specified the exchange rates and date of exchange to be used in the future payments, Bell et al. (2007: 7) refer to the Italian moneylenders as being at "the forefront of the development of... early derivative markets."

Members of royalty sometimes paid loans to the Italian financiers in wool as well, since some of the crown's wool tax was paid in kind (Gras 1918).

Moneylending for profit violated church canon against usury and was punishable by excommunication.[8] To cover their risks of church sanctions against usury, and because money was scarce, Italian merchant-bankers charged 30–40% interest rates (Schevill 1963). Among other ways, the Italian financiers circumvented church law against moneylending for profit by making loan contracts for an amount greater than the loan to hide the interest. Sometimes kings and other members of royal families paid, or promised to pay, interest hidden in contracts as "gifts" or "damages" to circumvent usury prohibitions (Hunt 1990).[9] With the rise of commerce in the thirteenth and fourteenth centuries, finance became commonly practiced in Europe with a distinction between legitimate interest and usury, and popes, bishops, and other clergy, as well as members of royalty, became regular borrowers (Schevill 1963). The elevation of the Italian merchant-bankers to papal revenue collectors increased their status from local bankers to "world-bankers" in Europe (Schevill 1963: 295).

Before proceeding to a description of the Florentine woolen merchant-bankers' restructuring of artisan textile production in Florence to capitalist production, the next section briefly describes the woolen textile industry in the three regions of Flanders, Italy, and England. The description lays out the early interconnections of the regional system in western Europe that undergirded the rise to woolen capitalist production in Florence. That is to say, from its early inception in a medieval prelude stage, capitalism developed through the dynamics of an interregional economy, and not through the social forces of a solitary culture.

2.2 Three Major European Areas of Woolen Production

Flanders, Italy, and England had the largest concentrations of woolen production in Europe in the late Middle Ages. The centers of woolen textile production included Ghent and Ypres in Flanders, Florence and Milan in Italy, and Northampton and London in England. In terms of sizes, the textile workforces in these urban centers were relatively small, since in the whole of Europe the urban population in this period never exceeded 10% of the total population (Pirenne 1937; Sjoberg 1960). Florence and Ghent, two of the largest textile production centers in medieval Europe, had textile workforces in the 1300s of about 30,000 and 25,000 workers, respectively (Gimpel 1976; Lopez 1967).

---

[8] Some priests would not give the final sacrament to moneylenders on their deathbeds until they arranged to return the interests paid by clients, or gave the ill-gotten gains to the church (Schevill 1963).

[9] A detailed study by Dorothy Hughes in the early twentieth century of historical records of the English wool trade concluded that there was widespread "cheating" and "swindling," including by Italian merchant-bankers (see Hunt 1990: 158–9).

The woolen industries in Flanders, Italy, and England were interrelated, and partly because of this relationship, the three areas enjoyed different periods of prosperity in woolen production. English wool was exported to Flanders and Italy for cloth production, and cloth manufactured in Flanders was sometimes exported to Italy for finishing processes, such as for fulling and dyeing (Hodgett 1972). The areas were also interrelated through the migration of Flemish woolen workers. Banished from Flanders because of their revolts, many of these workers migrated to England and some to Italy (Gimpel 1976). Finally, and very importantly, Italian banking capital contributed heavily to the development of the wool trade in England.

Of the three areas, Flanders was the first to reach its height of prosperity in woolen manufacturing. This prosperity lasted from the late twelfth century to the beginning of the fourteenth century (Hodgett 1972). But because of difficulties with English wool embargoes, interferences of the French crown in the Champagne fairs, and worker unrest, Flemish textile production declined in the early 1300s (Gimpel 1976). By the 1330s Italy, particularly Florence, achieved dominance in European clothing production. However, by the late fourteenth century, when the control of the English wool trade shifted to native hands, England took the lead in cloth production (Hodgett 1972). In so doing, its woolen industrial involvement changed from being primarily an exporter of wool to a producer of woolen cloth. While England's export of wool decreased by one-half (from 35,000 to 17,000 wool sacks per year[10]) in the last half of the fourteenth century, its production of cloth increased by 300%, to 45,000 pieces of cloth per year (Lopez and Miskimin 1962).

From a political-economic systems perspective, England went from being a peripheral source of raw wool in the interregional wool economy to becoming a core area of woolen production. As long as control of the English wool trade was in the hands of foreigners such as Italian merchant-bankers, England's primary role in the European wool economy was to provide raw wool to foreign manufacturing centers. But once the foreign production centers declined, and the English took control of the English wool trade, woolen production in England increased. This medieval situation of English woolen industrial development is suggestive of the dependency model of development that was constructed in the late twentieth century to describe underdeveloped economic conditions caused by foreign intervention in countries at the periphery of the world-economy (Cardoso and Faletto 1979).

---

[10] Carus-Wilson (1954) states that the actual amounts may be larger if the wool that was not passed through customs (to avoid taxes) is considered. Each wool sack weighed 365 lbs.

2.3 Capitalist Production and Class Structure in the Woolen Industry

The emergence of merchant-capitalists in Italy did not occur from a radical transformation of the previous putting-out system of artisan production. Instead, cloth-producing entrepreneurs acquired their capitalist status because of their gradual expansion in the control of cloth production.[11] This change can perhaps be understood as a quantitative–qualitative transformation where degrees of change result in a new quality.[12] Moreover, there is nothing to indicate that an ideological or conscious spirit of capitalism drove the merchant-entrepreneurs' to restructure production with owners/employers and wage labor. Capitalism had not existed before in industrial production, and thus, there was nothing to emulate. The word "capitalism" did not even exist. Until new historical evidence emerges to the contrary, we can assume that the woolen merchant-capitalists of Florence were among the original designers of the new capitalist system of industrial production.

Drawing from historical sources (e.g., Staley 1906; Carus-Wilson 1952; Hodgett 1972), the transformation of woolen production in Florence from the putting-out system based on artisan production to capitalist production using wage labor can be summarized as follows. In the late Middle Ages, cloth merchants belonging to family firms bought woolen cloth produced in town and rural households and sold the material in local markets and fairs abroad. Eventually, the merchants bought the wool themselves and put it out to artisan workshops where it was made into cloth. From the weaver workshops, the merchants next took the cloth to the shops of fullers and dyers. In this putting-out system of production the merchants cannot be considered capitalists because (1) they do not control the means of production (these are controlled by the craftworkers); (2) they lack an economic-class condition (the identity is mainly with the family unit and the determinants of social status are mainly family linage and position in the polity); and (3) there is an absence (or very low level) of capital accumulation derived from surplus value (textile production on an expanding scale is impossible, or very limited, given a static number of workshops and a limited amount of labor time that craftworkers are willing to devote to cloth production, fulling, etc.).

The merchants' acquisition of a capitalist status in Florence occurred as the following conditions developed over time. Firstly, the merchants created trade organizations (guilds) to further their collective interests through organizational

---

[11] While the entrepreneurs in cloth-production acquired a capitalist role in manufacturing, they did not acquire an identity as manufacturers. According to Schevill (1963: 298), "the leading men of [Florence] always presented themselves to view not as industrialists but as merchants."

[12] I have in mind Hegel's description of qualitative change as consisting of an alteration of a quantitative condition. To illustrate, Hegel (1975: 158–159) comments on the conversion of water into steam or ice as follows: "A quantitative change takes place, apparently without any further significance but there is something lurking behind, and a seemingly innocent change of quantity acts as a kind of snare, to catch hold of the quality."

codes and enactments of industrial regulations and labor-control laws. The important point here is that the merchants used their unity as a class to further their economic interests, particularly in relation to labor. Secondly, through their organizational laws, the merchants gained control of some of the instruments of production (e.g., cloth-stretching frames and fulling equipment). Control was obtained both by direct ownership and by enacting ordinances that regulated the artisans' use of their own tools. Thirdly, the merchants added a new item to the list of commodities they bought for production—wage labor. Instead of buying all the cloth from artisan producers, the merchants now hired workers, by the day or week, to produce cloth. It is important to understand that at this point in the late 1200s the merchant–entrepreneurs did not hire wage workers for all the work involved in cloth production. Of the many tasks involved in cloth production, they hired wage workers mainly for the work needing less skill (e.g., foot fulling).

The wage workers, who were also employed by the bigger cloth artisans, came from the ranks of propertyless apprentices, journeymen, and migrants from rural areas. By the early 1300s, these workers constituted a permanent class of producers who subsist only through the sale of their labor power. Depending on the area, different reasons existed for why journeymen and apprentices were not able to ascend to artisan status. In Florence, one reason was that artisans attempted to limit their own numbers in order to increase their value. Eventually, as the cloth merchants increased their manufacturing role, even some of the poorer artisans fell into the ranks of wage workers. Finally, by the 1330s, the merchant-capitalists in Florence operating in an organized class-for-itself manner so dominated the social relations of production between themselves and waged artisans and laborers that the woolen industry took on a significant capitalist character.

In the presentation below, the capitalist development of the Florentine woolen industry is described from the perspectives of the emergence of organized merchant-capitalists, the appropriation of artisan production, and the employment of propertyless wage workers. As explained below, Florence developed the highest level of capitalist organization the earliest, compared with Flanders and England. By the early 1300s, when Flemish woolen merchants still depended on artisans to hire and supervise the woolen workers, and when England was still primarily an exporter of raw wool, the Florentine cloth-manufacturers were directly employing through wages much of the textile labor force in their city.

2.3.1 Emergence of Merchant-Capitalists

Florentine woolen production in the thirteenth and fourteenth centuries was organized and controlled by the powerful *Arte della Lana* (the Guild of Wool) of merchant-entrepreneurs (Schevill 1963). The Arte was the organizational domain of merchants in Florence who became involved in the production of woolen cloth

2.3 Capitalist Production and Class Structure in the Woolen Industry

using imported wool.[13] Through the Arte, the merchants acquired a capitalistic role as they coordinated and monopolized the activities involved in producing woolen cloth. The Arte used the Code of Statues and the Court of Consuls to bolster its industrial domination (Staley 1906). The Code of Statues consisted of civil and criminal laws adopted by all the Florentine guilds in 1301–1309, and it was the regulatory source for all the economic and moral behavior within and between guilds. The Court of Consuls consisted of eight appointed master-merchants, and it had civil and criminal jurisdiction over all persons associated with the woolen industry (Staley 1906).

Membership in the Arte was based on qualifications of birth, education and parental income (Staley 1906). Workers were affiliated with the Arte in a subordinated status. The main subordinated groups of workers were as follows (Staley 1906; 142):

Shearers	Winders
Washers	Master-planners
Sorters	Carding-machine oilers
Carders	Combers
Spinners	Beaters
Weavers	Comb makers
Fullers	Curriers
Dyer	

Although they were subject to the Arte, these subordinated groups were excluded from participating in the decision-making of the guild. The forced affiliation of worker groups with the Arte appears to have been a tactic to prevent workers from also working for the Guild of Calimala, a guild of business families that dealt with the finishing of imported foreign cloth (Edler 1934).

In the division of labor of the Florentine woolen industry, the merchant-entrepreneurs had the tasks of buying wool and coordinating its circulation through the woolen production processes. Unlike members of the Calimala, the woolen merchants of the Arte did not travel abroad in search of raw materials. They obtained their wool supply and sold their wool products through firms that specialized in foreign trade (Hodgett 1972).

Apart from their activities in the division of labor of woolen production, the Florentine merchant-capitalists were also involved in acquiring ownership of the instruments of production. Of the 300 woolen workshops reported by a Florentine accountant and chronicler, Giovanni Villani,[14] to have existed in Florence in the first decade of the 1300s, many of the larger ones were owned by the Arte

---

[13] Prior to the rise in power of the Arte della Lana, the Arte de Calimala, which was a guild of merchant importers of Flemish and French cloth for finishing in Florence, had dominated the woolen-cloth industry in Florence in the 1200s (Schevill 1963).

[14] Villani's accounts are central to the historiography of Florence in the trecento (see Sapori 1970).

merchant-capitalists (Villani 1823). Some of these workshops were former church buildings, such as the monastery of Santa Maria della Disciplina, acquired by Arte merchants, sometimes through loan defaults, to house spinners and weavers. In addition, the Arte owned six large cloth-stretching areas around Florence (Staley 1906).

In the first decade of the trecento, the Florentine merchant-capitalists coordinated a level of production of more than 100,000 woolen pieces annually (Villani 1823). By 1315, the wool suppliers for the Florentine woolen industry included some 200 monasteries throughout Flanders, France, Portugal, Spain, and especially England. By comparison, in 1330 Ypres in Flanders had a production level of about 75,000 pieces annually, and England had a production level of fewer than 5000 pieces annually (Lopez and Miskimin 1962).

2.3.2 Expropriation of Artisan Production

The situation of the artisans in the Florentine woolen industry in the early 1300s can be described as contradictory and precarious. It was contradictory because, although the artisans owned the instruments of labor in the production stages not yet expropriated by the merchant-capitalists, their power within the woolen industry declined drastically (see Carus-Wilson 1952; Ferguson 1962). It was precarious because more and more the artisans became employees of the merchant-capitalists. In sum, it was a situation in which the woolen artisans lost control of the production process to the Arte. To understand the significance of this subordination, it is necessary to give some description of the Florentine woolen industry prior to the fourteenth century.

Early documents concerning the woolen industry in Tuscany indicate that in several towns and villages the majority of inhabitants were working in woolen production by the ninth century and that by the year 846 CE several woolen trade associations existed in the region (Staley 1906). There is mention of the Arte della Lana in Florence by the year 1212. The year 1238, however, is perhaps a more significant date in the history of the Florentine woolen industry because it is the year that the *Umiliati*, the Humble Fathers of Saint Michael of Alexandria, migrated to Florence and established their woolen industry in the city (Staley 1906).

Soon after arriving in Florence, the Umiliati acquired properties (e.g., convents and monasteries) for use as workshops and housing quarters for the families of workers that migrated with the Order (Staley 1906). In the 1250s, the Umiliati expanded their manufacturing areas with the building of more workshops, warehouses, and quarters for workers on the riverbanks of the Arno. With an increase in production, the Umiliati promoted the development of a bridge across the river in order to provide access to the workshops to people living in three poor suburbs. In the 1260s, the government of Florence gave permission to the Umiliati to expand their manufacturing to islands in the Arno. By the end of the thirteenth century, however, the industrial development of the Umiliati slowed down, and in 1330, the Order closed its workshops.[15]

The Umiliati likely provided an advantageous situation to the Florentine woolen artisans because the Order attracted both commerce and labor to Florence. But perhaps more beneficial for the artisans, the Umiliati very likely delayed the woolen merchants' rise to dominance in the industry. The promptness and facility of the monks in acquiring properties and expanding their manufacturing to the adjacent Florentine countryside indicated that they enjoyed substantial influence with the Florentine government and the local bishopric, and thus slowed the rise to power of the woolen merchants. After the decline of the Umiliati, the Florentine government and the local bishopric became allies of the Arte merchants (Carus-Wilson 1952).

The initial attempt of the Arte to subordinate the woolen artisans occurred in 1236 when the *Buonuomini* (representatives of city wards) met with merchants to decide on the rank and structure of the guilds in Florence (Staley 1906). Based on their collaboration with the merchants, the Buonuomini ruled that the city's guilds would be classified into two categories of different importance. The seven wealthiest and more influential guilds (e.g., the Guild of Judges and Notaries, the Arte della Lana, and the Guild of Bakers and Money-Changers) were classified "*Le Arti Maggiori,*" (the Greater Guilds), and the less influential guilds of shopkeepers and artisans (e.g., butchers, carpenters, and bakers) were classified as "*Le Arti Minori,*" (the Lesser Guilds) (Staley 1906). The critical significance of this determination of guild ordering for the woolen artisans was that they were not assigned to either of the two guild categories. In short, the woolen artisans were forced out of their trade associations and placed under the authority of the woolen merchants (see Hauser 1951; Schevill 1963).

Thirty years after the classification of the guilds, fighting between Guelph and Ghibelline groups in the commune severely weakened the government of the Buonuomini. In 1268, King Charles of Anjou took over the position of chief magistrate and added to the Buonuomini an advisory council composed exclusively of merchants from the Arti Maggiori (Staley 1906). This political ascendancy of the merchants sealed the subordinate condition of the woolen craftworkers, as well as for Florentine workers in general.

It was through the statutes of the Arte adopted in the early 1300s, however, that the subordination of the woolen artisans was solidified. As described by historians (Staley 1906; Carus-Wilson 1952; Hodgett 1972; Gimpel 1976), the statutes of the Arte restricted the woolen artisans in several ways. For example, the artisans were forbidden to make commercial transactions with anyone not associated with the Arte, they were forbidden to seek work (they had to wait for the merchants to bring work to them), and the artisans working in their own workshops were subject to inspections by Arte officials at any time. In some stages of woolen production, the artisans were forbidden to work in their private dwellings. The

---

[15] The Order was finally suppressed in 1564 by Pope Pius V.

artisans were forbidden to form groups not approved by the Arte, and they were also forbidden to emigrate from Florence without permission from the Arte. During times of economic slumps, the merchant-employers advanced goods or money to the workers that had to be repaid later in work (Gimpel 1976). Since workers were not allowed by the Arte to migrate in search of work, this truck system effectively kept the woolen workers dependent on their employers.

In addition to being subordinated by the laws of the Arte, the woolen craftworkers lost economic power as the Arte merchants-capitalists increasingly took control of production. By the end of the fourteenth century, this progressive appropriation of the labor process transferred 13 of the 19 occupations in the woolen industry to workshops owned by the Arte (Edler 1934). With the merchants' increasing ownership of the means of production, such as workshops, fulling equipment, and stretching grounds, the woolen industry became more concentrated, shifting to large-scale organization (Hodgett 1972). The movement toward large-scale organization was evident in the period 1308–1338 when the number of workshops contracted decreased from 300 to 200. Although the amount of total cloth production also decreased, the rate of pieces of cloth produced per workshop increased by 13%, and the quality of cloth produced in the larger workshops was twice as valuable as before (see Villani 1823). That is, more work was involved per cloth.[16]

The merchants' appropriation of the means of production increased their control of labor. Undoubtedly, it was easier for the merchant-employers to control production when the workers were assembled in large workshops than when they were scattered in hundreds of small domestic workshops throughout Florence. In addition, the centralization of woolen manufacturing subprocesses in large workshops also increased the coordination of production. Production in large workshops reduced the time spent putting out and then collecting materials among producers. Moreover, it was easier to maintain and introduce standards of woolen production in centralized workshops than in scattered domestic workplaces (Heaton 1959).

Undoubtedly, the increase of raw wool importation in Florence after the Italians dominated the wool trade in regions of Europe, especially in England, affected the merchant-capitalists' appropriation of control of the woolen labor process. By the late 1200s, the existing putting-out system using artisan production became inadequate to handle the increasing importation of raw wool. Under the putting-out arrangement, where the artisans owned the means of production and controlled the production process, there was a limit to how much the productivity of the woolen industry could be increased. The very arrangement of the productive forces (labor and other means of production) became a barrier to the enhancement of the woolen industry by the merchants.

Among the limitations to the enhancement of productivity that the merchants faced in the putting-out system were the following. Firstly, there was a limit to the number of households available for working on cloth (many of the rural and other

---

[16] Arrighi (2010) relates this change in production to a drop in the demand for coarse cloth and a rise in the buying of expansive clothing by the upper classes.

immigrants that came to Florence were not skilled in making cloth). Secondly, there was a limit to the length of time that workers were willing to spend working on cloth. Religious holidays, which reduced work time, were rigidly observed and certain noisy production process (e.g., wool-sorting and beating) were prohibited by Florentine ordinances from being conducted between mid-afternoon and daybreak (Staley 1906). Thirdly, there was a limit to the number of workers that were approved by the artisan guilds to work on cloth. Finally, there was a limit to the level of intensity at which artisans were willing to work in their domestic workshops.[17] Viewed from these limitations, the expropriation of artisan control of production by the merchant-capitalists was an attempt to increase productivity beyond the limits of the putting-out system.

Two other factors help to explain the artisans' loss in control and power in the late 1200s and 1300s. One factor was that the woolen artisans in Florence were completely dependent on the merchants for their supplies of imported wool, which was considered superior to native wool (Sée 1928). By comparison, English woolen craftworkers lived near wool suppliers, and Flemish cloth workers could depend on native and Italian suppliers for wool (Gimpel 1976). The second factor concerned the difference in the involvement of the state. In Italy in the late Middle Ages, the city-state was the principal state organization, and it was allied with the merchant class. The Catholic Church also had state authority and was a traditional ally of the merchants, who provided it with financial loans when needed (see Strayer 1970).

The importance of the merchants' closeness to the state and the church in Florence was that these alliances helped to implement the labor-controlling measures of the Arte. As described above, the city government of Florence was the authority through which the merchants forced the woolen workers out of the guilds, and, as I will describe later, the church used doctrinal authority to help discipline woolen workers in Arte workshops.

2.3.3 Development of Propertyless Wage Workforces

Actions by Florentine merchant-capitalists to expand woolen production through the appropriation of the means of production and the centralization of the cloth-making processes in large workshops led to the development of a propertyless workforce—the *sottoposti*—that was completely subordinate to the merchant-capitalists. In contrast to the artisans that acquired a partial-proletarian status because of their piece wages and loss of control of the production process, the sottoposti were true proletarians. For the sottoposti, the only means of income was the sale of their labor power. Before going further into the description of these

---

[17] The literature (e.g., Staley 1906; Carus-Wilson 1952) describes some methods used by woolen workers to shorten work and cheapen expenses. These included over-stretching pieces of cloth. Through this practice the artisans misrepresented both the labor time spent and the quantity of cloth produced.

workers, I will comment on the logical moment that their development constituted in the capitalist development of the Florentine woolen industry.

In the discussion above, I described the Arte merchants' increasing appropriation of the means of production and centralization of cloth making as actions taken to enhance work coordination, efficiency, and productivity. Weber's (1978) concept of historical rationalization in social institutional sectors is relevant in this regard. The rationalization of production by the merchant-capitalists in Florence's woolen industry was more than just a technical rearrangement of the forces of production. Above all, the rationalization was a social struggle. It was a social struggle not only because it involved a multitude of merchants trying to dominate the production process, but, more importantly, because it involved the Arte, acting politically as a group for itself, i.e., as a politically conscious class, trying to restructure the social relations of production to restrict the power of the artisans. As Weber (1978: 138) pointed out, the technical process of appropriation, i.e., of separating workers from the means of production, is related "to the structure of power relations in a society."

In the 1330s, the sottoposti constituted the bulk of the 30,000 workers in the Florentine woolen industry (Gimpel 1976; Ferguson 1962). Three sources supplied the growth of the sottoposti labor force. One source was the population of poor craftworkers. Members of this group could descend into the inferior category by failing to pay the bond of 310 florins required by the Arte, or by losing their tools (e.g., looms) to merchant pawnbrokers (Staley 1906; Hodgett 1972). Another source was the population of apprentices and journeymen, who by the 1300s had become laborers without opportunity to advance in their crafts. With the merchant-capitalists' increasing ownership of the means of production, and the abolishment by the Arte of free contracts between artisans and employees, apprentices and journeymen were effectively precluded from ever advancing into the master class, and thus became permanent wage workers (Hauser 1951; Chamberlin 1965). The third source was the in-migration of workers from the countryside and nearby communities. Former peasants, workers from neighboring towns, individuals who wandered unattached to any particular community—all added to the migrant workforces of propertyless wage workers in Florence (Schevill 1963).[18] With the merchant-capitalists' growing investments in the means of production in the fourteenth century the sottoposti became increasingly concentrated in the large workshops owned by Arte merchants.

As mentioned above, of the 19 different specializations that composed the woolen industry in medieval Florence, 13 could be found in large merchant-owned workshops by the end of the fourteenth century. These thirteen occupations of laborers were the following (Edler 1934):

---

[18] Cultural critics viewed the sottoposti as morally malignant (see Holme 1980). Writing in the late trecento and in the fourteenth century, Dante, who was born in Florence, referred to immigrants and the wealth-producing industry of the city as he described a journey to Hell in the *Inferno*: "The new inhabitants and the sudden gains, Pride and extravagance have in thee engendered, Florence, so that thou weep'st thereat already! (Alighieri 2016: 58)."

2.3 Capitalist Production and Class Structure in the Woolen Industry

Williers	Warpers
Sorters	Burlers
Beaters	Menders
Oilers	Wool washers
Combers	Cloth workers-fullers
Carders	Stretchers-dryers
Appennecchini	

The master craftworkers who worked at home on materials provided by Arte merchants were spinners, weavers, and sometimes warpers. Other master craftworkers who worked in their own workshops were dyers, teaslers, shearman, pressers, and sometimes menders (Edler 1934). The sizes of workforces hired by merchant-employers (and supervised by master craftworkers) varied from a few workers to over one hundred (Carus-Wilson 1952; Staley 1906). In their private shops, master craftworkers employed several workers, according to the amount and particularity of their work (Staley 1906; Thrupp 1971).

As throughout Europe, the workday of the woolen workers was from dawn until sundown. The workweek was from Monday until Saturday afternoon, which was the beginning of the vigil of the feast (Thrupp, 1971). Based on regulations of the Arte, all laborers and operatives in Florence's woolen industry were paid wages according to the time worked (Edler 1934; Carus-Wilson 1952). Master craftworkers working in their own shops were paid piece wages (Edler 1934).

The wages of the sottoposti have been described as submarginal and rarely rising above the bare minimum of subsistence (Schevill 1963; Ferguson 1962). Famine among the impoverished sottoposti, however, was not entirely the consequence of lean harvests. In a revolt of the city's poor in 1368, a crowd of five hundred persons stormed a granary and, carrying off sacks of wheat and flour, shouted, "Long live the *popolo minuto* and death to the *popolo grasso* who starve us and refuse to sell us grain" (Brucker 1962: 197–198). According to Schevill (1963: 265), for the merchant-capitalists of the Arte, "the wool workers were no better than human chattels required to subsist on a submarginal wage."

Wages were set by the Arte, and workers were prohibited from making wage demands. This measure was particularly important to the merchant-capitalists, since the cost of labor was 60% of production cost (Gimpel 1976). Workers were also prohibited from forming unions. Surviving judicial records indicate that when Florence experienced political and financial crises and labor unrest in 1343–1348 several workers were convicted, and some executed, for attempting to form worker unions (Brucker 1962). One case involved a wool carder named Ciuto Brandini who attempted to form a union of carders, combers, and other wool workers. A merchant named Francesco Duranti recorded the punishment carried out against the wool carder:

On May 24 1345, the captain of Florence…seized at night Cuito Brandini, carder, and his two sons, because Ciuto wished to organize a company at S. Croce and create a union with the other workers of Florence. On the same day, the Florentine workers, that is, the carders and wool combers, learned the news…and they stopped work and did not wish to continue until Ciuto was returned to them. These workers went to the priors and urged them to restore Ciuto safe and sound…and they also wished to be better paid. And Ciuto was then hung by the neck. (Brucker 1962: 110–111)

Arte statutes prohibited workers from having meetings of more than ten workers for any purpose whatsoever (Schevill 1963). Violating this rule was punished by the *divieto*, i.e., by exclusion of the workers from a list of approved workers for a period of one year or more. This blacklist was greatly feared because it was equivalent to a sentence of death by starvation. Furthermore, workers were not permitted to leave Florence without permission of the court of the Arte, and violations of this statute were punished by fines, postponement of wages, floggings, loss of a hand, and ultimately death (Carus-Wilson 1952).

Merchant-capitalists also sought control of the workers by pressuring the Bishop of Florence to direct the priests to preach three times a year that failure to obey employers was punishable by excommunication (Carus-Wilson 1952). Excommunication was a severe penalty that severed persons from the church and issued everlasting damnation after death. Some of the leading Florentine business families, taking the law into their own hands, sought to control their workers through terror. One such family, described by Villani, "in their own house in the Mercato Nuovo [New Market] in the centre of the city, hung men up in ropes, and at midday put them to the torture" (Holme 1980: 54).

Although Florentine woolen artisans lost substantial industrial control in the restructuring of their industry in the thirteenth and fourteenth centuries, in general the artisans did not descend to the conditions of the sottoposti. The statutes of the Arte segmented the woolen working class of Florence, giving the artisans some status and power as supervisors in the large workshops of the merchant-capitalists, and by allowing some artisans to keep their shops and workers, but under the regulations of the Arte. When joblessness increased among the sottoposti due to foreign competition and a drop in the sale of coarse cloth in the 1330–1370s, prosperity increased among artisans who produced expensive woolen clothing, which was increasingly demanded by upper-class families and ecclesiastical officials. Undoubtedly, due to their higher status in the working class and greater possibility for prosperity, artisans sided with the merchant-capitalists in their struggles with the sottoposti, including helping the Arte suppress the sottoposti and other propertyless workers in the *Ciompi* revolt of 1378 (Arrighi 2010).[19]

---

[19] The Ciompi revolt commenced with conflict among guild factions but drew in the involvement of workers in the summer of 1378. Woolen workers were among the most radical of the rebellious workers. The workers overthrew the Florentine government and briefly setup a new government representative of all the classes in Florence. A guild for workers was also organized but lasted only briefly before it was abolished by the established guilds (Arrighi 2010). Alfani (2013) describes developments that ended economic prosperity in Italian cities in the fifteenth and sixteenth centuries.

2.3.4 Women in Woolen Work

Cloth-producing labor forces in Florence and other regions in northwestern Europe involved major participation by women workers, who dominated some of the occupations in the production of cloth. The available historical surveys of censuses, guild registers, tax records, etc., however, are inadequate for a full accounting of women's work in textile production in these regions in the thirteenth and fourteenth centuries. One data problem is that the enumeration of workers was based on heads of households, which given the tradition of pater familias referred to men. For example, the enumeration of women textile workers increased after the Black Death when husbands or fathers died and women became heads of household, and then decreased years later when males reassumed the heads of the family household. Throughout the time span, however, the actual textile work of women could remain the same or even increase if more women and girls in the household worked in textile production. The inconsistency between enumerations and actual women work participation can lead to conflicting conclusions of the role that women played in textile production.

A second data problem is that men dominated the guilds, and so the business activity reflected by guild records concerned mainly men. All craftworkers, including women, were required to join guilds controlled by merchant-capitalists, and were required to pay a membership fee and agree to abide by guild work regulations and standards. However, guild rights and privileges of women workers were not always equal to those of men. While a guild code of ethics could require respect for all, guilds demonstrated prejudices against women as troublesome and in need of supervision in public life. One saying in Florence at the time was, "A good woman and a bad one equally require the stick! (Staley 1906: 91)."

The participation of women in woolen production in Florence in the thirteenth and fourteenth centuries can be summarized as follows based on historical materials (Staley 1906; Hanawalt 1986; Lindholm 2017). In the many subprocesses that were involved in the production of woolen cloth, women worked in spinning, warping, and weaving. Women, especially rural women, accounted for all the labor in spinning, for the vast majority of the labor in warping, and worked equally with men in weaving. As part of the putting-out system of production, most women worked at home and were paid piece rates for the cloth they produced, while men worked at home, in centralized and private workshops, and in rented spaces and were paid daily or weekly wages. In the occupations they shared with men, women received equal pay but had lower income than men because they usually worked on less valuable cloth and for less time (Lindholm 2017), because they were given fewer and shorter cloths to work on in the putting-out system. Among weavers, however, women sometimes did more work and thus had more income than men. Women were also recognized as especially skilled in the making of ecclesiastical and royal vestments involving elaborate embroidery and expensive adornment.

Women were more involved in part-time work than men because women also devoted time to household work and caring for children. Claudia Goldin (2014) has referred to women's irregular work patterns, such as in Florence woolen production, as "nonlinear work." In times of labor scarcity in Florence, more women worked in textile production but were not elected to official positions in the Arte della Lana, although a few women were listed in the guild as owners of business capital. It is likely that widows who took over woolen workshops after their husbands died became important members of the Arte even if they were not elected to guild offices, especially if their workshops were an important part of the Arte's overall business. In the woolen industry, there was the officially prescribed way of doing business, and then, there was the actual way things were done to meet lucrative and practical ends.

Conditions of women in textile production in the larger regions of northern and western Europe in the Middle Ages had similarities and differences. One overarching similarity was the patriarchal subordination of women in the larger economy (Hanawalt 1986). Women were usually relegated to the lower-status work even if sometimes they shared the work with men, and they were not elected to high offices in the guilds. Since the guilds maintained production standards, women's skills were equal to men's in the occupations they shared. Yet, men and women did not join guilds equally. In the Italian cotton industry, for example, men worked in guild occupations, but women worked with less-skilled men in seasonal and non-guild work.

Interregional differences in women's work in cloth production also characterized the working conditions of women. While in Florence women had pay equal to the men's in the same woolen occupations, in England guilds enacted laws to pay women less (Hanawalt 1986). Moreover, in the English silk cloth industry, women did not form guilds as the men did, and men refused to do the work done by women (Dale 1933). Florentine guilds, however, seem to have been more concerned than guilds in other European areas with the regulation of women's behavior and how they dressed in public. The Florentine guild of judges and notaries had many laws to regulate how women should dress when out in public, including the number of adorned rings that women could wear (Staley 1906).

One can summarize that while in some regions of Europe women workers fared better than women in other regions, overall women's work in the woolen industry remained segmented. The male-dominated trade organizations subordinated women workers in the economy, and governmental and ecclesiastic institutions reinforced the subordination of women.

2.4 Fleeing Harsh Economic Conditions

The hardships of manorial servitude in the late Middle Ages in Europe produced a large reservoir of potential migrant labor. Migration became a means, although a risky means, for serfs to resist the oppression of the manorial system. While social and economic differentiation existed among serfs, the outstanding characteristics of serfdom were impoverishing service and rent bondage to the seigniorial class (Dobb 1963; Weber 1950; Pirenne 1937). In describing the relation of the lord to

2.4 Fleeing Harsh Economic Conditions

the serf, Weber (1950: 71) cites Marx, "the walls of his stomach set the limits to his exploitation of the peasant."

Until feudalism became a less accommodating social system for the seignorial class, many manorial workers faced expanding condition of servile oppression. Partly to meet increasing revenue demands set by the Crown and partly for their own enrichment, lords continually augmented the requirements of services and payments from manorial peasants (Wallerstein 1974). In English manors, for example, to the obligatory work were added the requirements that peasants had to grind their grain in the lord's mill for a "multure" (a payment in kind); had to bake their bread in the manorial oven for a fee; had to work on holy days when demanded; had to pay tallages exacted at will, regardless of harvest conditions; and had to forfeit at death their best possessions to the lord (Bennett 1937).

In addition to describing how increased servile oppression sometimes forced whole peasant settlements to relocate, Dobb's (1963) description of the serfs' illegal flight from increased servitude depicts the supplying of labor to towns, tramping, and peasant outbreaks[20]:

> The result of this increased pressure was not only to exhaust the goose that laid the golden eggs for the castle, but to provoke, from sheer desperation, a movement of illegal emigration from the manors: a desertion en masse on the part of the producers [...]. This flight of villains from the land often assumed catastrophic proportions both in England and elsewhere, and not only served to swell the population of the rising towns but specially on the Continent contributed to a prevalence of outlaw-bands and vagabondage and periodic *jacqueries*. (1963: 46; italics in the original)

The penalties in England for runaway serf migration included imprisonment and branding on the forehead (Dobb 1963).

Peasants who fled manorial estates preferred to resettle in agricultural communities, rather than to look for a proletarian life in the city (Thrupp 1971). The preference was to have land to farm with some degree of control, and not have a wage-laborer's life of poverty and rigid control by employers in urban areas. Many of the peasants who abandoned manors became free settlers of new farming communities on royal and church lands. Pirenne's (1937) description of economic and social life in medieval Europe indicates that many of the rural workers who migrated to the cities came from the ranks of the poorer manorial emigrants, including second sons whose lower birth rank precluded inheriting the family's farming plot.

Wage workers also used migration to find better work conditions in Europe in the late Middle Ages. While woolen guilds in Florence prohibited the out-migration of woolen workers without guild permission, other wage workers had freedom of movement. Masons, for example, were another emerging group of

---

[20] Illegal flight from bounded labor continues into the present era. During the Bracero Program, which imported Mexican migrant workers into US farms during 1942–1964, braceros sometimes ran away from their contracted work crews to find work on their own (Ordaz 2021).

wage labor in the 1300s and used migration to improve their work conditions. According to Hodgett (1972: 135–136), these workers "were certainly in a better position to bargain over wages and conditions of labour than were most groups, for they were frequently able, when dissatisfied to pack up and go to another site." Undoubtedly, the most desperate wage workers to migrate in search of better working conditions were the propertyless, wage workers who were unattached from all social structures but the social relations of work. Pirenne (1915: 95) described the wretchedness of these wage workers in the medieval woolen industry in Flanders as follows:

> When work failed, the workmen everywhere lost all means of subsistence, and bands of the unemployed spread through the country begging the bread they could no longer gain by their labour. [...] These workers dwelt in the suburbs in miserable hovels hired by the week. They hardly ever owned anything but the clothes they stood up in. They wandered from town to town offering the labour of their hands for hire.

Socially unattached from all community social structures but work, migrant wage workers were the most vulnerable and dispensable laborers in times of economic downturns, which sometimes resulted from population decline in bad years of epidemics or crop failures (Wrigley 1969).[21]

2.5 Migration and the Development of Medieval Capitalist Production

The migration of merchant-bankers and workers played a major role in the development of woolen capitalist production in Florence in the thirteenth and fourteenth centuries. It was the migration of merchant-bankers that produced the commercial circuits, sometimes in the remittance form of papal revenue, across regions of Europe providing the raw wool material for production into woolen commodities for markets. Labor migration helped supply a labor force for the capitalist arrangement of employers and propertyless wage workers that emerged in production sites in Florence to produce woolen cloth and clothing in large volume.

Migration of Italian merchant-bankers across Catholic Europe as papal tax agents, and also as traders and financiers, involved more than business trips;

---

[21] Existing in primitive settings in the dawn of capitalist production, the category of migrant wage workers no doubt overwhelmed local sources of poor-relief if any existed (van Leeuwen 1994; 2010), or were disqualified from such local support given their migratory status. Rather than offers of charity, by the late 1400s beggars and other unemployed workers on the move in western Europe faced physical punishments for being out of work if they appeared able to work. In England, under Henry VIII legislation enacted in 1530 to force beggars to work mandated floggings until blood ran from their bodies and other corporal punishments ending with executions for beggars seemed fit to return work, ironically even when their work had disappeared through economic change (Marx 1967).

the journeys involved a relocation to live and conduct business abroad for central offices in Italy. Moreover, the international settlement became more involved when foreign governments appointed Italian merchant-bankers to official posts. Overall, the long-distance migrations of merchant-bankers in the thirteenth and fourteenth centuries sowed early seeds in Europe for the accumulation of economic wealth through interregional commerce and investment. This economic-spatial development became a central feature of capital accumulation in the capitalist world-system that emerged in the late long sixteenth century (Wallerstein 1979).

Across the woolen economy of northern and western Europe, and especially in the woolen-producing centers of Florence, Flanders, and England, governments and entrepreneurs supported labor migration to secure workers for economic development. In Florence, textile merchant-capitalists promoted the in-migration of workers, particularly those experienced in cloth production, and restricted their out-migration. The exception was the occasional passing of laws to restrict the in-migration of agricultural workers into the city, which was done to prevent a shortage of food producers for the city (Waley 1969). Examples of the Florentine support for the in-migration of cloth workers included the granting of resources by the city government to the arriving Umiliati monks in 1238 to provide for the monks' immigrant-worker families and enable the monks to attract other workers from nearby communities (Staley 1906).

Other actions that illustrated the Florentine policy of developing the city's textile workforce partly through immigrant labor were the forced migration of Sicilian weavers from the captured city of Lucca into the Florence in 1315 and the passage of laws in the 1350s to relax citizenship standards in the post-Black Death decade to attract workers from abroad (Issac 1947; Schevill 1963; Whewell 1977). As described above, Arte ordinances restricted worker out-migration in Florence's woolen industry, and Arte merchant-capitalists created economic dependence among the workers through a truck system that indebted workers and kept them in the city.

In Flanders, by comparison, the actions of woolen capitalist entrepreneurs regarding labor migration underwent a transformation in the late Middle Ages. Initially, around the tenth century, when Flanders was an unrivaled producer of cloth in Europe, the view of the merchant class in Flemish towns (such as Ghent, Burger, and Ypres) toward immigrant labor was the same as the views that existed in other nascent industrial centers in Europe: Immigrant workers were desirable because they were a means to economic development and to circumvent the guilds of craftworkers (Pirenne 1915; Weber 1950).

As was the practice in many European towns, Flemish town governments passed laws to incorporate serfs who ran away from manors into their workforces by granting citizenship in the towns to anyone who resided within the city walls for a year and a day (Pirenne 1937). "City air makes a man free" is an adage from this era (Pirenne 1937: 51; Weber 1950: 132). However, by the fourteenth century, Flemish textile capitalists were endorsing forced labor emigration (i.e., banishment) as a means of quelling outbreaks of worker rebellion (Hodgett 1972). In 1328, after the defeat of a Flemish worker-peasant army at Cassel by French forces, about one thousand workers, equally divided between weavers and fullers, were banished from Ypres alone, many of whom migrated to Florence and England (Carus-Wilson, 1952, p. 415). Another conflict in 1344 resulted in the exile migration of weavers from Poperinghe to England (Hodgett 1972).

Migration was a more complex factor in the development of the cloth industry in England than in Florence and Flanders. In the initial commercial development of the industry in English towns in the 1200s and early 1300s, labor in-migration from the countryside was a source of unskilled labor (Ashley 1925). Similar to other urban communities in Europe, English towns offered citizenship to anyone—including runaway serfs—who remained within the towns for a year and a day (Bennett 1937). In the fourteenth century, however, the prominent pattern of migration that developed in the woolen industry was the movement of commercial cloth production by capitalist entrepreneurs from the town to the countryside (Hodgett 1972).

Artisan cloth workers in the English towns resisted the migration of the woolen industry to the countryside because it took woolen production out of their guild control in the towns. Capitalist entrepreneurs sought to relocate their industries especially to areas where supplies of wool and fuller's earth existed close to swift streams and rivers, which were used to power waterwheels, and where unorganized rural labor was plentiful (Carus-Wilson 1952). In the initial stage of the industry's relocation, when capitalist entrepreneurs in the towns started sending their cloth to rural mills for fulling, weavers and fullers in many English cities obtained ordinances to restricted city-produced cloth to fulling in the cities. For example, in 1298 London cloth makers secured an ordinance from the Crown to prohibit the sending of cloth outside the city for fulling and appointed six men to watch the city gates for violators (Carus-Wilson 1954).

Despite the town ordinances, in the fourteenth century, capitalist entrepreneurs relocated the English woolen industry to the countryside. The relocation was particularly effective in the West Riding of Yorkshire, the marches of Wales, the Cotswold Hills, and the valleys in Wiltshire and Berkshire. Freed from the control of urban guilds, the English woolen industry developed into a source of cloth for Europe by the latter part of the century (Hodgett 1972). Furthermore, the industry's transition to the countryside appears to have included an urban to rural migration of cloth workers as well. Concurrent with the growth of worker settlements in the rural mill sites, a rapid diminution of cloth workers occurred in the major cloth-producing cities (Carus-Wilson 1954). For example, in the early fourteenth century, the number of looms in London dropped from 380 to 80, and by the second decade of the century the city, which once had two hundred weavers, had no weavers left (Lipson 1915).

In the English medieval scene of nascent capitalist woolen production, the state, in the form of the Crown, also played a significant part in the migration of cloth workers and entrepreneurs. Partly as a policy to strengthen the developing native industry (and enhance revenues for royalty) and partly as a strategy to counter pro-France industrialists in Flanders, the English kings Henry III and Edward III issued proclamations to promote the immigration of Flemish cloth workers. As early as 1271 Henry III issued the decree that, "all workers of woolen cloths, male and female, as well as of Flanders as of other lands, may safely come into our realm, there to make cloths" (Lipson 1915: 397). The decree also contained the provision that immigrant cloth workers would be free from taxation for five years (Lipson 1921).

Edward III initiated his policy to attract Flemish cloth makers in 1331 when he gave special permission to a Flemish entrepreneur to bring his manufactory, workers, and servants to England (Salzman 1923). In 1337, at the beginning of the Hundred Years' War, the king issued special letters of permission to immigrate to Flemish dyers and fullers and sent an agent to Flanders to encourage a group of English immigrant cloth makers to return to England (Gibbins 1916). More Flemish cloth-entrepreneurs migrated to England when the king gave special immigration permission to the cloth burghers of Ghent in 1343 (Salzman 1923).

Unlike the welcome given by the kings, English towns treated the Flemish cloth workers and entrepreneurs with hostility and pressured them to follow local guild regulations (Gibbins 1916). To relieve the Flemish who had settled in Bristol from some of this adverseness, in 1340 Edward III ordered the mayor of the city to cease imposing a loom-tax on foreign weavers. Twelve years later, the king issued a general proclamation that forbade the compelling of foreign cloth makers to join guilds (Salzman 1923).

The migration of workers into the urban woolen-producing centers in Europe in the late Middle Ages constituted a process of proletarianization. Labor migration was no longer just a means to increase the number of cloth producers; it was also a means to further cloth production using propertyless wage workers controlled by merchant-capitalists, and not by the artisan guilds. The purpose of this new labor force was to raise production beyond the limits of using craftworkers in the putting-out system. Migrant labor thus became a resource to advance the accumulation of economic wealth. Whether they went to work for master craftworkers, who by the fourteenth century were rapidly taking on a foreman status in the industry, or for merchant-capitalists in centralized workshops, as occurred in Florence, migrant workers became members of a permanent class of laborers that subsisted through the sale of their labor power, and who were thus dependent on the employing class for survival.

As the Flemish and English cases demonstrated, migration was not solely a self-activity of workers. In Flemish towns, migration was a process imposed by the ruling class on rebellious cloth workers. In England, migration was also an activity of capitalist-employers undertaken partly to avoid the power of organized cloth workers in the towns. Moreover, as the actions of Henry III and Edward III demonstrated, migration also was used as an economic strategy of the state. Considering that the kings made special concessions (e.g., tax exemptions) to immigrant cloth-entrepreneurs and prohibited native cloth producers from organizing immigrant workers, it is reasonable to regard the king's actions as precursory of capitalist-state actions to promote economic development with the use of migrant labor.

2.6 Conclusion

Both Marx and Wallerstein emphasized the agricultural transformation to capitalist production as the crucial step for capitalist development. For Marx (1967: 713), the driving off the peasantry from their lands and into wandering workforces looking for wage work was the stage of "primitive accumulation," that is, the "starting point" of the capitalist mode of production. For Wallerstein (1974), the entrance of the agricultural sector into interregional commerce for profit to accumulate capital had major importance for the beginning of capitalist development.[22] The perceptions of Marx and Wallerstein are logical given that the vast majority of the European population lived in rural areas laboring in agricultural production during the historical periods they analyzed. The dominance of the agricultural economy, however, concealed the dynamics of production in pre-industrial cities (Sjoberg 1960). Consequently, the significance of migration for medieval urban settings remained understudied and inadequately theorized (Glick Schiller 2012).[23] But the social path to capitalist production in Europe traveled along both urban and rural settings, and, while the former was much smaller and limited, in some cases it was ahead of the latter on the road to capitalism.

The historical accident that initiated the concentration of tax revenues for the papacy as an original form of capital accumulation concealed the medieval rise of capitalistic social forces in Europe. It was a Catholic pope who faced financial needs after going to war against a German emperor that led to the collection of papal war taxes by Italian merchant-bankers. Accepting tax payments from bishoprics in the form of raw wool, the merchant-bankers acquired commercial dominance in the wool trade in areas of Catholic Europe and this eventually led to woolen capitalist production in Florence. In several ways, Catholic financial, material, and moral resources helped propel the medieval development of woolen capitalist production in Florence and in other areas of Europe in the thirteenth and fourteenth centuries.

Migrating in search of wealth or for work to survive, merchant-bankers, investors, and workers—all helped lay the social structures of capitalist development and demonstrated the importance of spatial mobility for the expansion of commerce and production for profit to accumulate private wealth. While feudalism centered economic production in the family household in fixed manorial clusters, the emerging merchant-capitalist class in the thirteenth and fourteenth centuries in Florence and other European areas sought expansion of their wealth partly through migration across regions. By the long sixteenth century, the capitalistic mode manifested in the interregional woolen commerce and production

---

[22] Wallerstein's (1974) subtitle to his first volume of *The Modern World-System*—"Capitalist Agriculture and the Origins of the European World-Economy in the Sixteenth Century"—illustrates the importance he gives to the agricultural sector for capitalist development.

[23] "Migrants were pictured as part of the urban industrial workforce but not theorized as constitutive of transnational processes within which cities are situated," according to Glick Schiller (2012: 26).

in Europe in the thirteenth and fourteenth centuries expanded to other industrial sectors and reached the level of the world-economy in the long sixteenth century.

References

Abu-Lughod, Janet. 1989. *Before European Hegemony: The World System A.D. 1250–1350*. Oxford: Oxford University Press.

Alfani, Guido. 2013. *Calamities and the Economy in Renaissance Italy: The Gran Tour of the Horsemen of the Apocalypse*. New York: Palgrave Macmillan.

Alighieri, Dante. 2016. *The Divine Comedy,* Volume I, *Hell*. Trans. by Henry Wadsworth Longfellow. Overland Park, Kansas: Dirireads.com Publishing.

Arrighi, Giovanni. 2010. *The Long Twentieth Century: Money, Power and the Origins of Our Times*. New York: Verso.

Ashley, Sir William. 1925. English Economic History and Theory. Part II, The End of the Middle Ages. London: Longmans, Green.

Bell, Adrian R., Chris Brooks, and Paul R. Dryburgh. 2007. *The English Wool Market, c.1230–1327*. Cambridge, UK: Cambridge University Press.

Bennett, H.S. 1937. *Life on the English Manor: A Study of Peasant Conditions 1150–1400*. Cambridge: Cambridge University Press.

Britnell, R. 2004. *Britain and Ireland 1050–1530: Economy and Society*. Oxford: Oxford University Press.

Brucker, Gene A. 1962. *Florentine Politics and Society, 1343–1378*. Princeton: Princeton University Press.

Cardoso, Fernando Henrique, and Enzo Faletto. 1979. *Dependency and Development in Latin America*. Berkeley: University of California Press.

Carus-Wilson, E. M. 1952. "The Woolen Industry." In *The Cambridge Economic History of Europe, II, Trade and Industry in the Middle Ages*, ed. M. Postan, and E. E. Rich, 354-429. Cambridge: Cambridge University Press.

Carus-Wilson, E. M. 1954. *Medieval Merchant Venturers*. London: Methuen.

Chamberlin, E.R. 1965. *Everyday Life In Renaissance Times*. New York: Perigee Books.

Dale, Marian K. 1933. The London Silkwomen of the Fifteenth Century. *Economic History Review* 24 (3): 324–335.

Dobb, Maurice. 1963. *Studies in the Development of Capitalism*. New York: International Publishers.

Edler, F. 1934. *Glossary of Medieval Terms of Business: Italian Series 1200–1600*. Cambridge: The Medieval Academy of America.

Ferguson, Wallace K. 1962. *Europe in Transition, 1300–1520*. Boston: Houghton Mifflin.

Gibbins, Henry De Beltgens. 1916. *Industry in England*. New York: Charles Scribner's Sons.

Gimpel, Jean. 1976. *The Medieval Machine*. New York: Penguin Books.

Goldin, Claudia. 2014. A Grand Gender Convergence: Its Last Chapter. *American Economic Review* 104 (4): 1091–1119.

Gras, N.S.B. 1918. *The Early English Customs System*. Cambridge: Harvard University Press.

Hanawalt, Barbara A. 1986. *Women and Work in Preindustrial Europe*. Bloomington: Indiana University Press.

Hauser, Arnold. 1951. *The Social History of Art*, vol. 1. New York: Random House.

Heaton, Herbert. 1959. "History of Factory Production." *Encyclopaedia Britannica,* Vol. 9, 10th ed.

Hegel, G.W.F. 1975. *Logic. Translated by William Wallace*. Oxford: The Clarendon Press.

Hodgett, Gerald A. J. 1972. *A Social and Economic History of Medieval Europe*. New York: Harper & Row.

Holme, Timothy. 1980. *'Vile Florentines': The Florence of Dante, Giotto, and Boccaccio*. New York: St. Martin's Press.
Hunt, E. 1990. A New Look at the Dealings of the Bardi and the Peruzzi with Edward III. *The Journal of Economic History* 51 (1): 149–162.
Issac, Julius. 1947. *Economics of Migration*. London: Kegan Paul, Trench, Trubner & Co.
Leeuwen, Van, and H.D. Marco. 1994. Logic of Charity: Poor Relief in Preindustrial Europe. *The Journal of Interdisciplinary History* 24 (4): 589–613.
Lindholm, Richard T. 2017. *Quantitative Studies of the Renaissance Florentine Economy and Society*. New York: Anthem Press.
Lipson, E. 1921. *The History of the Woolen and Worsted Industries*. London: A & C Black Ltd.
Lipson, E. 1915. *Economic History of England, Vol I, The Middle Ages*. London: A & C Black, Ltd.
Lopez, Robert S. 1967. *The Birth of Europe*. New York: M. Evans and Company.
Lopez, R. S., and H. A. Miskimin. 1962. "The Economic Depression of the Renaissance." *The Economic History Review* 2nd ser., 14 (London): 408–426.
Lunt, William E. 1965. *Papal Revenues in the Middle Ages*, vol. 1. New York: Octagon Books Inc.
Marx, Karl. 1967. *Capital*, vol. I. New York: International Publishers.
Ordaz, Jessica. 2021. *The Shadow of El Centro: A History of Migrant Incarceration and Solidarity*. Chapel Hill: The University of North Carolina Press.
Pirenne, Henri. 1915. *Belgian Democracy: Its Early History*. London: Longmans, Green & Co.
Pirenne, Henri. 1937. *Economic and Social History of Medieval Europe*. New York: Harcourt, Brace & World.
De Roover, R. 1965. "The Organization of Trade." In *The Cambridge Economic History of Europe, Vol. 3, Economic Organizations and Policies in the Middle Ages*, edited by M. M. Postan, E. E. Rich, and Edward Miller, 42–118. Cambridge: Cambridge University Press.
Ryder, M.L. 1984. Medieval Sheep and Wool Types. *Agricultural History Review* 32: 14–28.
Salzman, L.F. 1923. *English Industries of the Middle Ages*. Oxford: Clarendon Press.
Sanderson, Stephen K. 1999. *Social Transformation: A General Theory of Historical Development*. Lanham, MD: Rowman & Littlefield Publishers Inc.
Sapori, Armando. 1955. *Merchants and Companies in Ancient Florence*. France: Ulan Press.
Sapori, Armando. 1970. *The Italian Merchant in the Middle Ages*. New York: W.W. Norton.
Schevill, Ferdinand. 1963. *Medieval and Renaissance Florence, Vol. 2, The Coming of Humanism and the Age of the Medici*. New York: Harper Torchbooks.
Schiller, Nina Glick. 2012. "Transnationality, Migrants and Cities: A Comparative Approach. In *Beyond Methodological Nationalism: Research Methodologies for Cross-Border Studies*, edited by Anna Amelina, Devrimsel D. Nergiz, Thomas Faist and Nina Glick Schiller, 23–40. New York: Routledge.
Sée, Henri. 1928. *Modern Capitalism: Its Origin and Evolution*. New York: Adelphi Company.
Sjoberg, Gideon. 1960. *The Preindustrial City, Past and Present*. New York: The Free Press.
Staley, Edgcumbe. 1906. *The Guilds of Florence*. London: Methuen & Co.
Strayer, Joseph R. 1970. *On the Medieval Origin of the Modern State*. Princeton: Princeton University Press.
Thrupp, Sylvia. 1971. "Medieval Industry 1000–1500." In *The Fontana Economic History of Europ, Vol. 1, The Middle Ages*, edited by Carlo M. Cipolla, 221–273. London: Fontana/Collins.
Villani, Giovanni. 1823. *Cronica Di Giovanni Villani: A Miglior Lezione Ridotta. Coll' Aiuto De' Testi A Penna*, Tomo II. Firenze: Peril Magheri.
Waley, Daniel. 1969. *The Italian City-Republics*. New York: McGraw-Hill.
Wallerstein, Immanuel. 1974. *The Modern World System: Capitalist Agriculture and the Origins of the European World-Economy in the Seventeenth Century*. New York: Academic Press.
Wallerstein, Immanuel. 1976. From Feudalism to Capitalism: Transition or Transitions? *Social Forces* 55 (2): 273–283.
Wallerstein, Immanuel. 1992. "The West, Capitalism, and the Modern World-System." *Review* 15 (4): 561–619.
Weber, Max. 1950. *General Economic History*. Glencoe, IL: The Free Press.

References

Weber, Max. 1978. *Economy and Society*. Berkeley: University of California Press.
Weber, Max. 1958. *The Protestant Ethic and the Spirit of Capitalism*. Translated by Talcott Parsons. New York: Charles Scribner's Sons.
Whewell, C. S. 1977. "Textile Industry." *Encyclopaedia Britannica*. 15th ed., Vol. 18: 170–189.
Population and History. New York: McGraw Hill Book.

Migration and Dutch Capitalist Development 3

In the long sixteenth century of 1450–1640, a world-economy emerged in Europe with the "distinctive feature of the modern world-system" (Wallerstein 1974: 15). At the beginning, the social system did not extend to the whole world, but to the world most western Europeans knew at the time, and it was larger than any political domain in the region. Increasingly, the pursuit of economic gain through investment, commerce, and production expanded the new world-economy into domestic and foreign regions. It was a capitalistic social system imbued with a ceaseless drive to accumulate economic wealth. The capitalistic spirit of economic accumulation that drove Italian merchant-bankers to expand their woolen commerce and financial investments in European regions in the thirteenth and fourteenth centuries now advanced to a world scale. In 1625–1675, the Dutch gained economic and military dominance in this new world-economy, and Dutch hegemony reached into eastern Europe, Africa, and Asia, and into the Western Hemisphere such as the western Atlantic and the Caribbean (Wallerstein 1974).

From the perspective of Arrighi's concept of hegemony as involving leadership in addition to economic and military dominance, the United Provinces reached hegemonic status "by leading a large and powerful coalition of dynastic states towards the liquidation of the medieval system of rule and the establishment of the modern interstate system" (2010: 44).[1] As Arrighi (2010) explains, the Dutch had also demonstrated intellectual and moral leadership in northwestern Europe through their fight for independence from Spanish rule, which benefited other states in northwestern Europe.

In this chapter, I argue that migration of capital and labor was critical for the development of the United Provinces (the northern Netherlands) as a hegemonic core state of the capitalist world-system. Firstly, I sketch the development of Dutch

---

[1] The Peace of Westphalia signed in 1648 in the Westphalian cities of Osnabrück and Münster is considered to be the cornerstone of the modern interstate system.

© The Author(s), under exclusive license to Springer Nature Switzerland AG 2023
N. Rodriguez, *Capitalism and Migration*, World-Systems Evolution and Global Futures,
https://doi.org/10.1007/978-3-031-22067-8_3

hegemony by describing various dimensions of economic growth and commercial expansion that the Dutch undertook in their emergence as a hegemonic power. Secondly, I describe patterns of migration in the northern Netherlands during the period under investigation, focusing mainly on Holland, which was the central industrial area of the United Provinces in the seventeenth century. Thirdly, I describe labor migration that occurred in the Dutch expansion to the peripheral areas of the East Indies, the West Indies, and to the Pernambuco region in Brazil. This migration included the forced labor transfers of the African slave trade into New World regions. It also included the migration, or attempted migration, of native populations away from colonial areas. Finally, I will discuss the overall significance of migration for the Dutch rise to hegemony in the world-system.

3.1 Dutch Hegemony

The productive efficiency that thrust the United Provinces into economic ascension in the late 1500s and into hegemonic status during 1625–1975 involved principally the fishing, shipbuilding, textile, and agricultural industries (Wilson 1957; Wallerstein 1980), all of which depended, to one degree or another, on migration as a labor source.

3.1.1 Industrial Development

In the fishing industry, the productive superiority of the Dutch, compared with other European countries, was markedly evident in herring fishing. By the end of the seventeenth century, the Dutch were gaining dominance in the North Sea herring fishery (the Grand Fishery) with unrivaled production based on three herring-fishing seasons per year. From a study of salt-tax records, Michell (1977) estimates that in 1599 the Dutch fishing industry produced 18,000 lasts (about 78 million pounds) of salted herring. This Dutch success in herring fishing was particularly attributed to their use of the *haringbus*, a "factory ship" designed with wide decks to enable curing on board (Michell 1977). Combining on-board processing with a barreling method discovered in the thirteenth century in the Dutch town of Biervliet, the Dutch were able to conduct large-scale fishing far from their shore for weeks at a time (Barker 1906; Michell 1977).

The superiority of the Dutch in the fishing industry, as well as in their commerce as a whole, was based mainly on their advancement in shipbuilding. In this industry, the Dutch led in the design of ships as well as in their construction (Wilson 1957).[2] As described below, by the early seventeenth century the Dutch were designing cargo ships, e.g., the fluyt, that needed less than half the crew of

---

[2] "The real instrument of Dutch greatness was a fleet the equivalent of all the other European fleets put together (Braudel 1984: 190)."

other European merchant vessels (Kindleberger 1975). This reduced labor costs and enabled the Dutch to acquire shipping contracts in many places in Europe (e.g., English and Italian ports) by offering freight rates that were one-third to one-half lower than those of other shippers (Kindleberger 1975). Sir George Downing, an English observer and reluctant admirer of Dutch industrial growth in the seventeenth century, assessed the importance of efficient shipping for the Dutch as follows: "In this very thinge is the Mystery of their state and by this Means doe they gayne all their wealth" (quoted in Wilson 1965: 168).

Using standardized and repetitive construction methods, as well as labor-saving machinery such as wind-driven sawmills and great cranes for lifting, Dutch industrialists developed the most efficient shipbuilding industry in seventeenth-century Europe (Kindleberger 1975). Working with an inventory of millions of tons of timber imported mainly from the Baltic, workers in the yards of Saardam could build fluyts at the rate of one a day (Wallerstein 1980; Kindleberger 1975). Wallerstein (1980: 55) views this efficiency in Dutch shipbuilding as having had a spiral effect: "[C]heaper freights led to control of the Baltic trade, which led to cheaper timber, which led to cheaper costs in shipbuilding, which led to cheaper freights."

Another industry in which the Dutch surpassed other developing industrial areas in Europe in the seventeenth century was textile production. In this industry, which was centered in Leiden, the Dutch owed their superiority to the immigration of cloth workers and entrepreneurs from the war-torn southern Netherlands and to the situation that European cloth makers sent their materials to Holland for finishing and dressing processes (Wilson 1965, 1968). Beginning in the 1570s, the declining textile industry of Leiden was revitalized by the immigration of thousands of cloth workers who fled the southern Netherlands to escape the Spanish repression of the Dutch revolt against the rule of the Roman Catholic Habsburg King Philip II of Spain (Barker 1906). Not only did the immigrant workers provide a large supply of labor power for Leiden's textile production, they also introduced the profitable "new draperies" (e.g., bays, says, camlets, and fustians) to the city's textile industry (Wilson 1967; Coleman 1969).[3]

The advancement of the Dutch in agriculture during their interval of hegemony consisted mainly in draining wetlands, industrial-crop production, and improved agricultural techniques (Wallerstein 1980). Projects of land reclamation from the sea undertaken by the Dutch to enlarge agricultural areas were comparable in economic importance to today's most impressive industrial undertakings (De Vries 1974). Financed by urban capitalists, the largest projects involved thousands of laborers and required the ingenuity and coordination of many surveyors and hydraulic engineers. For example, a reclamation project started in 1596 in an inundated coastal area of the Zijpe involved over 3000 workers and 1000 horses and was encouraged by tax exemptions from various taxes for up to twenty years in

---

[3] Coleman (1969: 421) hypothesizes that the new draperies originated in Flanders from "commercialization of peasant techniques" and from "copying, and adaptation, of Italian textile models."

some cases (De Vries 1974). The Dutch achieved the highest level of polder development between the first and fourth decades of the seventeenth century when the amount of reclaimed land averaged 1762 ha per year (De Vries 1974). There is a Dutch saying derived from this history: "God made the sea; we made the land" (Barker 1906: 12).

Much of the reclaimed land was not suitable for arable agriculture. The Dutch, however, turned this disadvantage into an economic gain. By shifting to industrial crops such as flax, hemp, hops, and particularly those used for the making of dyes, the Dutch were able to advance the growth of their industries and then trade advantageously for much of the grain they needed (Wallerstein 1980). Other innovations that made the United Provinces the leading agricultural area in Europe for much of the seventeenth century were rotation systems, cultivation of fodder crops, bed and row cultivation, the use of light plows, and the use of urban refuse and cattle manure for fertilizer (Slicher van Bath 1960). During the "Dutch agricultural century," visitors from Great Britain, France, Germany, Italy, and Sweden traveled through the United Provinces to study the agricultural innovations of the Dutch (Wallerstein 1980: 41–42; Slicher van Bath 1960).

3.1.2 Commercial Expansion

During their hegemonic status, the Dutch "spread everywhere" in the pursuit of economic gain (Coornaert 1967: 244). Vlekke (1951) captured the spirit of Dutch commercial expansion in the East Indies, the West Indies, the Atlantic, the Mediterranean, and the Baltic in the following comment:

> Everywhere and always the sole concern of XVIIth century Dutch capitalism was "profit making," whether under the Netherland flag or that of some other nation or even under the black flag of piracy. [...] Gold was their sole aim and many did not hesitate to sell Spain ammunition and war equipment that, a few days later, might be used against Netherland towns and troops. A popular story told of a sea captain who said that "he would sail into hell and trade with the devil were it not that his sails might catch fire." (Vlekke 1951: 180)

The first appearance of Dutch trading vessels in the East Indies occurred on June 5, 1596, when four Dutch ships approached the west coast of Sumatra (Vlekke 1945). Dutch motivation to go to the East Indies came partly from the war with Spain, which made Lisbon, the chief European spice port, inaccessible to them (Wallerstein 1980). Following the principle of going around intermediaries, the Dutch bypassed India and went directly to the Indonesian sources of spices (Parry 1967). But if the original intention of the Dutch in the East Indies was to gain access to spice trading, it soon changed. Organized through the East India Company (*Vereenigde Oost-Indische Compagnie*), which was established in 1602 mainly by investors from Amsterdam, the Dutch undertook actions that by the early 1620s gave them a monopoly of the spice trade, as well as shipping control in much of the inter-Asiatic trade. Under conditions of ongoing warfare with Portuguese, British, and native forces in Java, the Moluccas, and the Banda Islands, the Dutch

3.1 Dutch Hegemony

established a commercial network in the Indian Ocean and in the Far East by 1623. In the region, the Dutch traded for such items as spices, silk, cloth, porcelain, and copper in the ports of India, Ceylon, Indonesia, Formosa, and Japan (Vlekke 1945; Hyma, 1942).

In the Atlantic, Dutch commercial expansion was carried out through the West India Company. Similar to its sister company in the East, the West India Company was a joint-stock venture organized by investors from different parts of the United Provinces, with Amsterdam investors constituting the majority of shareholders (Boxer 1965). However, in contrast to its sister company, the West India Company had a diversity of religious and political factions among investors, some of which favored colonizing and privateering as a means to wealth (Wallerstein 1980). Chartered in 1621, the West India Company also had a major mission of raiding Spanish shipping in the New World (Boxer 1965; Geyl 1961). Its biggest success in this mission occurred in 1628 when the Dutch captured a Spanish fleet carrying Mexican silver valued in the millions (Boxer 1965). By 1636, the West India Company had captured or destroyed 547 Spanish ships (Geyl 1961). In carrying out its other projects of colonizing and trading, including involvement in the "triangular trade" based on slave transfers, the Company reached its zenith in 1640. By this time, it had gained several possessions, including the Pernambuco sugar industry in Brazil, fur-trading colonies on the Hudson River, the islands of Curacao and Aruba in the Caribbean, trading posts on the Gold Coast, and the slave market in Angola (Van Hoboken 1960).

The entry of the Dutch into the Mediterranean trade was intense and forceful, particularly in northern Italy.[4] For example, of the 15,000 tons of grain transported to Leghorn in 1593 from more than ten northern European ports, Amsterdam alone was the source for close to 40% of the tonnage (Braudel 1972). With superior ships and the ability to reach northern Italy in five weeks, the Dutch were able to gain control of the larger trade between the Mediterranean and northern Europe by the early seventeenth century (Parry 1967). The success of the Dutch in the Mediterranean trade, however, was heavily dependent on their Baltic trade, which was the source of timber and grain.

The Dutch trade in the Baltic involved trading cloth and draperies from the Netherlands, salt from Biscay and Portugal, and herring from the North Sea for iron and copper from Sweden, timber from Norway, and grain and timber from Poland (Wilson 1968; Boxer 1965). Based partly on their efficient shipping, which enabled cheap freights, and on their supply of silver in times of currency devaluation in the Baltic, the Dutch were able to control about 60% of the Baltic shipping in the sixteenth century and through the 1660s (Wallerstein 1980). This dominance included transporting three-fourths of the rye and wheat that was exported from the Baltic (Glamann 1974). Danzig (Gdansk) was the principal source of grain. Connected to the rich hinterland by the Vistula River and its tributaries, Danzig

---

[4] According to Fernand Braudel (1972: 634), "the Dutch swarmed into the Mediterranean like so many heavy insects crashing against window panes."

supplied about 70% of the rye and 64% of the wheat in the Baltic trade (Glamann 1974).

While foreign trade with Asia and the New World extended the economic reach of the Dutch, it was the river trade between Holland and other areas in the Netherlands and western Europe that became the chief commerce of the Dutch in their era of hegemony. According to Wallerstein (1980), Dutch trading in the East Indies, the Mediterranean, and the Atlantic did not generate the level of commerce achieved by the Dutch in the inland river trade in Europe. Of great importance for the industrializing cities in Holland, the river trade was the source of peat fuel (De Vries 1974). For the agricultural industry, the river trade was the source of urban manure (Wilson 1968). With the construction of the first *trekvaart* (a channel for passenger boats) in 1632, the river commerce accelerated through intensive capital funding and reached its height of prosperity in the 1660s (Wallerstein 1980). Water transportation grew in financial importance because it was cheaper than land transportation.

3.2 Migration in the Northern Netherlands

The migration of capital and labor was a central force of the Dutch rise to hegemony in the young capitalist world-economy. It enabled the United Provinces to reach a height of economic development beyond what existed in neighboring countries. Two patterns of capital migration particularly spurred economic development in the northern Netherlands. One pattern was the migration of capital to the Dutch countryside before and during the rise to hegemony, which gave capitalist entrepreneurs an opening for growth in the craft trades. A second pattern was the migration of refugee business families from the southern Netherlands to the northern Netherlands to escape the devastation brought by Spanish forces in the southern region. This refugee migration helped to amass capital wealth especially in Holland (Amsterdam), which helped to expand investment enterprises in land reclamation, shipbuilding, agricultural industrialization, etc., in the United Provinces.

3.2.1 Capital Migration in the Northern Netherlands

In the late sixteenth and early seventeenth centuries, emerging Dutch capitalist entrepreneurs lacked the power to counter the craft guilds in the established trade industries that produced cloth, hats, shoes, etc. (Barbour 1950; Geyl 1961). The majority of the guilds in Holland were recently formed and thus did not have an official voice in government, but they gained influence through the support of town officials, who viewed the guilds as sources of jobs ('t Hart 2001). Craft guilds in towns regulated work standards and working conditions, e.g., the number of work hours per day and the number of workers per workshop (Geyl 1961).

3.2 Migration in the Northern Netherlands

Dutch urban centers also had acquired decrees to restrict the out-migration of craftwork to the countryside, but by the late sixteenth and early seventeenth centuries, the decrees became ineffective (Hoppenbrouwers 2001). Similar to actions taken by cloth merchant-capitalists in England in the fourteenth century (see Chap. 2), Dutch entrepreneurial capital circumvented the power of craft guilds by establishing craft production in rural areas, particularly in the low-wage countryside outside Holland (Van der Woude 1975). Examples of the rural transfer of craft production by capitalist entrepreneurs included the decline of textile manufacture in Haarlem and Leiden and its growth in rural Twente and North Brabant; the decline of pottery-making in Delft in southern Holland and its growth in Friesland; and the transfer of commercial-baking from northern Holland to rural places outside the province (Van der Woude 1975).

The relocation of industries to the countryside provided advantages for employers. Urban industries in Holland were re-established in rural areas outside the urban radius of business taxes and in other provinces where wages were lower than in Holland (De Vries 1974; Van der Woude 1975; Hoppenbrouwers 2001). One example was the relocation of linen production in rural areas of the province of Overijssel. Labor conditions in the countryside of this province could not have been more attractive for textile entrepreneurs. An expanding rural population accompanied by a declining agricultural (grain) economy made the hinterland of Overijssel a prime area for the putting-out system in the latter part of the seventeenth century (De Vries 1974). Textile production became an occupation of the province's rural poor, and, conducted on a family basis, it involved the labor of children (Van der Woude 1975).

In the late sixteenth century, Roman Catholic Hapsburg King Philip II of Spain undertook a violent repression of Calvinist and other forces that opposed his rule in the southern Netherlands. The Spanish repression took tens of thousands of lives, including the lives of 8000 citizens in Antwerp and thousands more through the Inquisition (Barker 1906; Helleiner 1967). The resulting refugee exodus helped concentrate business capital in the northern Netherlands, especially in the financial center of Amsterdam in Holland and in Zeeland (Vlekke 1945). Among the 180,000 inhabitants who fled the southern Netherlands were members of once-powerful merchant and industrialist families from Antwerp, Brussels, Ghent, and other cities in the southern Netherlands (Norwood 1942; Vlekke 1945). Some of these refugees were families that had earlier migrated to the southern Netherlands (particularly to Antwerp) for business purposes or to escape religious persecution in Germany, France, and England (Barker 1906). The refugees from the southern Netherlands also included Jewish merchants and financiers who had originally fled persecution in Portugal and Spain.

By 1610, the business families from the southern Netherlands accounted for more than half of the 320 greatest depositors in the exchange bank of Amsterdam, and in 1631 for one-third of the richest citizens in Amsterdam (Barbour 1950). The migrant business families became an aggressive investment source for joint-stock ventures in the Dutch trade in Russia, the Mediterranean, the East Indies, and the West Indies. Investment for ventures in the latter two regions involved the funding of the East Indies and the West Indies quasi-governmental companies and the funding of other smaller joint-stock enterprises that sought to gain economic profit from the expansion of Dutch trade and colonialism to the East and to the Americas (Barbour 1950). The profit sources included trade in commodities (e.g., spices, raw sugar, and slaves) and speculative trading in stock and shares in the companies that ventured to faraway regions.

In addition to being a financial source for the joint-stock companies involved in trading and other profit-seeking activities abroad, capital migration from the southern provinces helped give rise to business institutions in the northern Netherlands, including the Exchange Bank and the Loan Bank in Amsterdam, both established after the Italian bank model (Wilson 1968). The Exchange Bank and other smaller business institutions, such as trading clubs and finance houses, played a central role in organizing trade and financial exchanges among Dutch investors and between Dutch and other business investors in the expanding world-economy. The Exchange Bank, later rename the Brouse, was founded in 1609 and was administered by the city of Amsterdam. In 1611, it had 708 depositors and the number grew to 2698 by 1701, with florin deposits growing from f. 925,562 to f. 16,284,849 during this period (Barbour 1950). More than just a place for buying and selling commodities, or for investing in projects for production, the Amsterdam financial district, which was centered on the Exchange Bank, advanced speculative trading such as in commodity futures, company shares, public loans, annuities, and insurance (Barbour 1950). According to Braudel (1982: 535), by the late seventeenth century the distinction in Amsterdam "between wholesale merchants and banker-financiers grew wider... and the gap... rapidly expanded." To a significant extent, capital migration to the United Provinces helped make Amsterdam the core financial center of the world-economy in the period of Dutch hegemony.

3.2.2 Labor Migration in the Northern Netherlands

Labor migration was a principal element supporting the United Provinces' economic development in the seventeenth century. Four patterns of migration were key sources of labor for economic development in the United Provinces from the late sixteenth century to the end of Dutch hegemonic status in the 1670s. These patterns were rural to urban migration, immigration of workers from the southern Netherlands, importation of child labor, and migration between rural areas.

Rural to Urban Migration. During Dutch economic ascension in the late 1500s and early 1600s and throughout the Dutch interval of hegemony, Holland was the center of economic growth in the United Provinces. In addition to being the most industrialized province in the Dutch Republic during its "Golden Age," it was also the most urbanized. By the start of Dutch hegemony in the 1620s, a time when Europeans lived predominantly in rural areas, 60% of Holland lived in urban areas (De Vries 1974). While natural population increase contributed to this urbanization, the high rate and uneven growth patterns in the province's urban

3.2 Migration in the Northern Netherlands

centers indicated that in-migration was also a source of urban growth (see De Vries 1974). Among the urban centers in Holland, the most industrialized cities, e.g., Amsterdam and Leiden, grew at a higher rate (Price 1974). At the beginning of Dutch hegemony in the early 1620s, about 57% of Holland's 397,307 urban inhabitants lived in the five leading commercial centers of Amsterdam, Rotterdam, Leiden, Haarlem, and the Hague. By the end of the hegemonic era in the 1670s, these five cities accounted for about 68% of Holland's urban population (De Vries 1974).

People who left the countryside to work in the towns and cities were those who lost or sold their lands, came from impoverished areas, or lived in areas of surplus population (Van der Woude 1975; Lambert 1971; De Vries 1974). Impoverished peasants in industrializing agricultural areas sold their land to town merchants and moved to towns and cities in search of livelihoods in fishing or urban industries (Van de Woude 1975). Men from the economically less-developed rural areas in northern Holland (e.g., Westfriesland, Waterland, and the Zaanstreek) migrated permanently or seasonally to work in the merchant and fishing fleets in such ports as Amsterdam, Monnickendam, and Edam (Lambert 1971). The surplus working population in rural areas was partly a consequence of a political situation in which urban centers in Holland had obtained a decree (the *Order op de Buitennering*) in 1531 to prohibit many urban industries from relocating to the countryside (Lambert 1971; 't Hart 2001; Hoppenbrouwers 2001).[5]

Immigration from the Southern Netherlands. The immigration of workers from the southern Netherlands was part of the mass exodus that ensued after Philip II of Spain sent 10,000 Spanish soldiers to the region in 1567. Philip II wanted to keep the Netherlands in the Habsburg Empire by suppressing agitation for self-government and rising Protestantism (Vlekke 1945). It is estimated that 180,000 inhabitants of the southern Netherlands fled the Spanish suppression, migrating especially to the textile centers of Leiden and Haarlem and to Amsterdam (Geyl 1966; Van Houtte 1977).[6] Antwerp, which had been the commercial and industrial center for much of western Europe in the first half of the sixteenth century, suffered the severest depopulation during the Spanish invasion with the loss of about 50,000 inhabitants from 1568 to 1589 (Helleiner 1967).[7]

---

[5] Dutch textile industrial production was originally established in the southern Netherlands as a rural industry; as demand for textile increased, it became an urban industry in Flanders in the twelfth century (Harreld 2004). In a description of production in Holland in the sixteenth through the early eighteenth centuries, 't Hart (2001: 89) describes the putting-out system of textile production as being "concentrated among urban spinners and weavers."

[6] Different figures have been given for the number of refugees that fled the Spanish Inquisition in the southern Netherlands. I use Van Houtte's conservative estimate of 180,000 because it is more soundly derived.

[7] Barker (1906) describes that 19,000 people from Antwerp went to Holland (especially to Amsterdam) following a Spanish attack on Antwerp on November 4, 1576. De Vries (1974) describes that after Antwerp was captured by the Duke of Alva in 1585 there was a rapid loss of 30,000 of the city's inhabitants, who either emigrated or died.

The situation from which the northward migrants fled was that of a war-torn region in social and economic turmoil. Thousands of lives were taken by the Spanish force, which sacked and plundered in the southern Netherlands. Barker (1906: 95) described the devastation as a situation in which "Murder and rapine reigned supreme." The Inquisition accounted for another 7000 victims between 1568 and 1573 (Helleiner 1967).[8] The Spanish campaigns against rebel forces also produced much destruction in the industries in the southern provinces, and by 1584, only the fulling mills of Blendecques were left standing in all of Flanders (Cipolla 1980).[9]

In Holland, workers and other emigrants from the southern provinces found a liberal and economically attractive atmosphere. By the late 1580s, the seven northern provinces of Holland, Zeeland, Gelderland, Friesland, Overijssel, Groningen, and Utrecht, which composed the United Provinces, had achieved substantial success against the Spanish forces and were in a stage of rebuilding and expanding their industries (Price 1974). In the period 1612–1632, the municipal government of Amsterdam enacted a policy to provide housing and other inducements to skilled, immigrant workers from the southern provinces and other countries that came to work in the city's industries of silk-finishing, cloth-making, cloth-dressing, leather-gilding, glass-blowing, mirror-manufacturing, salt-refining, and shipbuilding (Barbour 1950).

Immigrant labor from the southern Netherlands expanded cloth production in the major textile center of Leiden (Spooner 1970; Price 1974). From the latter 1500s and throughout most of the seventeenth century, immigrant Flemish textile workers (particularly from the area around Hondschoote) increased the city's cloth production from 27,000 pieces in 1584 to 144,000 pieces by 1664 (Price 1974). But the most cited contribution of immigrant textile workers from the southern Netherlands was the introduction of new draperies, i.e., fabrics that were smoother and lighter than those previously produced in the textile centers of the United Provinces (Price 1974). Immigration of more than 400 silk workers from Antwerp and other towns of the southern Netherlands in the years 1585 to 1606 also helped develop silk industries in Amsterdam, Utrecht, and Haarlem (Norwood 1942; Barbour 1950). The establishment in Haarlem of linen bleacheries that treated yarns from various parts of Europe, e.g., England, Germany, and Baltic countries, is also considered to have resulted from worker immigration from the southern Netherlands (Lambert 1971).

Child Labor Importation. Labor migration in the United Provinces in the form of child labor importations concerned mainly the industrializing towns and cities

---

[8] The figure of 7000 victims is a conservative estimate. As described by Barker (1906), other estimates range from 50,000 to 100,000 victims, and the military commander of the repression, the Duke of Alva ("the Iron Duke"), claimed 18,000 executions. Gruesome effects of religious persecution were omnipresent: "Gallows, wheels, stakes, and trees in the highways were laden with carcasses or timber of such as had been hanged, beheaded, or roasted" (Brandt 1720: 112).

[9] The economy of the southern Netherlands suffered additional damage when the Spanish forces seized the properties of suspected Anabaptists, Calvinists, and Lutherans, exacted special tributes from towns, and levied a 10% tax of the value of any article sold (Geyl 1966).

in Holland. In such industrial centers of the province as Haarlem and Leiden, child workers, which in some cases included young girls, were especially sought by the larger textile manufacturers (Murray 1967).[10] To supplement the supply of child workers from local working-class families, big textile manufacturers obtained child workers, supposedly to work as apprentices, from orphanages and almshouses in Holland and abroad (Geyl 1961). Between the years 1608 and 1643, textile manufacturers in Leiden employed 1542 orphans of the town (Van Houtte 1977). Between 1638 and 1664, the number of native and foreign child workers registered by cloth manufacturers in Leiden totaled 7500 (Van Houtte 1977). The manufacturers of Leiden sought orphans and other child workers outside of the United Provinces in such areas as the Rhineland, Westphalia, Norwich, and Douai (Lambert 1971; Van Houtte 1977). Liege alone is considered to have been a source for over 4000 of Leiden's child workers (Lambert 1971).

Child labor became a part of the silk industry in Amsterdam that developed in the early seventeenth century with the establishment of regular supplies of raw silk from the Far East. The child workers were primarily used in spinning and spooling tasks of the silk industry, which consumed about 120,000 pounds of raw silk annually (Van Houtte 1977). As described by Vlekke (1951: 178), the lives of child workers in the urban industries of seventeenth-century Holland were harsh: "children six years of age and over were forced to work as long as daylight permitted, and then set free to be on the streets." The use of child labor was not restricted to the textile industry. Throughout Europe, child labor was used in the seventeenth century in printing, mining, and metallurgy industries (Kellenbenz 1977). It is likely that child labor was also used in Holland's expanding printing industry, which produced maps and charts for the United Provinces' expansion of world trade.

Rural to Rural Migration. The commercial and industrial development in the urban centers of the United Provinces during its development as a hegemonic state is also seen as having significantly affected labor migration in rural sectors (Lambert 1971). One way in which urban economic growth influenced rural migration was by the movement of urban industries to the countryside. Once relocated in rural areas, these industries attracted the in-migration of rural labor if they were not located next to a labor supply. A second way by which urban economic growth influenced rural labor migration was by the development of rural industries that produced goods for urban areas. Like some of the urban industries that were re-established in the countryside, the growth of these rural industries relied on the in-migration of rural labor if they were not located among populations of workers.

---

[10] As Van Nederveen Meerkerk (2004) explains, Dutch orphan boys and girls did not receive the same work educational opportunity. Boys placed with master craftworkers received the training of regular apprentices and could advance in the trade with their education, while girls remained spinners from childhood until adulthood, unprepared for higher skill work. Gender labor segmentation characterized the Dutch textile industry, producing the situation that women had inferior working conditions and pay compared to men (Van Nederveen Meerkerk 2010).

According to De Vries' (1974) analysis of Dutch rural development in the seventeenth century, even before the United Provinces' ascension as a world power in the late sixteenth and seventeenth centuries, labor migration was a significant feature of the Dutch countryside. A survey undertaken in 1540 of the population living within the immediate rural vicinity of Leiden showed that of the 52 respondents only eight had lived in the area all of their lives (De Vries 1974). Although the majority of the respondents were over 40 years of age, half indicated that they had moved to their 1540 residence within the previous ten years, and many indicated that they had lived in more than one village prior to moving to the vicinity of Leiden.

A description of the residence of older children recorded in the probate records of deceased farmers in the rural district of Hennaarderadeel in the province of Friesland illustrates the nature of Dutch rural migration in the mid-seventeenth century. According to the description, of 127 children over the age of 20 in 34 households recorded in the probate records in the period 1651 to 1655, 25 lived in their parents' villages; 19 lived elsewhere in the rural district; 40 lived elsewhere in rural Friesland; 27 lived in cities in Friesland and Holland; and 16 had unknown residency (De Vries 1974). Even if it is assumed that the 16 with unknown residency lived in their parents' villages or migrated to cities, the proportion of the children that migrated to other rural localities is almost one-half. De Vries (1974: 113) comments on Dutch rural migration in the sixteenth and seventeenth centuries as follows:

> This information is not consistent with the frequently evoked image of the stable rural society of the ancient regime, where sons succeeded their fathers on ancestral homesteads. Such a stable succession hardly characterized the landed farmers, surely we cannot suppose it characterized the growing rural proletariat of the northern Netherlands.

Dutch economic development contributed to the proletarianization and migration that had begun to characterize rural sectors even before the Dutch rise to hegemony. The development furthered a rural social dynamic different from earlier conditions where much of rural life was based on a sedentary culture.[11]

By the latter part of the seventeenth century, there was also a movement trend of Holland's urban shipbuilding industry relocating to the countryside, where lower wage levels existed (Van de Woude 1975). In the same period, the linen industry declined in Haarlem and Leiden and redeveloped in the countryside of Twente, the easternmost region of the province of Overijssel. Linen manufacturing and its ancillary (labor-intensive) flax farming in Twente depended heavily on the labor of poor rural families (Van der Woude 1975). Another example of the ruralization of urban industries was the movement of the herring-packing industry from Rotterdam to settlements downstream on the Maas (Meuse) River. In the first quarter

---

[11] Yet, as Adams (1994) points out, feudalism never fully characterized the northern provinces that constituted the United Provinces, or never to the extent that it characterized the southern provinces and other European areas.

3.2 Migration in the Northern Netherlands

of the seventeenth century, Rotterdam developed into the greatest herring-packing center on the Maas estuary (Lambert 1971); however, as the town expanded its trade in tobacco, coal, and lead, and developed distilling and shipbuilding industries, its herring-packing industry passed to settlements around Scheidam, "where a poverty-stricken, peaty hinterland furnished a large, cheap labour force" (Lambert 1971:186).

Two major rural industries that were linked to urban economic growth and that depended heavily on the migration of workers were land reclamation and peat production. Land reclamation, both through the dyking of coastal lands (*bedijkingen*) and through the drainage of lakes (*droogmakerij*), was closely associated with Dutch urban economic growth in the seventeenth century. It was an industry in which urban capitalists invested and that enabled the development of farms to produce industrial and food crops consumed in the cities (Wagret 1968). In the seventeenth century, land reclamation, which was related to the grain prices in the market of Amsterdam (Spooner 1970), reached a boom in the 1615–1640 period with a total reclamation of 111,407 acres (Minchinton 1976). This amount was not achieved again until the mid-1800s (Wagret 1968). Even with the use of windmills for draining water, land reclamation remained a labor-intensive industry in the seventeenth century. The basic tools used in reclamation projects consisted of wheelbarrows, spades, mattocks, and pile drivers operated by teams of 30–40 men (Lambert 1971).

Land reclamation attracted thousands of workers to the drainage sites (the drainage of the Zijpe in the late 1590s involved a workforce of over 3000 workers), and it also brought the in-migration of families that came to farm on the reclaimed lands. Indeed, in trying to gain support for drainage projects, capitalists stressed that reclaimed lands attracted workers and farmers that otherwise would emigrate to other regions, "to the detriment of the tax revenue" (De Vries 1974: 194–195). In the Noorderkwartier, after the drainage of six of the larger lakes in the first half of the seventeenth century, the in-migration of agricultural people led to the development of 1402 new farms (De Vries 1974).

The peat industry affected the rural migration of workers in much the same way as land reclamation did. A consortium of capitalists would organize a peat excavation project and recruit thousands of workers to build the infrastructure for peat production.[12] This consisted of such work as building windmills for lowering the surface water on peaty grounds; constructing canals for carrying away the water; and laying out farm plots on which settlers could farm and produce peat-fuel blocks for the market (Lambert 1971; De Vries 1974). After the construction of the peat plots was completed, settlers arrived to farm and dig for peat.

---

[12] As described by the economic historian Carlo M. Cipolla (1980), in the United Provinces in the seventeenth-century peat was used not only for home purposes but also in the industrial production of such things as brick, glass, beer, and pottery. According to Cipolla, in the mid-seventeenth century, the Dutch were burning peat at an amount of 6000 million kilo-calories per year.

The need for the in-migration of labor in the peat industry was a consequence not only of the expansion of the industry but also of its production methods. Preparation of the infrastructure for peat production and the production process itself was labor-intensive. Women and children worked in the final processes of treading and piling the peat blocks (Lambert 1971).[13] The construction of the infrastructure (building windmills, digging canals, etc.) involved the same labor-intensive work as land reclamation.

As explained by De Vries (1974), the peat industry's impact on the development of rural communities extended beyond the people who migrated to farm and work the peat bogs.

The opening of new peat-production sites further necessitated labor in-migration for the construction of ships and the building of large water-transportation networks to deliver the peat fuel to urban markets. In peat-producing areas such as in the southern rural part of the province of Groningen, labor migration contributed to the development in the early part of the seventeenth century of industrial workforces for shipbuilding and transportation industries.

3.3 Migration in the Periphery

In comparison with the patterns of migration in the northern Netherlands, Dutch capital and labor migration to the newly peripheralized areas of the emerging world-economy was much less dynamic. During the Dutch period of hegemony, only a few thousand Dutch migrated from the United Provinces to the largest colonial settlements in the East Indies, the West Indies, the Hudson River region, and Africa. In terms of capital, the quasi-governmental Dutch East India and West India Companies were invested with 6.5 and 7.0 million guilders,[14] respectively, with the largest sums of capital invested by Amsterdam funders (Barbour 1950; Boxer 1965). In terms of magnitude, the largest migration in the periphery related to Dutch expansion was not of Dutch immigrants, but of African slaves imported into the West Indies. Jan Pieterszoon Coen, who was appointed Governor-General in the Dutch East Indies in the early seventeenth century, blamed the rural migration to drained lands in the northern Netherlands for the lack of Dutch labor emigration to colonial areas (Geyl 1961).

---

[13] Production of peat-fuel blocks consisted of several processes (Lambert 1971). First, peat was dredged with a long-handled tool (the *baggerbeugel*) from the bog. Second, the peat was raked, mixed with water, mashed, and spread on a layer of reeds to drain. Third, the peat was treaded. Finally, the dried and compressed peat was cut into blocks and piled for storage to be later sent to the towns.

[14] The Dutch name "guilder" (Dutch medieval meaning: "golden") is symbolized by "f" or "fl." which is derived from the old currency of the *florin*. Guilder and florin (f) have often been used interchangeably (Krause and Mishler 2003).

3.3.1 East Indies

The migrations involved in the Dutch East Indies trade during the Dutch period of hegemony included the arrival of Dutch East Indies Company traders and administrators, Chinese merchants and workers, and imported slaves. The number of Dutch who settled in Batavia (now Jakarta), the center of Dutch administration in the East Indies colonial zone, has been described as a few hundred Dutch aristocratic traders, some of who brought their families.[15] A Dutch military force of about 1200 soldiers was also transferred to Batavia (Vlekke 1945). Throughout the seventeenth century, the number of Europeans (Dutch, British, and Portuguese) in Batavia varied from five to ten thousand (Vlekke 1945).

Chinese migrants played an intermediary role for the Dutch East India Company in the Malay Archipelago. Chinese traders conducted business between Company posts and the small ports in the Archipelago that were not visited by Dutch ships. The Chinese also became entrepreneurs in the Archipelago's sugar-growing and milling industries (Masefield 1967). In addition, the Chinese worked as fishermen, tailors, bricklayers, and carpenters (Vlekke 1945). Migrating alone to the Archipelago, Chinese men married native women or bought slave women. The number of Chinese in Batavia grew from eight hundred in the early 1620s to two thousand a decade later.

Men and women slaves were brought to the Dutch trading centers in the East Indies from local islands and from the coast of India (Vlekke 1945; Rich 1967). Their number, however, never approached the number of African slaves used in the West Indies. The slaves worked as house servants and as sanitation and agricultural workers (Rich 1967). About one hundred slaves were used to clean and to maintain the drainage canals of Batavia (Vlekke 1945). In the absence of the immigrant women from the United Provinces, Dutch personnel took slave women as wives, much to the displeasure of colonial officials (Geyl 1961).

3.3.2 Atlantic Peripheral Zone

Migration related to Dutch expansion in the Atlantic peripheral zone of the emerging world-system was greater than in the East Indies. Control of areas in the Atlantic periphery by the Dutch West India Company ranged widely. Above the equator, the West India Company gained control of a small trading colony, New Netherlands, on the island of Manhattan, and control of islands in the West Indies, and slave trading ports on the western African coast. Below the equator, the Dutch gained control of a northern region of Brazil and more slave trading ports on the African coast. The most active Dutch expansion in the Atlantic area during the

---

[15] Batavia was originally a fortress. The Dutch captured the fortress in a 1618–1619 conflict with English and native forces. After capturing the fortress, the Dutch called it Batavia, "as Holland used to be called in days of antiquity" (Vlekke 1945: 87). Batavia became the capital of the Dutch East Indies.

period of Dutch hegemony was in northeastern Brazil, particularly in the captaincy of Pernambuco. For many Dutch who migrated to Brazil during its possession by the Dutch from 1630 to 1654, the source of attraction was the sugar industry. But sugar production was dependent on another commerce—the African slave trade. In the era of Dutch hegemony, it was the forced transfer of slaves from western Africa to sugar-producing Pernambuco and islands in the West Indies that constituted the largest patterns of labor movement in the Dutch-controlled peripheral areas.

3.3.3 Colonizing Northeastern Brazil

After waging a six-year struggle for control of the Portuguese-occupied eastern coast of Brazil, the Dutch West India Company finally took possession of Pernambuco's capital, Olinda, and a nearby harbor, Recife, in 1630. The Heeren XIX, i.e., the nineteen-men directorate of the Dutch West India Company, envisioned several advantages that the Company could derive from the possession of northeastern Brazil (Boxer 1957). Firstly, the region's coast was an excellent base for the Company's pirating operations in the Caribbean. Secondly, Recife would provide the Company's forces a strategic position to attack sources of Spain's wealth in the Americas. Thirdly, Dutch Brazil would enable the Dutch to create colonies where Dutch immigrants "of modest means" could work in sugar and tobacco planting and set up small shops.

Fourthly, from ports in northeastern Brazil the company would be able to control Brazil's slave trade with Cape Verde, Guinea, and Angola in Africa. Finally, according to optimistic Dutch calculations, it was estimated that the trade in northeastern Brazil would yield the Dutch about 8 million guilders yearly, with about 60% coming from the sugar trade alone (Boxer 1957).

The optimism of the Heeren XIX for profitable involvement in northeastern Brazil was based on the knowledge that the Portuguese had built 137 sugar mills in Pernambuco, producing about 22.4 million pounds of sugar yearly, and that the Portuguese brought 8000 slaves from Angola to Brazil yearly and about an equal number to Spanish America (Boxer 1957). When the Dutch took possession of Pernambuco, however, they found that the Portuguese had implemented a "scorched earth" policy in their retreat inland. Many of the sugar mills and sugarcane fields had been burned to the ground (Vlekke 1951). It was not until the late 1630s that the Dutch were able to raise sugar production and, hence, the slave trade to profitable levels, although at levels less than what had been expected.[16] Whereas the Portuguese had been able to export more than 20 million pounds of

---

[16] A decade and a half after taking possession of northeastern Brazil, the Dutch West India Company remained optimistic about investing in Brazil and in the African slave trade of the West Indies. In 1644, the West India Company projected that a capital outlay of 1,430,000 guilders in Dutch Brazil would produce an 89% profit. For the African part of the triangular trade, it was estimated that an outlay of 144,000 guilders would produce an 859% profit of 1,238,000 guilders.

sugar a year from Brazil, mostly from the northeastern regions, the Dutch could only reach a sugar export level of about 8 million pounds (Vlekke 1951; Boxer 1957).

Frequent raids by guerilla bands from the two to three thousand Portuguese that fled inland, and the lack of an adequate labor supply limited Dutch economic development in Brazil. The emigration of agricultural labor from the Netherlands to Dutch Brazil that some members of the Heeren XIX had envisioned did not materialize at the expected level. Although some Dutch farmers did migrate to Brazil (mainly to Pernambuco), many more immigrated as merchants and artisans (Boxer 1957). In addition, most of the immigrants in Dutch Brazil stayed in or near the colony at Recife. That is, they did not go into the agricultural lands where workers were needed as mill craftworkers and planters. With an inadequate supply of Dutch immigrant labor, the region's sugar production remained largely in the hands of Portuguese planters and mill owners (Geyl 1961).

A census of Dutch Brazil conducted by the West India Company in 1645 counted a total of 12,703 persons. As tabulated by Wiznitzer (1954), the breakdown of the 1645 census count was as follows: (a) Company soldiers, 3050; (b) wives and children of Company employees, 500; (c) non-Company civilians (White Hollanders, Portuguese Jews), 2899; and (d) indigenous people, 3583; African slaves, 2671. Of the non-Company civilians, 1704 lived in the region of Recife and consisted of 855 men, 452 women, and 397 children. The remaining non-Company civilians lived in the regions of Maurícia (685), Itamaracá (150), Paraíba (160), and Rio Grande (200).

Non-Company immigrants (i.e., the *vrijluyden*) consisted of merchants, sugar planters, manual laborers, retired soldiers, and artisans (e.g., smiths, masons, builders, and cobblers) (Boxer 1957). The 1645 Company census indicated that the majority of the non-Company immigrants settled in the colony at Recife. Johan Maurits, the Governor-General of Dutch Brazil from 1637 to 1644, described the vrijluyden in Recife as a burden on the Company who were unwilling to undertake agricultural work. At one point, he asked the Heeren XIX to recruit workers for Dutch Brazil from among German refugees of the Thirty Years War in the Netherlands. As an alternative, he also petitioned the Prince of Orange for workers: "The soil needs nothing but inhabitants and cries out for colonists to people and till this solitude.... I wish that the Amsterdam workhouses would be opened and the galley-slaves released so that they could here till the soil...." (quoted in Boxer 1957: 71–72).

Jews, both Sephardic and Ashkenazim, reached their greatest number in Dutch Brazil in the mid-1640s, constituting about one-half of the vrijluyden population (Witznitzer 1954). Viewing Dutch Brazil as a refuge from persecution and as an opportunity for prosperity, Jews emigrated to Pernambuco from Amsterdam and from other parts of Europe and Portuguese territories. While some Jews arrived in

---

A detailed breakdown of this tentative accounting is found in Boxer (1957). Nonetheless, scholars have debated the profitability of the Atlantic slave trade for Dutch investors and the economic impact of profits from the slave trade for the overall Dutch economy (Emmer 1975).

Pernambuco "with nothing but the little torn garment which they wore," according to one observer (see Boxer 1957: 134), others came with financial power or quickly achieved it. The Jews that prospered played an important intermediary role in the Dutch rebuilding of the region's economy. Since many of the Jews that emigrated from Holland were refugees from Spain and Portugal who spoke Spanish, Portuguese, and Dutch, the Jewish community served as a linguistic bridge between the Dutch and the Portuguese populations in Pernambuco (Witznitzer 1954). The Jews also played an intermediary role in Dutch Brazil's industrial reorganization. Jews bought two-thirds of the sugar plantations abandoned by the Portuguese and sold by the Dutch West Indies Company (Vlekke 1951: 214). Later, when the Company began the importation and sale of African slaves and demanded full payments in cash, Jewish speculators bought most of the slaves and resold them to planters that paid in installments of sugar, at three or four times the original price (Boxer 1957).

The solution that was implemented for Dutch Brazil's labor shortage is well known—the importation of African slaves. After losing hope that the Heeren XIX would recruit workers for Dutch Brazil from among German refugees in the Netherlands, Johan Maurits accepted the prevailing view that without African slaves Pernambuco would not succeed as an economic settlement. Occasional attempts were made to enslave the indigenous Tupi and Tapuya people that lived in northeastern Brazil, but they proved to be highly resistant, especially the Tapuya, who were fierce jungle fighters (Boxer 1957). As the Dutch colonizers later learned, these indigenous groups worked out much better as allies against Portuguese guerilla bands.

Even before Maurits' appointment as Governor-General, the Heeren XIX had decided on the use of African slaves for Dutch Brazil. The Heeren XIX had consulted Protestant theologians regarding the trade in slaves and had received favorable responses, with the condition that the slaves should not be sold to Spanish or Portuguese masters where they would be exposed to "the perils of Popery" (Boxer 1957: 83). The large-scale Dutch importation of African slaves in Pernambuco started in 1636. In the years 1636–1645, a total of 23,163 African slaves were imported into Recife and sold for a total of 6,714,423 guilders (Boxer 1957). Following the example in the East Indies of capturing the source of the trade, in the late 1630s and the 1640s the Dutch captured several slave-trading stations in western Africa (e.g., Elmina, Axim, and Luanda) from the Portuguese (Davidson 1961).

There is a large difference between the reported number of African slaves imported into Dutch Brazil from 1636 to 1645 and the number of African slaves recorded in the region's 1645 Company census. The literature is silent on this difference of about 20,000 slaves. It is not difficult to suggest plausible explanations for this difference. Firstly, it is likely that slaves were resold outside Dutch Brazil. Despite Protestant theologians' warnings, it is likely that speculators in Pernambuco sold slaves to the Portuguese in other parts of Brazil after the Portuguese lost control of the slave trade in western Africa. Secondly, slaves frequently escaped from plantations into the forest. From their communal agricultural settlements (*quilombos*) in the forests, runaway slaves additionally contributed to the reduction of slave population by raiding outlying plantations for women and recruits (Boxer 1957). Thirdly, the mortality rate of slaves in sugar plantations was very high. According to Dunn (1972: 301), in sugar plantations slaves "died much faster than they were born." In some plantations, the slaves did not survive over twenty years (Davidson 1961).

3.3.4 Settlement in New Netherlands

The establishment of the colony of New Netherland on the northeast coast of North America in 1610–1614 was the northernmost expansion of the Dutch into the Atlantic peripheral zone. Initially, labor migration to the colony was very low since the main activities of the colony were trading in furs and smuggling goods into New England (Rich 1970; Wilson 1965). In 1628, the colony had only about 300 inhabitants (Rich 1970). Beginning in 1629, however, the Dutch West India Company attempted to encourage agricultural people to settle in the Hudson River Manhattan region. A plan, "Privileges and Exemptions," was developed whereby any shareholder of the Company who started a settlement with at least fifty immigrants was given a sizable land grant, with what came close to being seigniorial authority (Geyl 1961). Later in 1639, the plan was changed to give land to any individual, Dutch, or other foreigners, who settled in the region to farm. In addition to the Dutch, this plan attracted Englishmen, Germans, Huguenots, Piedmontese, Waldensian, Scots, Anabaptists, and Jews to the region (Rich 1967). From 1653 to 1664, the number of inhabitants in the New Netherland colonial region grew from about 2000 to almost 10,000 (Rich 1967). The English captured the New Netherland settlements in 1664.

3.3.5 Migration to the Caribbean

Dutch migration in the Caribbean during the period of Dutch hegemony included the immigration of agricultural people from the Netherlands to a few islands in the Caribbean and the importation of African slaves into sugar-producing islands of the West Indies. In the 1630s and the 1640s, the Dutch acquired several islands in the Caribbean, e.g., Tobago, Curacao, and St. Eustatius (Davidson 1961). The islands were used by the Dutch West India Company mainly as entrepôts, but they also attracted farmers and farm workers from Zeeland (Rich 1970; Vlekke 1951).[17] As occurred in Dutch Brazil, the Dutch migration to islands in the West Indies never reached a sufficient number to establish large productive settlements.

---

[17] Entrepôts were valuable resources for stockpiling commodities in this historical era when transportation across world regions was irregular and subject to disruption by a variety of factors (Israel 1989).

Adversities such as subtropical diseases, Spanish attacks, and raids by Carib tribes decimated the Dutch immigrants on the islands. For example, of the more than seven hundred Dutch immigrants that settled in Tobago in the first half of the seventeenth century, fewer than seventy survived (Vlekke 1951).

Importation of African slaves in the West Indies was part of the West India Company's extensive involvement in the trade of these islands. In the early 1640s, at a time when sugar production in Dutch Brazil was at its highest level and just prior to the Pernambuco Portuguese revolt of 1645, the Dutch in Brazil showed the English in Barbados how to develop the sugar industry. Several reasons have been proposed to explain why the Dutch sought to establish a rival sugar industry in the English West Indies (i.e., Barbados, the Leeward Islands, and Jamaica) at a time when the Dutch West India Company controlled the (Brazilian) sugar trade with Europe. Dunn (1972) suggests that the Dutch considered the European sugar demand to be large enough to enable them to play a lucrative intermediary trading role between the English West Indies and Europe. Since the 1630s, Dutch traders had carried much of the tobacco and cotton produced in the English islands to Amsterdam (Dunn 1972). Wallerstein (1980) suggests that the Dutch were reasoning from the standpoint of the exhaustibility of sugarcane plantations and, thus, were seeking to continue the sugar trade in the more favorable physical environment of Barbados. These are plausible explanations for why the Dutch helped the English develop a sugar industry in the West Indies, but important too must have been the prospect of a lucrative African slave trade with the English West Indies. The prospects of a profitable slave trade with the English islands (mainly with Barbados at first and later with other islands) must have been particularly attractive for Dutch investors, since in the early 1640s the Dutch were in control of sixteen slave posts in western Africa (Rich 1967).[18]

Prior to Dutch involvement, the English-controlled Barbados economy had consisted mainly of tobacco small holders that depended on indentured-worker immigration for their labor supply.[19] According to Dunn (1972: 52), this imported servile labor consisted of two sorts: "temporary, youthful laborers from the middling classes and permanent drudges from the lower orders." The former category included the children of English yeomen, husbandmen, and artisans; the latter category consisted of the laboring poor, as well as convicts. London port records of 1635 describe characteristics of 985 emigrants that embarked for Barbados as follows: 91% of the emigrants were single persons in their teens and twenties, 29% were aged ten to nineteen, 47% were aged twenty to twenty-four, and 6% were women (Dunn 1972). An increase in the number of women going to Barbados is shown in Bristol records for the 1654–1686 interval in which 24% of the 2678

---

[18] The profitability of the Dutch slave trade is debated by historians; for example, see Emmer (2006) and Fatah-Black and van Rossum (2015).

[19] Estimates differ as to the size of the early English settler population in Barbados. Rich (1967) gives a figure of 6000 English settlers by 1636. Dunn (1972), using discovered poll tax returns for Barbados in the 1630s, estimates the English settler population to have increased from 1227 in 1635 to 8707 in 1639.

who left the port for Barbados were women (Dunn 1972). The women became wives and household workers in the rising planter class on the island. About one-third of the Bristol emigrants to Barbados during 1654–1686 were artisans such as "carpenters, coppers, smiths, and masons" (Dunn 1972: 71).[20]

The Bristol records indicate that the West Indies' conversion to sugar production did not stop the immigration of workers from Britain. It did, however, slow down the migration; of the 2678 migrants that left Bristol (the main center of indentured labor) for Barbados during 1654–1686, only 12% emigrated after 1669, by which time the island's sugar industry was developed enough to export ten thousand tons of sugar to England yearly (Dunn 1972).

Partly through Dutch involvement in the slave trade and in the introduction of sugar production in the West Indies, the forced transfers of African slaves became the dominant pattern of labor movement in the Atlantic peripheral zone of the expanding capitalist world-system. According to Curtin's estimations (1969), about 1,316,000 slaves were imported in major regions of the New World (e.g., Spanish America, and Brazil) in the seventeenth century.[21] About one fifth of the slaves were imported into the sugar-producing British West Indies islands of Barbados, Leeward Islands, and Jamaica (Curtin 1969). Two-thirds of the slave importations into the British West Indies in the seventeenth century occurred in the last quarter of the century. The number of slave importations in the British American slave trade continued to grow in the eighteenth century and reached an estimated 1,247,400 imported slaves from 1701 to 1775 for all British possessions in the American continent (Curtin 1969).

Feminist research since the 1970s, and the creation of the Trans-Atlantic Slave Trade Database, has produced new findings that contradict the conventional belief that males predominated the African slave trade to the Americas in a 2:1 gender ratio (Morgan 2004). Through a summary of several studies and original analysis, Donato and Gabaccia (2015) demonstrate that the gender composition of the trans-Atlantic slave trade varied across time. Female predominance or gender balance characterized the slave trade prior to 1650, and this profile continued for 16 more years after 1650 for which data are available, as the number of imported slaves in the Americas climbed into the tens of thousands per year (Donato and Gabaccia 2015). Males predominated after 1700 when the number of slaves began climbing to 100,000 and more per year. A number of factors affected the selling and buying of females in the slave trade, including gender conditions in slave-exporting African areas and the attraction of buyers for female slaves to produce offspring

---

[20] Eric Williams (1966) states that between 1654 and 1685 ten thousand indentured servants sailed from Bristol alone, chiefly for the West Indies and Virginia. Dunn (1972) tabulates the number of indentured servants shipped from Bristol to the West Indies (Barbados, Nevis, Jamaica, and other islands) between 1654 and 1686 to have numbered 4526.

[21] Curtin (1969: 57) cautions that data on slave importations "are faulted to an uncertain extent by inter-island migration." Some slaves were enumerated more than once when they were taken from one island to be sold again in another island. As Donato and Gabaccia (2015: 63–64) explain, for a number of reasons the data on the trans-Atlantic slave trade "are far from perfect."

to enlarge their workforces or to sell in slave markets (Morgan 2004; Donato and Gabaccia 2015). Thus, males were bought for work, but women were bought for work and for reproduction of labor to use or sell.

Although English, French, Danes, Swedes, and Genoese entered the Caribbean slave trade from the 1640s onward, the Dutch were the region's principal transporters of forced African labor until the creation of the English Royal African Company in 1672 (Curtin 1969; Rich 1967). Moreover, the significance of the Dutch as conveyors of slave labor in the New World extended beyond the Caribbean-Brazil region, as sometimes Dutch traders sold African workers in other English or Spanish colonial settlements (Boxer 1965; Rich 1967). There is also a likelihood that some of the slaves sold in the West Indies by the Dutch were eventually taken to other colonies (e.g., Virginia in North America) through the intercolonial trade (Curtin 1969; Rich 1967).

3.4 Indigenous Migration in the Periphery

Many patterns of indigenous migration ensued as European powers developed colonial social structures in the extension of the capitalist world-system to the Western Hemisphere and regions in Asia (Geyl 1961; Robinson 1990; Lal 2006). In settings where indigenous populations were not spatially concentrated, the process of colonialization by Europeans brought the forced migration of scattered indigenous communities into centralized settlements for more efficient and effective social control. In Spanish America, these new settlements took such forms as *congregaciones* and *reducciones* for carrying out religious indoctrination and the extraction of tribute and forced labor from the colonized populations.

Patterns of indigenous migration that emerged with colonialization varied by the conditions of voluntary/involuntary, permanent/temporary, and rural/urban destinations (Robinson 1990). Voluntary migration included the indigenous accompaniment of European colonizers to new regions such as to overthrow an indigenous center of power, or indigenous migration to towns or districts of growing prosperity, while involuntary migration included the forced movement to centralized settlements, as well as the movement to work projects under the *encomienda* and later the *repartimiento* system of forced labor.[22] Permanent migration was the means for developing centralized settlements such as congregaciones and reducciones (Lovell and Swezey 1990), and temporary migration included migrations for labor servitude in public works, mines, and other settings controlled by colonial overseers (Cook 1990; Zulawski 1990). Until colonial areas developed major economic centers and Catholic evangelizing *pueblos*, much of indigenous migration occurred among rural areas, while towns attracted indigenous persons with artisan

---

[22] According to Mexican historian Federico Navarrete (2019), the Tlaxcala, Campoala, Texcoco, Chalco, and many other indigenous populations did not merely accompany the Spaniards in their conquest after the destruction of México-Tenochtitlan in 1519–1521 but undertook their own indigenous "conquest" of Mesoamerican regions during 1521–1545.

3.4 Indigenous Migration in the Periphery

skills, women for service work, and youth for religious and other school-based training (Castañeda 1990; Lovell and Swezey 1990; Malvido 1990).

Another type of indigenous migration consisted of the movement *away from* colonial settlements (Lowery 1959; Borah 1970; Parry 1981). Fugitive migration by natives was a constant reaction to colonial administration and exploitation (Robinson 1990; Watson 1990).[23] Given the oppression imposed by European colonizers on indigenous communities, the movements away from colonial settlements represented a strategy of resistance to the imposition of tribute and forced labor, and to overall colonialization. The indigenous strategy of resistance through migration was ever-present and a constant concern of colonial officials, including the clergy, who saw the *fugados* as acting stubbornly toward the "civilizing" designs of colonialism (Watson 1990). To be sure, some indigenous populations were never completely colonized, since they fought the European colonizers or out-migrated from their areas of dominance from the start. Examples of these populations include the Tupi and Tapuya who fought against the Dutch in jungles of Pernambuco in northeast Brazil (Boxer 1957) and the Mapuche who resisted the Spaniards for more than 300 years in the Araucanía (Bengoa 2003).

The flight of native workers from the Potosi silver mines in the Viceroyalty of Peru during the first half of the seventeenth century was an example of indigenous workers using migration as a strategy to resist labor exploitation. As described by Borah (1970), the Potosi mines were operated by the Spaniards through the *mita* system, which was originally a mode of labor used in the Inca Empire. In the mita system, Spaniards compelled native populations to provide quotas of men to work in the mines for months at a time. Although the workers were paid wages, the native people much hated the forced labor service because mine work was increasingly harsh, and it separated the men from their families. By the mid-1600s, the number of workers supplied to the mines by the mita system was only about half the 4400 quota of 1610. According to Borah (1970), worker out-migration contributed more than mortality to this diminution of mita workers. Workers and their families moved beyond the reach of the colonizers. But migrating away from colonial areas did not guarantee survival.

Lowery (1959: 108) describes how the strategy of resistance through migration brought the end of a native population in the colony of Hispaniola:

> Disease, hunger, enforced labor in the mines far beyond their untrained capacity, indiscriminate and wholesale slaughter on the bare suspicion of revolt, had decimated [the natives] by the hundreds and thousands until, desperate and at the limit of all human endurance, *they had been forced to take refuge in the mountains and to die of starvation, refusing to till the soil in the vain hope of also starving out their conquerors* (my italics).

A massive migration of agricultural workers away from Dutch colonization in the Banda Islands in the East Indies also illustrated the desperate, fatal attempt to

---

[23] "Invasion and immigration for whites often meant retreat, and emigration for Indians," according to Robinson's (1990: 1) discussion of indigenous migration in colonial Spanish America.

emigrate away from colonialism. In the process of subjugating Bandanese workers to the authority of the Dutch East India Company, the Governor-General, Coen, attempted to transfer them to the Company headquarters in Batavia. According to Geyl (1961), 789 Bandanese were transferred, but thousands more fled to the mountains, and a few to other islands. The Dutch blockaded those that fled and launched a deadly attack against them. Governor-General Coen described the end of the Bandanese refugees:

> About 2,500 are dead either of hunger and misery or by the sword. So far we have not heard of more than 300 Bandanese who have escaped from the whole of Banda. It appears that the obstinacy of these people was so great that they had rather died all together in misery than give themselves up to our men. (Quoted in Geyl 1961: 178)

This repression of Bandanese was an unsuccessful attempt of capital to bring peripheral labor under control through human oppression.[24]

In outlying Asian and New World regions of the emerging world-economy, the Dutch East India and West India Companies extended the networks and circuits for economic profit based not infrequently on human oppression and exploitation. In the Dutch West Indies, the transfer of enslaved African people became a central means to establish colonial workforces and became an investment enterprise in itself. Colonial subjugation of native populations became another means to develop labor systems in the periphery. Both means involved forced migration.

3.5 Class Struggle

Relations between capital and labor are central to the conditions of capitalist production. Historically, workers have undertaken struggles to improve their working conditions in response to the capitalist exploitation of labor.[25] One approach taken by capitalist employers to counter worker struggles, or the potential for worker struggles, has been to combine or supplement local workforces with migrant labor. By employing migrant labor that is socially dissimilar from local workforces, employers can segment workers to lessen their ability for collective resistance

---

[24] A criticism of Wallerstein's world-system has been that it focuses on the expansion of trade relations at the expense of the relations of production. In the article "Structural Transformations of the World-Economy," Hopkins and Wallerstein (1981), however, explore the importance of a labor force in newly incorporated areas. In the current chapter, I highlight the repression of labor, which, in my view, has often been a characteristic of peripheral areas incorporated into the world-system.

[25] By capitalist exploitation of labor, I mean that workers are paid less than the value of commodities and services they produce. As found today in high-tech or professional work, the exploitation of labor is not necessarily abusive, but it is the source of profit, which capital seeks to maintain or enlarge. At times, collective-bargaining strategies, such as in Keynesianism, have been used to link higher wages to increased productivity (Cleaver 1979), but state policies, such as Reaganomics and Thatcherism, and economic restructuring, including at the level of the world-system, have made these strategies less useful for labor, especially as the rate of organized labor decreases.

against exploitation (Gordon et al. 1982). Employers also may resort to migrant labor, especially foreign-born labor, to fill undesirable occupations where work is hard, wages are low, and jobs are unattractive to domestic labor (Piore 1979).

During the period of Dutch hegemony, Holland's industrial centers, e.g., Amsterdam, Leiden, and Rotterdam, had the highest wages and level of worker activism in the United Provinces. Kindleberger (1975) describes the wages of Holland and Zeeland as having been higher than in the provinces of Utrecht, Friesland, Overijssel, Gelderland, and Groningen. Based on such evidence as income tax records (*Familie-geld*), Price (1974: 47–48) describes the artisans and laborers in Holland as being "among the best paid in Europe." While in the early seventeenth century the cost-of-living index generally exceeded the wage index in Holland,[26] by the latter part of the century wage increases exceeded cost of living increases, according to historical wage and price data for Holland (De Vries 1974).

The claim can be made, as Price (1974) does, that the higher wage levels in the industrial centers of Holland were a consequence of labor scarcity, and thus not of working-class pressure. But as I have described above, in the first half of the seventeenth century Holland was characterized by an abundance of labor, including immigrant labor, and not by a lack of it. A Dutch pamphleteer writing in 1623 described the overpopulation of labor: "Our land teems with people, and the inhabitants run each other's shoes off in looking for work. Wherever there is a penny to be earned, ten hands are at once extended to get it" (see Boxer 1965: 58). The forced labor of the destitute, i.e., beggars and vagrants, also increased the number of workers in industrializing Holland (Kossman 1970). In the United Provinces, as in other European societies undergoing capitalist development, the state declared non-participation in the labor force to be a crime:

> Nowhere in the world was as large a production in proportion to the number of the people. Nowhere were so few unproductive consumers. Everyone was at work. Vagabonds, idlers, and loafers such as must be in every community, were caught up by the authorities and made to earn their bread by work. (Quoted in Barker 1906: 123–124)

In Amsterdam, following the passage of a city ordinance in 1614 against mendicancy, male beggars and vagrants (some as young as ten and twelve years of age) were imprisoned in the Rasphuis, a "house of corrections," and were required to do weaving and rasping of dyewoods (Sellin 1944: 41–48). Women vagrants were imprisoned in the Spinhuis and did spinning, sewing, and knitting of nets (Sellin 1944). Other unemployed poor in Holland were less fortunate; they were sentenced to be galley slaves (Dobb 1963).

Wallerstein (1980: 62–64) describes the lower strata in the Netherlands during the period of Dutch hegemony as having been "less turbulent" and "less rebellious" than in England and France. Nevertheless, historical works indicate that sectors of

---

[26] An exception was the wage index of unskilled laborers, which increased from 100 in 1580–1584 to 361 for 1625–1649, while the cost-of-living index grew from 100 to 211 in the same time period (De Vries 1974).

the emerging Dutch proletariat brought pressure to bear on the capitalists. Wilson (1968) describes the industrializing Dutch economy as being subject to periodic strikes. In Leiden, the cloth workers "would turn on their masters, denouncing them as blood-suckers and hinting darkly at communist solutions" (Wilson 1968: 56). Workers in the brewery and cloth industries in Amsterdam also made wage demands with some success (Boxer 1965). In what must have been a major barrier to large-scale, capitalist production, the craft guilds stubbornly resisted changes to their regulation of work hours, wages, and number of workers (Geyl 1961). The guilds also refused to accept immigrants (Vlekke 1951). Capitalists in Holland's cloth industry attempted to counter the power of the workers by forming an intercity association (the so-called *droogscheerdersynoden*) in nine towns of the province. According to Barbour (1950), the capitalists' association had the goals of establishing a common wage and employment policy and of repressing unrest among cloth workers.

Rural to urban migration in the northern Netherlands (especially in Holland) gave employers a means to circumscribe the requirement of guilds. Rural migrant workers in the towns did not benefit directly from the improved conditions (e.g., higher wages) brought about by guilds. The emerging working class in the industrializing centers of Holland was divided into two basic sectors. One sector consisted of the workers organized in guilds who had considerable control in their industries and gained benefits (e.g., higher wages) from their collective power. Based on 1688 records (see Murray 1967), some of Amsterdam's largest craft guilds and membership sizes were as follows: tailors, 881; cobblers, 658; ribbon and lace-makers, 645; glass, pottery, and tankard makers, 604; house carpenters and furniture makers, 600; hatters, 521; master ship carpenters, 400; and coopers and wine cast makers, 362.

Rural migrant workers in the urban centers, however, were incorporated in a second sector. This sector consisted of poor workers, who usually were unskilled in urban industries. These workers, called the *grauw*, labored for master artisans and in the new industries that developed because of Dutch trade hegemony (Garraty 1979). Examples of these industries, called *trafieken*, which were not under guild authority, were sugar refining, the working of tobacco, and the making of earthenware goods (Price 1974). The grauw constituted what Marx (1967) later called an industrial reserve army that could expand or contract according to the needs of capital. To use Wilson's (1968: 57) words, the grauw was "a floating mass of humanity" that "drifted from town to town." This second sector of workers included rural migrants, the unemployed, and other urban poor, and "lived on the brink of penury and were liable to frequent unemployment, owing to their dependence on ill-paid labor and the impossibility of saving money" (Boxer 1965: 58).

3.5 Class Struggle

While guild workers were not considered a threat to the established social order,[27] the grauw was looked on with contempt and fear. These workers in this lower stratum of the working class were viewed as being riotous and a threat to established authority. One Leiden industrialist, De la Court, writing in the mid-seventeenth century warned that with the presence of "very many poor people" in times of economic hardship there "might easily arise a general uproar, with the plunder, and subversion of the whole state" (1972: 119–120).[28] As explained by Wallerstein (1980), the ruling stratum bought social peace from the potentially disruptive sector through the development of what were perhaps the most advanced social welfare measures in the core states of the emerging world-system. The social welfare measures for the poor, who suffered the most from the price revolution that peaked in the mid-seventeenth century, included lodging, hospitalization, and monetary payments for some (Murray 1967; van Leeuwen 1994). Funds for the operation of these welfare measures, which benefited thousands in such towns as Amsterdam, Leiden, and Haarlem, were obtained from private and public sources, e.g., the poor rate, and from revenues derived from confiscated properties of the Catholic Church (De Vries 1974; Norwood 1942).

Moreover, the social welfare measures helped to sustain the poor in the labor force. A severely weakened workforce that lived in squalor and with sickness and little money to buy food was, to some extent, a disadvantage to the emerging capitalistic industries. While no doubt the capitalist entrepreneurs in the trafieken industries gained an economic advantage from the vulnerability of their workers; nevertheless, beyond a certain point the workers' wretchedness could jeopardize the labor supply of the expanding capitalist economy.

While worker activism could pressure wages to rise, the most rebellious workers were not among the most prosperous. Sea workers were among the most involved in worker struggles, but they did not achieve the most prosperous conditions. In contrast to other Dutch workers, ship workers in the Dutch sea trade were known for their rebelliousness. Boxer (1965: 69) comments on this characteristic of the sea workers as follows:

> The Dutch seafaring communities were, or the whole, much less resigned to their hard lot than were the more submissive urban workers and agricultural labourers. Mutiny was far from uncommon, and when sailors felt defrauded of their wages they were apt to riot in ways which frequently worried the regent class in the seaports.

The working conditions of ship workers could be more severe than the conditions of workers in Dutch industries on land. Sickness and death were constant dangers on ships. In addition, ship owners kept wages low in order to offer lower freight

---

[27] This was not always the case. Recall that Chap. 2 mentions the banishment of rebellious artisans in Flanders in the thirteenth century.

[28] De la Court's manuscript "The True Interest and Political Maxim of the Republic of Holland" was circulated, edited, and published without his consent. The 1972 version cited here is a reprint of a 1746 edition.

rates, and ship captains sometimes sold portions of a crew's food rations for extra profit (Lambert 1971; Boxer 1965).[29]

Severe forms of punishments were used aboard Dutch ships to control the sea workers, who sometimes seized vessels and attacked ship captains and other officers. The disciplinary measures included ducking from the yard arm, imprisonment in irons on bread and water flogging from ten to five hundred lashes, kneel-hauling, nailing of the hands to the mainmast, and execution (Boxer 1965).

The large workforces of the Dutch fisheries and sea trade during the seventeenth century employed from sixty to eighty thousand sea workers, and Dutch ship officers used foreign-born workers to segment and control their work crews.[30] Ship officers hired Dutch workers that emigrated from impoverished rural areas (e.g., northern Holland) to the seaports, but they also hired large numbers of foreign-born workers (Vlekke 1951). Going against company orders that foreigners and Roman Catholics should not be used as ship workers, the ship officers in the East India and West India Companies hired French, English, Scot, Portuguese, and Spanish workers. Foreign workers served to alleviate the problem of finding adequate crews for the trade with the faraway regions in the Far East and in the New World. But according to Boxer (1965: 71), foreign-born workers also were employed in the belief that "the mixture of nationalities on board a ship lessened the chances of a successful mutiny being hatched among the men."

The extensive use of foreign child labor in the cloth industry of Leiden—the most important Dutch textile center in the mid-seventeenth century—represented more than a need for a labor supply. It also represented a need to counter the power of cloth workers.[31] Although the weavers' guild had been abolished in Leiden in 1561 (Van Nederveen Meerkerk 2004), cloth workers had made advances in their economic struggles in the city by the seventeenth century, so much so that it forced

---

[29] It is likely that the worst working conditions of workers on Dutch ships occurred in the long-distance, sea voyages. Wallerstein (1980: 55) points out, however, that Dutch freight shippers fed their crews "probably better than other shippers," because Dutch freight ships in the Europe trade required smaller crews than ships of other countries.

[30] Vlekke (1951) states that in the first decade of the century the Dutch fisheries occupied 20,000 sea workers, the trade with Spain and Portugal another 20,000, and the Baltic trade more than 20,000. The figure of 80,000 was given by a Dutch pamphleteer in 1644 and is cited in Boxer (1965: 69). However, Boxer (1965) cautions that the estimate may include an element of "patriotic exaggeration." As with many historical figures, different observers give different estimates. For example, Sir Walter Raleigh complained that in 1603 the Dutch fishing workforces off the coast of England, Scotland, and Ireland totaled to 50,000 workers (Barker 1906).

[31] It was principally in Leiden's cloth industry where some grounds existed for suspecting that the importation of foreign child labor was related to resistance of organized craftworkers. To an extent, the child workers (mainly orphans) constituted an alternative supply of labor. Yet, research by Ruben Schalk (2016) has found that guild masters did not oppose the hiring of orphaned children although many eventually became regular apprentices in the crafts. As described above, in the silk industry in Leiden many orphan-child workers were used in the spinning and spooling stage of the production process that required minimal skill, and thus, they did not immediately serve to increase the supply of skilled labor in order to reduce its value.

capitalist entrepreneurs to form a united front of opposition. Using child labor was a way for capitalist entrepreneurs to attempt to lessen worker advances in textile workplaces. As described above, Leiden's cloth industry used thousands of local and foreign-born child workers between 1638 and 1664.

It was not necessary for native workers to actually be successful in their struggles for higher pay or to improve other working conditions for employers to become motivated to hire foreign labor. Employers could use foreign-born labor proactively to prevent successful worker struggles. The fact that contentious Dutch sea workers did not make advances in improving their severe working conditions of very low wages, inadequate food, and constant danger was likely due in some part to the practice by Dutch ship officers of mixing their crews with English, French, and other foreign-born workers (Boxer 1965). While Dutch ship officers did not hire foreign workers to fill their total labor needs, the numbers they hired may have been sufficient to produce a divisive segmentation in their crews.

Worker resistance in the periphery has also been cited as one motivation for the importation of slave labor into the West Indies sugar plantations. As Dunn (1972) describes the thousands of indentured workers that were part of the sugar-producing labor force in the West Indies often engaged in acts of rebellion. In some cases, indentured workers were executed for participating in rebellions. Thus, as Dunn (1972: 72–74) argues, the sugar planters may have turned to slaves partly because slaves were considered to be "a more settled, more dependable workforce."[32] Yet, the impetus of trying to reduce worker resistance through the use of slave labor should not be stressed too strongly. From the perspective of the West Indies' incorporation into the world-system, slavery was the most "effective" labor system for the planter class. As Padgug (1976) explains, slaves were the only workers that could be obtained in sufficient quantities in order for the sugar-producing colonies to establish commercial ties with the world-system.

3.6 Technological Development

Historically, capital has used technological development to counter the power of craft labor when craft guild workers fought to maintain control of their industries. Capital used technological innovations such as mechanization of production and detailed divisions of labor to deskill artisan production and thus reduce the need for craftworkers. By deskilling the production process, employers were able to switch to labor not controlled by craft guilds, such as the labor of women, children, and migrant workers. Later, labor-saving technology was introduced to save on the amount of labor needed for production. The deskilling of the production process by breaking up of artisan work into sub-processes that could be carried out by less-skilled workers also attracted migrant workers such as from the countryside.

---

[32] Needless to say, slaves were never a passive, docile labor force. Slaves revolted in Barbados in 1649 and engaged in many forms of resistance (Parry 1981).

Moreover, some displaced craftworkers emigrated to other areas of the country or abroad where their handicraft work was still in demand.

Capitalists also have used technological development in their "industrial war" to advance production (Marx 1973). That is, they have introduced social and mechanical technology to increase productivity in order to sell more cheaply than competitors and dominate markets. The capitalists' goals of using technology to replace skilled workers, reduce the amount of labor needed, or dominate a market are not mutually exclusive. Given the different stages and industries involved in capitalist expansion in different regions of the world-system, the levels of technological development and the effects on migration vary considerably. Within this variation, presently we find agricultural migrant farmworkers working in low-level, technological environments in Asian and Latin American peripheral regions, and migrant workers from these regions working in high-tech, software-design offices in core countries of the world-economy such as in Europe and North America.

Wallerstein (1980) highlights Dutch "productive efficiency" due to technological advancement as a major factor enabling the northern Netherlands to gain hegemonic status in the emerging world-system for close to half of the seventeenth century. The United Provinces' (and especially Holland's) technological superiority in such industries as land reclamation, agriculture, shipbuilding, shipping, and fishing enabled the Dutch to surpass rival core states in world trade (Wilson 1968; Wallerstein 1980). These industries depended partly or mostly on migrant labor.

Although land reclamation was labor-intensive, depending mostly on migrant labor, reclamation projects involved aspects of technological sophistication. One example was the use of windmills in multiple-pumping systems to drain the water (De Vries 1974). Another example was the use of the bucket dredger and the wheelbarrow, a recent innovation in the Netherlands in the 1600s that must have been a considerable technological advancement over the use of wicker baskets (Lambert 1971). Undoubtedly, technological developments in the drainage projects were used primarily to shorten drainage time, and not to fight labor, which consisted mainly of migrant workers (De Vries 1974). Some drainage projects took five to six years to complete, and time also had to be spent laying out agricultural and peat lots before the reclaimed lands could become economically productive. The use of technological innovations thus was a means to hasten financial returns from investments in the polder industry. Nevertheless, land reclamation brought together thousands of workers in a single site, so reducing drainage time in reclamation projects also reduced the opportunity for wage workers to resist the primitive and harsh working conditions of the times.

For the sea trade, on the other hand, a plausible argument can be made that the capitalists' use of technological innovations was at least partly motivated by worker unrest. As described above, Dutch sea crew, composed of migrant workers, frequently undertook mutinous actions against their employers. For reasons related to their harsh working conditions, they seized vessels at sea and attacked ship officers. On land, the workers also attacked the offices and warehouses of shippers. In one of the more serious outbreaks in Amsterdam, soldiers fired on sea workers and hung two of their leaders (Boxer 1965).

3.6 Technological Development

Dutch shippers started the seventeenth century with new shipping technology, a highly specialized cargo-carrier, the *fluyt*, that was designed with features that were "great labour savers" (Parry 1967: 211). The design of the fluyt, which according to Parry (1981) amounted to "little more than floating holds," enabled Dutch shippers to reduce the size of their crews to as few as ten workers, while other European competitors still required thirty workers per vessel (Kindleberger 1975). One way the fluyt reduced the number of workers was through an extensive use of pulleys and tackles for control of the yards and sails (Unger 1980). Another way was by carrying few or no guns (Parry 1967). The sail divisibility of the fluyt also helped to save labor in two ways. In contrast to the traditional square rig, sails divided into sections could be handled by fewer workers (Parry 1965). Sail divisibility also increased maneuverability, which decreased the time spent in harbor waiting for the right wind, and thus decreased the time workers spent on board (Unger 1980).

A counterargument may be offered that the design of the fluyt was not motivated by worker struggles, but solely by the desire to increase efficiency in sea transportation. There is little support for this view in historical works. In the first place, the fluyt did not contain any distinctively new innovations. For the most part, it brought together in one design feature that had been used in other cargo ships (Unger 1980). Thus, if production efficiency was the sole motivation for its construction, then it very likely would have been designed earlier. Secondly, the fluyt did not represent an unequivocal advance in efficiency. The design of the fluyt maximized cargo space, but, on the other hand, the smaller sails made it a slower ship. According to Unger (1980: 263), in the construction of the fluyt, Dutch shippers sacrificed speed for the advantage of hiring fewer workers: "The fluyt was slower... but builders did not design the fluyt for speed. The goal was to minimize costs... The final result was a slow, light ship, with good handling qualities which could be and were traded off for smaller crews." For Dutch shippers in the seventeenth century, labor cost consisted of more than the wages they paid; it also included the cost of worker unrest.

Dutch fishing industries experienced some of the largest patterns of labor migration in the seventeenth century.[33] The technological advances that were accomplished in this industry in the seventeenth century appear to have been made primarily to increase production in order to win the industrial war in Europe's fish trade. Fish, particularly herring, was an important part of the diet in the Catholic south of Europe, and especially for the poor classes (Barker 1906; Wilson 1968).

Two particular technological advances enabled the Dutch to dominate commercial fishing in the North Sea for over six decades in the seventeenth century. One advancement was the construction of a fishing ship called the buss (*buizen*). The second innovation was a new method of transporting fish to market. The buss was

---

[33] Immigrant labor was also used in the newly created trafieken industries. But the development of these industries did not represent attempts to simplify (deskill) craftwork in order to appropriate its control from skilled workers. The trafieken industries were created by capitalist entrepreneurs based on the availability of raw products (e.g., sugar and tobacco from the West Indies) and thus, from the start, were under the control of entrepreneurs.

a factory ship. In addition to being used to catch fish with a new type of large drag net, the buss was large enough to enable the cleaning and barreling of the fish to be done on board (Wallerstein 1980). Thus, the factory ship carried three kinds of workers on board: fisherman, gippers to remove fish intestines, and curers to add salt to the fish (Michell 1977). The Dutch increased this technological advantage through the use of fast ships, known as *ventjapers* (sale-hunters), that transported the salted and barreled fish from the busses to harbors in the Netherlands and other countries (Parry 1967). By using ventjapers to take the fish to market, the factory ships could remain at sea for six to eight weeks during a season (Wallerstein 1980).

The impoverished Dutch hinterland was a major source of migrant labor for the 37,000 workers that were used in the Dutch fishing industry until its decline in the 1660s (Wilson 1968; Lambert 1971).[34] Working in over 500 busses from Holland, Friesland, and Zeeland, by the 1630s the fishing workforce constituted from one-fourth to one-third of the United Provinces' sea labor force (Michell 1977).[35] With a production of over 36,000 tons of fish annually, based on the exploitation of three fishing seasons in different parts of the North Sea, the fishing "factory workers" played a crucial role in the expansion of the Dutch fish trade in the Baltic, the Mediterranean, and in other regions of Europe (Glamann, 1974; Michell 1977).

The introduction by the Dutch of technological innovation in the Dutch period of hegemony does not appear to have caused the displacement and emigration of skilled workers in the northern Netherlands. Colonies of skilled Dutch workers existed in England and other European countries, but they did not represent displacement by technological development (Murray 1967; Wilson 1968). Similar to Dutch drainage experts recruited by the princess of northern Germany (Vlekke 1951), and Dutch cloth makers recruited by an English clothier to Edinburgh (Barbour 1950), the instances of Dutch skilled-labor emigration were mainly movements to more advantageous business positions, not flights from technological development that deskilled work. It should be noted that during the Dutch period of hegemony the capitalist mode of production was still in an early stage. Commercial capitalism had blossomed, but industrial capitalism was still in a budding stage. In the towns of Holland, the typical unit of industrial production was still a workshop with six to ten workers (Barbour 1950; Murray 1967). Although Dutch craftworkers were attached to capitalist entrepreneurs through wages, they still controlled much of the production in their trade.

---

[34] Wilson (1968) divides the number of workers as 32,000 workers employed in herring fishing and 5000 in the Dogger Bank fisheries of cod and ling.
[35] Parry (1967) and Wilson (1957) estimate that the number of busses was closer to one thousand. Michell (1977) makes a strong argument for the 500 figure. Writing in the 1660s, De la Court (1972) estimated the total fishing-related labor force (at sea and on land) constituted about one-fourth of the employed population in Holland.

3.7 The Economic Cycle

As discussed in Chap. 1, areas of capitalist production with cyclical upturns may attract labor immigration from less-developed areas. A twofold logic can be offered for this proposition. Firstly, skilled workers may migrate to areas of increasing prosperity expecting to find higher wages and greater availability of use-values (e.g., food, clothing, etc.). While foreign workers without specialization may be relegated to the inferior sectors of the labor force, nevertheless, in comparison with their prior situation, their new work positions may constitute an economic improvement (Piore 1979). Secondly, in times of economic expansion, employers may seek foreign workers in order to increase the size of the labor force to slow the growth of wages by increasing the supply of workers.[36] Employers may also use immigrant workers with tenuous status, such as undocumented migrant workers, to increase productivity by increasing the work pace.

In a description of cycles and secular trends of the capitalist world-economy, Hopkins, Wallerstein, and other world-system researchers give the following cyclical breakdown for the Dutch period of hegemony (Research Working Group 1979):

1575–1590	Ascending hegemony
1590–1620	Hegemonic victory
1620–1650	Hegemonic maturity
1650–1672	Declining hegemony

The years of ascending hegemony, 1575–1590, involved the expansion of Dutch industries described above, e.g., cloth production, land reclamation, foreign trade, and so forth. Declining hegemony in the post-1650 period involved the stagnation and decline of many of these industries and of population growth in urban areas. Examples of this Dutch economic slowdown were a decline in shipbuilding (to five ships a year in some yards), and a decline in the amount of herring caught per fishing vessel (Hobsbawm 1965; Price 1974; Van der Woude 1975).[37] In Leiden, the post-1650 decline involved a drop in cloth production from a peak of 144,000 pieces in 1664 to 85,000 in 1700 (Price 1974). In addition, some urban population levels reached in the 1670s dropped and were not reached again until the nineteenth century (Price 1974; Wallerstein 1980). In the latter part of the period of Dutch hegemony in 1625–1675, the Dutch experienced substantial social and

---

[36] This economic proposition does not consider the influence of the state, which may produce immigration policies based on political interests. In the Western Hemisphere and Europe, governmental immigration policies rose in the late nineteenth and early twentieth centuries (e.g., see FitzGerald and Cook-Martín 2014).

[37] There is a difference of opinion concerning the significance of this economic decline. For Hobsbawm (1965), it was part of a "general crisis" in which the European economy completed its final phase of transition from a feudal to a capitalist economy. In contrast, for Wallerstein (1980) the decline represented a stagnation (the first crisis) of an already established capitalist economy.

economic deterioration, i.e., a French invasion into areas of the United Provinces, a multitude of bankruptcies, a collapse of the stock of the East India and West India Companies, and, with the French threat, the transfer of millions of guilders from the Bank of Amsterdam to London, Hamburg, and other financial centers in Europe (Barbour 1950).

The logic of foreign workers migrating either by their own initiative or by recruitment to areas experiencing economic upturns is partly demonstrated by the migration of workers from the southern to the northern Netherlands. This migration included Flemings, Walloons, Brabants, and other workers from the southern Netherlands, as well as other Europeans who had earlier fled religious persecution into the southern Netherlands. The argument may be proposed that these workers were not attracted to the northern Netherlands by expanding economic conditions, but by a social environment that accepted Protestantism. A twofold counterargument, however, can be made against reasoning solely from the perspective of religion. Firstly, with their new-draperies technology many of the textile workers that came to Holland from the southern Netherlands were able to create an industrial niche and prosper from the expanding economy of Holland. Secondly, some of the emigrants went first to other countries and later migrated to industrializing Holland. For example, the Flemish cloth workers that settled in Leiden in the late 1570s and the 1580s during Dutch economic ascendancy had first settled in England (Colchester) and left only after the ruling elite in Leiden (the *Vroedschap*) recruited them with attractive economic inducements (Lamet 1981).

This illustration is not meant to imply that a liberal atmosphere was not significant in the migration of the refugees from the southern Netherlands. Reformation refugees sought a favorable religious environment, but the craftworkers among them also represented an economic force that prospered in the rising economy of the northern Netherlands. This economic factor was more evident for the refugees that went first to other areas in Europe and later migrated to industrializing Holland. Of the two factors of settling in a Protestant environment or gaining economic opportunity, it is safe to assume that the former factor was of greater importance for the emigrants from the south during the height of the ravages of the Spanish Inquisition in the southern Netherlands, which lasted until the late sixteenth century. After the Spanish-Dutch war ended in 1609 with a twelve-year truth, emigration from the southern Netherlands to Leiden and other industrial centers in Holland was probably associated more with the pursuit of economic opportunities (Dunn 1970).[38]

The reasoning that employers may promote the immigration of foreign workers in order to arrest labor advances during economic upturns has limited applicability to explain the presence of foreign workers in industrializing Holland. As mentioned above, in the early stage of Holland's industrial capitalism in the seventeenth

---

[38] As a testament to the capitalistic entrepreneurship in the northern Netherlands, Dunn (1970: 44) notes that "[t]he northern provinces flourished *mightily* during the war; [while] the south was in economic collapse" (my italics).

3.7 The Economic Cycle

century, many of the production processes in urban areas were still controlled by craftworker guilds. In the towns where craft guilds maintained control of their industries, the crafts regulated work hours, wages, and the employment of workers (Geyl 1961). Predictably, the craft guilds did not permit the use of immigrant labor in their industries (Vlekke 1951). Hence, in towns where craft guilds regulated industries, foreign workers were likely of little help to capitalist entrepreneurs. But there were important exceptions, such as in the production of the new draperies introduced by immigrants from southern Netherlands and the trafieken enterprises that developed with the importation of raw materials from the colonies.

Foreign-born workers were an important source of labor power for employers in the trafieken industries. Through the use of foreign workers, capitalist employers in these newly developed industries were able to create unskilled workforces whose members did not have the sympathy of native guild workers (Vlekke 1945). It is interesting to note that in the post-1650 decline of Dutch hegemony some trafieken industries, e.g., sugar refining, tobacco-curing, and distilling of gin and brandy, held their ground (Price 1974). This should not be surprising. If we view the Dutch economic decline in the post-1650 period as being partly an outgrowth of the organized craftworkers' opposition to the emerging capitalist-entrepreneurial sector (such as occurred in the cloth industry), then we should not expect such an economic decline in the trafieken industries. These new industries were not controlled by guilds, and thus, their employers hired unskilled, migrant workers.

It is logical to expect that in times of an economic downturn native workers may view foreign workers as a cause of deteriorating job conditions and create pressure for the removal of foreign labor. There is no indication in historical sources, however, that a major out-migration pattern of foreign workers developed in the United Provinces during the post-1650 period of economic decline. Two reasons can be suggested as to why such a pattern may not have occurred. Firstly, it is likely that in this stage of early industrial capitalism, worker struggles were very industry specific. That is, workers in this phase of class struggle strived separately for economic goals in their own industries. Historical sources (e.g., Barbour 1950 and Kellenbenz 1977) support this view. Hence, since foreign workers were not accepted in guild-controlled industries, it is likely that they generally were not seen as an economic threat by Dutch craftworkers.

Secondly, the post-1650 Dutch economic decline was not a clear-cut contraction of the economy. According to Price (1974), while some industries (e.g., fisheries and shipbuilding) underwent an absolute decline in production, others only experienced a relative decline in business, i.e., they lost some ground in their position in the market. In Wallerstein's words (1979b: 77), "It was less that the Dutch had lost so much than that the English and French had advanced so far...." With this condition of relative decline in the economy (in contrast to an absolute contraction) and with the development of social welfare programs, it is likely that economic pressures in the post-1650 slump were not severe enough for Dutch workers to view foreigners as a problem. It was semi-proletarian, rural labor, not foreign workers, that became rivals of urban Dutch craftworkers when capitalist entrepreneurs established industries in the countryside using rural labor.

The absence of an out-migration of foreign workers in the United Provinces during the post-1650 economic decline should not be interpreted to mean that these workers were completely accepted. As explained by Norwood (1942) in his analysis of the economic impact of the Reformation, refugees from the southern Netherlands were permitted to settle in many places of Europe but encountered opposition from native workers whenever they attempted to introduce labor-saving machines. For example, refugees from the southern Netherlands faced native opposition in London, Cologne, and Strasbourg in the late 1500s when they attempted to use technologically advanced looms ("greate looms") and dyeing processes (Norwood 1942:154–155). Native craftworkers in cloth production viewed these new technologies as a threat to their work security.

Finally, the "context of reception" should be considered to understand how more than just economic cyclical conditions may affect the reaction to newcomers (Portes and Rumbaut 2014). Given that the Counter-Reformation took thousands of Protestant lives and destroyed many Protestant communities, one could expect that Protestant foreign workers received better treatment than Catholic foreign workers in the United Provinces during the seventeenth century. For example, as described above, the official position of the Dutch East and West India Companies was not to allow Catholics as ship workers. The fact that Dutch ship officers disobeyed policy and hired Catholics anyway very likely to create ethnic divisions among their sea crews illustrates the unfavorable view of Catholic workers. There was also the non-acceptance of Jewish workers. While Jewish families of Portuguese or Spanish origin figured among the emerging bourgeoisie of industrializing Holland in the seventeenth century (Barbour 1950), it is unlikely that Jewish foreign workers achieved a similar level of acceptance in the Dutch working class. In this historical era, Jewish workers in Europe had severely limited opportunities regarding the trades they were allowed to practice, and they were often forbidden to work for non-Jewish employers (Wischnitzer 1954). Hence, it is likely that given these conditions Protestant foreign workers were more attracted than Catholics or Jewish workers by the economic prosperity of the United Provinces in the first half of the seventeenth century. Yet, perhaps this point should not be stressed too strongly, for Dutch industrialists were very aware of the advantages of having large worker populations available, which invariably included immigrants (De la Court 1972).

3.8 The State

In the era of Mercantilism, the state is concerned above all with the wealth of the nation based on a favorable balance of commerce (Issac 1947). To this end, the mercantile state regards migration as a means of increasing the national wealth through an increase in the supply of labor. Thus, the migration policy of the mercantile state is to encourage the immigration of workers and to restrict their emigration. According to Wallerstein (1980), in the period of Dutch hegemony the United Provinces was a "great exception" to this mercantilist philosophy. In contrast to other core powers, the Dutch state existed as a liberal decentralized structure, with the Estate-General (the central government) composed of representatives from the provinces and one from the noble class. This decentralized condition, as Wallerstein (1980: 60) explains, should not be misinterpreted as one of weakness: "the decentralized structure, which gave much legal power to local governments, created the condition for the success of private enterprises."[39] In regard to labor migration, thus, the formulation of immigration policy occurred at the local level and sometimes at the level of the enterprise, as in the cases of the East and West India Companies (Arrighi 2010).

The discussion in this chapter showed three ways in which local governments dealt with migrant workers. One policy was the passage of vagrancy laws in the towns. These laws attempted to make migrants "productive" and not dependent on social welfare programs that existed at the local level. A second approach was to place unemployed migrants who wandered into towns in workhouses. While these "houses of reform" were never developed at the level that was achieved later in England, nevertheless, those that were built were considered to be work-training institutions. The third approach was geared to attract skilled labor through the offering of incentives by the local governments to foreign craftworkers. An illustration of this approach was the offering of housing by the town government of Leiden to Flemish cloth workers who earlier had emigrated to England. To an extent, the regulations of the East and West India Companies prohibiting the use of foreign workers aboard ships can be considered quasi-governmental policy, since the two companies were chartered with powers that were usually reserved for government branches. From this perspective, although the Atlantic slave trade was authorized as a commerce in commodities, and not as a governmental labor policy, the Dutch transfer of enslaved African laborers to the West Indies represented a course of action undertaken by an organizational body chartered with state-making authority (Arrighi 2010).

3.9 Conclusion—Interrelation of Migration

The overall significance of migration for the development of Dutch hegemony rested on two interconnections. One interconnection concerned the interrelationship between capital and labor migration. Simply put, capital often depended on voluntary or forced migrant labor to accomplish its industrial enterprises. The second interconnection concerned the linkage of different labor migration patterns in the circuits of capital accumulation. For example, the forced transfer of African labor to colonial plantations in the West Indies enabled the industrial production

---

[39] From another perspective, Barbour (1950: 40) describes the central government as being weak for not being able to prevent the sale of arms by Dutch entrepreneurs to the enemy. See Julia Adams (1994, 2005) for lengthy discussions of the Dutch state during the period examined in this chapter, as well as for a critique of Wallerstein's world-system theorizing of the state's role in the rise of Dutch hegemony.

of raw materials that were exported to industrial centers in Holland for production into finished commodities often by migrant labor. Some of these commodities were then exported to different destinations in the Dutch world trade through the use of Catholic, English, and other migrant labor on ships.

Another example of the interconnection of labor migration patterns involved rural and urban migration. As described above, rural migration provided labor power for lake drainages and the subsequent industrial-crop and peat-fuel production. The industrial crops and peat fuel produced in the reclaimed lands were sent to urban markets for usage in industrial production in industries that depended on immigrant workers in varying degrees.

Some patterns of labor migration enabled capitalist production to grow in a quantitative manner, while other patterns affected the growth in a qualitative manner. For example, the migration of rural workers to seaports provided the labor power for the enlargement of the fishing industry. By comparison, the immigration of Reformation refugees in the northern Netherlands and the forced transfer of African workers to the West Indies led, respectively, to the development in Holland of the lighter fabrics called new draperies and of the trafieken industries that converted raw materials into finished products.

The migration of capital and labor in the Atlantic triangular circuit, and in other inter-regional trade, represented the *mobile* nature of capital as it circulated across investment and geographical domains of accumulation. This mobility demonstrated (and continues to demonstrate) the social character of capital that it grows through an organic relationship with labor in the circuits of accumulation (Marx 1967; Harvey 1982). In the settings of Dutch and other European colonialism in the seventeenth century, this motion often transpired in the periphery of the world-system through coercive and brutal social processes, often with ruinous outcomes for the affected populations.

References

Adams, Julia. 1994. Trading States, Trading Places: The Role of Patrimonialism in Early Modern Dutch Development. *Comparative Studies in Society and History* 36 (2): 319–355.
Adams, Julia. 2005. *The Familial State: Ruling Families, and Merchant Capitalism in Early Modern Europe*. Ithaca: Cornell University Press.
Barbour, V. 1950. *Capitalism in Amsterdam in the Seventeenth Century*. Baltimore: The Johns Hopkins Press.
Barker, J.E. 1906. *The Rise and Decline of the Netherlands*. London: Smith, Elder & Co.
Bengoa, José. 2003. *Historia de los antiguos mapuches del sur: desde antes de la llegada de los españoles hasta las paces de Quilín*. Santiago, Chile: Catalonia.
Borah, W. 1970. Latin America 1610–60. In *The New Cambridge Modern History, IV: The Decline of Spain and the Thirty Years War*, ed. J.P. Cooper, 707–726. Cambridge: Cambridge University Press.
Boxer, C.R. 1957. *The Dutch in Brazil, 1624–1654*. Oxford: The Clarendom Press.
Boxer, C.R. 1965. *The Dutch Seaborne Empire: 1600–1800*. New York: Alfred A. Knopf.
Brandt, Geeraerdt. 1720. The History of the Reformation and Other Ecclesiastical Transactions in and About the Low-Countries, from the Beginning of the Eighth Century, Down to the Famous

References

Synod of Dort, Inclusive. In Which all the Revolutions that Happened in Church and State, on Account of the Divisions Between the Protestants and Papists, the Arminians and Calvinists, are Fairly and Fully Represented ... Faithfully Translated from the Original Low Dutch. London: Printed by T. Wood, for T. Childe, 1720–1723.

Braudel, Fernand. 1972. *The Mediterranean and the Mediterranean World in the Age of Philip II*, vol. I. New York: Harper & Row.

Braudel, Fernand. 1982. *Civilization and Capitalism 15–18 Century. Vol. 2: The Wheels of Commerce.* New York: Harper & Row, Publishers.

Braudel, Fernand. 1984. *Civilization and Capitalism 15–18 Century. Vol. 3: The Perspective of the World.* New York: Harper & Row, Publishers.

Castañeda, Carmen. 1990. "Student Migration to Colonial Urban Centers: Guadalajara and Lima. In *Migration in Colonial Spanish America*, ed. David R. Robinson, 128–142. Cambridge: Cambridge University Press.

Cipolla, C.M. 1980. *Before the Industrial Revolution: European Society and Economy, 1000–1700*, 2nd ed. New York: W. W. Norton.

Cleaver, Harry. 1979. *Reading Capital Politically*. Austin: University of Texas Press.

Coleman, D.C. 1969. An Innovation and Its Diffusion: The "New Draperies. *The Economic History Review* 22 (3): 417–429.

Cook, Noble David. 1990. Migration in Colonial Peru: An Overview. In *Migration in Colonial Spanish America*, ed. David R. Robinson, 41–61. Cambridge: Cambridge University Press.

Coornaert, E.L.J. 1967. European Economic Institutions and the New World: The Chartered Companies. In *Cambridge Economic History of Europe, IV, The Economy of Expanding Europe in the Sixteenth & Seventeenth Centuries*, ed. E.E. Rich and C.H. Wilson, 220–274. Cambridge: Cambridge University Press.

Curtin, Philip D. 1969. *The Atlantic Slave Trade: A Census*. Madison: University of Wisconsin Press.

Davidson, Basil. 1961. *The African Slave Trade: Precolonial History 1450–1850*. Boston: Little, Brown and Company.

De la Court, Pieter. 1972. *The True Interest and Political Maxim of the Republic of Holland*. Translated by John De Witt. New York: Arno Press.

Dobb, Maurice. 1963. *Studies in the Development of Capitalism*. New York: International Publishers.

Donato, Katherine M., and Donna Gabaccia. 2015. *Gender and International Migration*. New York: Russell Sage Foundation.

Dunn, Richard S. 1970. *The Age of Religious Wars, 1559–1689*. New York: W. W. Norton & Company Inc.

Dunn, Richard C. 1972. *Sugar and Slaves: The Rise of the Planter Class in the English West Indies, 1624–1713*. New York: W. W. Norton & Company Inc.

Emmer, Pieter C. 1975. Surinam and the Decline of the Dutch Trade. *Revue Française D'histoire D'outre-Mer* 62: 245–251.

Emmer, Pieter. 2006. *The Dutch Slave Trade, 1500–1850*. New York: Berghahn Books.

Fatah-Black, Karwan, and Matthias van Rossum. 2015. Beyond Profitability: The Dutch Transatlantic Slave Trade and its Economic Impact. *Slavery & Abolition* 36 (1): 63–83.

FitzGerald, David, and David Cook-Martín. 2014. *Culling the Masses: The Democratic Origins of Racist Immigration Policy in the Americas*. Cambridge: Harvard University Press.

Garraty, John A. 1979. *Unemployment in History: Economic Thought and Public Policy*. New York: Harper & Row.

Geyl, Pieter. 1961. *The Netherlands in the Seventeenth Century*. New York: Barnes & Noble.

Geyl, Pieter. 1966. *The Revolt of the Netherlands, 1555–1609*. London: Ernest Benn.

Glamann, Kristof. 1974. European Trade 1500–1750. In *The Fontana Economic History of Europe, II, The Sixteenth and Seventeenth Centuries*, ed. C.M. Cipolla, 42–526. Glasgow: Collins.

Gordon, David M., Richard Edwards, and Michael Reich. 1982. *Segmented Work, Divided Workers: The Historical Transformation of Labor in the United States*. Cambridge: Cambridge University Press.

Harreld, Donald. 2004. Dutch Economy in the "Golden Age" (16–17 Centuries). In EH.Net Encyclopedia, ed. Robert Whaples. Accessed August 12, 2018. http://eh.net/encyclopedia/the-dutch-economy-in-the-golden-age-16th-17th-centuries/

Harvey, David. 1982. *The Limits to Capital*. Chicago: University of Chicago Press.

Helleiner, K. 1967. The Population of Europe from the Black Death to the Eve of the Vital Revolution. In *Cambridge Economic History of Europe*, Vol. IV, *The Economy of Expanding Europe in the 16th and 17th Centuries,* ed. E.E. Rich and C.H. Wilson, 1–95. London: Cambridge University Press.

Hobsbawn, E.J. 1965. The Crisis of the Seventeenth Century. In *Crisis of the Seventeenth Century*, ed. Trevor Aston, 5–58. New York: Basic Books.

Hopkins, Terence, and Immanuel Wallerstein. 1981. Structural Transformations of the World-Economy. In *Dynamics of World Development*, ed. Richard Rubinson, 233–261. Beverly Hills: Sage Publications.

Hoppenbrouwers, Peter C.M. 2001. Town and Country in Holland, 1310–1550. In *Town and Country in Europe*, 1300–1800, ed. S.R. Epstein, 54–79. Cambridge, UK: Cambridge University Press.

Hyma, Albert. 1942. *The Dutch in the Far East: A History of the Dutch Commercial and Colonial Empire*. Ann Arbor, MI: George Wahr Publishers.

Israel, Jonathan I. 1989. *Dutch Primacy in World Trade, 1585–1740*. Oxford: Oxford University Press.

Issac, Julius. 1947. *Economics of Migration*. London: Kegan Paul, Trench, Trubner & Co.

Kellenbenz, H. 1977. The Organization of Industrial Production. In *Cambridge Economic History of Europe*, Vol. V, *The Economic Organization of Early Modern Europe,* ed. E.E. Rich and C.W. Wilson, 462–548. Cambridge: Cambridge University Press.

Kindleberger, Chales P. 1975. Commercial Expansion and the Industrial Revolution. *Journal of European Economic History Review* 4 (Winter): 613–654.

Kossmann, E.H. 1970. The Low Countries. In *New Cambridge Modern History,* Vol. IV, *The Decline of Spain and the Thirty Years War, 1609–48/59,* ed J.P. Cooper, 359–384. Cambridge: Cambridge University Press.

Krause, Chester, and Clifford Mishler. 2003. *Standard Catalog of World Coins, 1601–1700: Identification and Valuation Guide 17th Century.* Iola, WI: Krause Publications.

Lal, Brij V. 2006. *The Encyclopedia of the Indian Diaspora*. Honolulu: University of Hawaii Press.

Lambert, Audrey M. 1971. *The Making of the Dutch Landscape: An Historical Geography of the Netherlands.* London: Seminar Press.

Lamet, Sterling A. 1981. The *Vroedschop* of Leiden 1550-1600: The Impact of Tradition and Change on the Governing Elite of a Dutch City. *The Sixteenth Century Journal* 12 (Summer): 15–42.

Van Leeuwen, Marco H.D. 1994. Logic of Charity: Poor Relief in Preindustrial Europe. *The Journal of Interdisciplinary History* 24 (4): 589–613.

Lovell, George, and William R. Swezey. 1990. Indian Migration and Community Formation: An Analysis of Congregación in Colonial Guatemala. In *Migration in Colonial Spanish America*, ed. David R. Robinson, 18–40. Cambridge: Cambridge University Press.

Lowery, W. 1959. *The Spanish Settlements Within the Present Limits of the United States, 1513–61.* New York: Russell & Russell.

Malvido, Elsa. 1990. Migration Patterns of the Novices of the Order of San Francisco in Mexico City, 1649–1749. In *Migration in Colonial Spanish America,* ed. David R. Robinson, 182–192. Cambridge: Cambridge University Press.

Marx, Karl. 1967. *Capital*, vol. I. New York: International Publishers.

Marx, Karl. 1973. *Grundrisse.* Translated by Martin Nicolaus. New York: Vintage Books.

Masefield, G. B. 1967. Crops and Livestock. In *Cambridge Economic History of Europe,* Vol. IV, *The Economy of Expanding Europe in the Sixteenth and Seventeenth Centuries,* ed. E.E. Rich and C.H. Wilson, 275–301. Cambridge: Cambridge University Press.

Van Nederveen Meerkerk, Elise. 2004. Textile Workers in the Netherlands. Part 1: 1650–1810. National Overview Netherlands, Textile Conference IISH, 11–13 November. Amsterdam, The

Netherlands. Accessed June 15, 2019. https://www.academia.edu/2118043/Textile_workers_in_the_Netherlands._Part_1_1650-1810

Van Nederveen Meerkerk, Elise. 2010. Market Wage or Discrimination? The Remuneration of Male and Female Wool Spinners in the Seventeenth-Century Dutch Republic. *The Economic History Review* 63 (1): 165–186.

Michell, A.R. 1977. The European Fisheries in Early Modern History. In *Cambridge Economic Organization of Early Modern Europe*, ed. E.E. Rich and C.H. Wilson, 134–184. Cambridge: Cambridge University Press.

Minchinton, Walter. 1976. Patterns and Structure of Demand 1500–1750. In *The Fontana Economic History of Europe*, Vol. 2, *The Sixteenth and Seventeenth Centuries,* ed. C.M. Cipolla, 82–176. Glasgow: Collins.

Morgan, Jennifer L. 2004. *Laboring Women: Reproduction and Gender in New World Slavery.* Philadelphia: University of Pennsylvania Press.

Murray, J.L. 1967. *Amsterdam in the Age of Rembrandt.* Norman: University of Oklahoma Press.

Navarrete, Federico. 2019. *¿Quién conquistó México?* Ciudad de México: Penguin Random House Grupo Editorial.

Norwood, Frederick. 1942. *The Reformation Refugees as an Economic Force.* Chicago: The American Society of Church History.

Padgug, Robert A. 1976. Problems in the Theory of Slavery and Slave Society. *Science & Society* 40 (Spring): 3–27.

Parry, J.H. 1965. *The Establishment of the European Hegemony.* New York: Harper & Row.

Parry, J.H. 1981. *The Age of Reconnaissance.* Berkeley: University of California Press.

Parry, J.H. 1967. Transport and Trade Routes. In *Cambridge Economic History of Europe,* Vol. IV, *The Economy of Expanding Europe in the Sixteenth and Seventeenth Centuries,* ed. E.E. Rich and C.H. Wilson, 155–219. Cambridge: Cambridge University Press.

Piore, Michael. 1979. *Birds of Passage: Migrant Labor and Industrial Societies.* Cambridge: Cambridge University Press.

Portes, Alejandro, and Rubén G. Rumbaut. 2014. *Immigrant America: A Portrait,* 4th ed. Oakland, CA: University of California Press.

Price, J.L. 1974. *Culture and Society in the Dutch Republic During the 17th Century.* London: Batsford.

Research Working Group on Cyclical Rhythms and Secular Trends. 1979. Cyclical Rhythms and Secular Trends of the Capitalist World-Economy: Some Premises, Hypotheses, and Questions. *Review* II (Spring): 483–500.

Rich, E.E. 1967. Colonial Settlement and Its Labour Problems. In *The Cambridge Economic History of Europe,* Vol. IV, *The Economy of Expanding Europe in the Sixteenth and Seventeenth Centuries,* ed. E.E. Rich and C.H. Wilson, 308–373. Cambridge: Cambridge University Press.

Rich, E.E. 1970. The European Nations and The Atlantic. In *The New Cambridge Modern History,* Vol. IV, *The Decline of Spain and the Thirty Years War 1609–48/59,* ed. J.P. Cooper, 672–706. Cambridge: Cambridge University Press.

Robinson, D.J., ed. 1990. *Migration in Colonial Spanish America.* New York: Cambridge University Press.

Schalk, Ruben. 2016. From Orphan to Artisan: Apprenticeship Careers and Contract Enforcement in The Netherlands Before and After the Guild Abolition. *The Economic History Review* 70 (3): 730–757.

Sellin, Thorstem. 1944. *Pioneering in Penology.* Philadelphia: University of Pennsylvania Press.

Slicher van Bath, B.H. 1960. The Rise of Intensive Husbandry in the Low Countries. In *Britain and the Netherlands,* ed. J.S. Bromley and E.H. Kossmann, 130–153. London: Chatto & Windus.

Spooner, Frank C. 1970. The European Economy, 1609–50. In *New Cambridge Modern History,* Vol. IV, *The Decline of Spain and the Thirty Years War, 1609–48/59,* ed. J.P. Cooper, 67–103. Cambridge: Cambridge University Press.

t Hart, Marjolein. 2001. Town and Country in the Dutch Republic, 1550–1800. In *Town and Country in Europe, 1300–1800,* ed. S.R. Epstein, 80–105. Cambridge: Cambridge University Press.

Unger, R.W. 1980. *The Ship in the Medieval Economy, 600–1600*. Montreal: McGill-Queen's University Press.
Van der Woude, A.M. 1975. The A.A.G. Bijdragon and the Study of Dutch Rural History. *Journal of European Economic History* 4 (Spring): 215–241.
Van Hoboken, W.J. 1960. The Dutch West India Company: The Political Background of its Rise and Decline. In *Britain and the Netherlands*, ed. J.S. Bromley and E.H. Kossman, 41–62. London: Chatto & Windus.
Van Houtte, J.A. 1977. *An Economic History of the Low Countries, 800–1800*. London: Weidenfeld and Nicolson.
Vlekke, Bernard H.M. 1945. *The Story of the Dutch East Indies*. Cambridge: Harvard University Press.
Vlekke, Bernard H.M. 1951. *Evolution of the Dutch Nation*. New York: Roy Publishers.
Vries, De. 1974. *The Dutch Rural Economy in the Golden Age, 1500–1700*. New Haven: Yale University Press.
Wagret, Paul. 1968. *Polderlands*. London: Methuen & Co.
Wallerstein, Immanuel. 1974. *The Modern World System: Capitalist Agriculture and the Origins of the European World-Economy in the Seventeenth Century*. New York: Academic Press.
Wallerstein, Immanuel. 1979. "Underdevelopment and Phase-B: Effect of the Seventeenth-Century Stagnation on Core and Periphery of the European World-Economy. In *The World-System of Capitalism: Past and Present*, ed. Walter L. Goldfrank, 73–84. Beverly Hills: Sage Publications.
Wallerstein, Immanuel. 1980. *The Modern World-System II: Mercantilism and the Consolidation of the European World-Economy, 1600–1750*. New York: Academic Press Inc.
Watson, Rodney. 1990. Informal Settlement and Fugitive Migration Amongst the Indians of Late-Colonial Chiapas, Mexico. In *Migration in Colonial Spanish America*, ed. David R. Robinson, 238–278. Cambridge: Cambridge University Press.
Williams, Eric. 1966. *Capitalism & Sugar*. New York: Capricorn Book Editions.
Wilson, Charles H. 1957. *Profit and Power: A Study of England and the Dutch Wars*. New York: Longmans, Green and Co.
Wilson, Charles H. 1965. *England's Apprenticeship, 1603–1763*. London: Longmans.
Wilson, Charles H. 1968. *The Dutch Republic and the Civilisation of the Seventeenth Century*. London: Weidenfeld & Nicolson.
Wilson, Charles H. 1967. Trade, Society and the State. In *Cambridge Economic History of Europe, Vol. IV, The Economy of Expanding Europe in the Sixteenth and Seventeenth Centuries*, ed. E.E. Rich and C.H. Wilson, 487–575. Cambridge: Cambridge University Press.
Wischnitzer, Mark. 1954. Origins of the Jewish Artisan Class in Bohemia and Moravia, 1500–1648. *Jewish Social Studies* 16 (October): 335–350.
Wiznitzer, A. 1954. The Number of Jews in Dutch Brazil (1630–1654). *Jewish Social Studies* XVI (April): 107–114.
Zulawski, Ann. 1990. Frontier Workers and Social Change: Pilaya and Paspaya (Bolivia) in the Early Eighteenth Century. In *Migration in Colonial Spanish America*, ed. David R. Robinson, 112–127. Cambridge: Cambridge University Press.

British Hegemony and Migration

4

After the period of Dutch hegemony, Britain became the second hegemonic power in the capitalist world-system during the interval between the end of the Napoleonic Wars in 1815 and the Great Depression of 1873 (Wallerstein 1979a, b). Similar to the rise of Dutch hegemony in the seventeenth century, migration played a critical role for the development of British dominance in the world-economy. Migration was particularly important to fill the ranks of factory workforces during British industrialization, which made Britain the industrial powerhouse of the world. Development of the factory system became a means for British capitalists to dominate industrial world trade and further incorporate peripheral regions into the capitalist world-economy, as these regions became buyers of British products and sources of raw materials for British industries. In Britain, the expansion of agricultural capitalism and the rise of the factory system stimulated emigration, providing human resources for economic development in the United States and other world regions. In Ireland, economic restructuring by British landlords in the late eighteenth and nineteenth centuries, along with famine, brought about large-scale Irish emigration to Britain and other countries, especially the United States.

According to Arrighi (2010), British dominance in the world-economy involved a synthesis between capitalism and territorialism that was not as present during Dutch hegemony. While Dutch hegemony involved the establishment of a seaborne empire to dominate trade,[1] British and other European investors and state powers took control of vast territories, cultures, and populations in far-flung regions of the world, such as the British colonial control of large areas in the Indian subcontinent. By the end of British hegemony in the 1870s, Western powers controlled about two-thirds of the earth's land surface (Magdoff 1978). According to Arrighi (2010), a new method of military training enabled the British and other European powers

---

[1] The Dutch acquisition by force of the Pernambuco region in northeastern Brazil in the seventeenth century is an exception to their seaborne empire (Boxer 1957).

to create armies abroad of native subjects to control lands taken into the European empires.

Arrighi (2010) cites settler colonialism, capitalist slavery, and economic nationalism as three central elements undergirding the synthesis of European capitalism and territorialism beginning in the eighteenth century. Settler colonialism provided a major resource for establishing economic enterprises and networks abroad—as well as for establishing imperial domination—to link to the home country. Capitalist slavery using foreign or native populations provided the labor power for settler enterprises, which often struggled to obtain labor forces, and the commerce in the slave labor itself became a profitable investment. The support of capitalistic world expansion by European states was geared to promote the development of the home economy through "free-trade imperialism" (Gallagher and Robinson 1953), which expanded interstate and interregional commerce much to the economic and political advantage of the European powers. War-making associated with colonial expansion also did much to support growth in the home economy, as the equipment for war was often produced in the home country with financial support gained from colonial tributes (Arrighi 2010).

The systemic relation between migration and capitalist development across regions of the world-system demonstrated new patterns and reached new levels in the era of British hegemony. One new pattern was the international displacement of Irish rural labor by British rearrangement of agricultural production in Ireland. Large numbers of displaced Irish migrated to Britain, creating one of the initial massive labor flows from a peripheral region to a core state in the capitalist world-system.[2] A second feature was the much larger sizes of the new migration patterns compared with earlier periods. During Dutch hegemony, the number of international migrants in the United Provinces was counted in streams of hundreds or thousands, but in the period of British hegemony international migrant streams reached *continual flows* of tens of thousands, hundreds of thousands, and over a million in the case of Irish migration to the United States in the 1850s (US DHS 2010: Table 2). One reason for the enlarged flows was simply that national populations grew larger, putting more people at risk of migration. But another reason had to do with how pervasive the effects of capitalism had become in society, reaching beyond a limited number of industries in earlier centuries to many sectors of society by the late eighteenth and nineteenth centuries. In the context of large populations, the transformative effects of capitalist development hurled massive numbers of people into migrant streams.

The discussion in this chapter is divided into four major sections. The Sect. 4.1 describes the condition of British hegemony, including the industrial transformation in Britain and cases of British capitalist expansion in peripheral and semiperipheral regions to gain markets for British industrial products. The Sect. 4.2

---

[2] In terms of absolute numbers the forced migration by European investors of African slaves remained the largest pattern, but this coerced migration was directed mainly to other peripheral areas in Latin America and the Caribbean and not to core states in Europe. In the United States, the importation of African slaves occurred before the country gained core status.

describes major patterns of labor migration that were a resource for British industrialization. The Sect. 4.3 analyzes the patterns of migration from the standpoint of class struggle, technological development, economic cycles, and the state. The chapter concludes by discussing how British economic development during its period of hegemony affected rural migration in the periphery, including massive emigration from Ireland, and also the emigration of skilled workers from Britain.

4.1 British Hegemony, 1815–1873

The decades that separated the end of the Napoleonic Wars in 1815 and the Great Depression of 1873 are among the most change-laden in British history.[3] Britons who lived through this time interval can be considered to have lived in two different worlds. It was the interval in which the Industrial Revolution and related social transformations were completed. The large numbers of factories, machines, and railroads that filled economic life in the 1870s had existed mainly in the imaginations of inventors and entrepreneurs in the second decade of the nineteenth century. Social change was just as dramatic. The economic center of gravity completed the transition from agricultural and household handicraft production to industries with workplaces outside the home. Populations also shifted to urban centers where industrial capital was concentrated.[4] Manufacturing cities such as Birmingham, Leicester, and Manchester reached prominence in Britain and in the world-economy.[5] The technological change brought about by the Industrial Revolution has been characterized as "a far more dramatic break with the past than anything since the invention of the wheel" (Landes 1965: 275).[6]

British hegemony involved the furtherance of capitalism at the world level. For analytical purposes, a country's domestic and external economic developments can be differentiated, but in the workings of the capitalist world-system, a country's domestic economic growth and economic expansion abroad can have an integral interconnection as different parts of the same system. For industrial development to proceed in Britain, raw materials, food, and markets had to be obtained abroad, sometimes by force. Moreover, as Frank (1969) has explained, the process of world capitalist development proceeded dialectically: economic development in the core meant the development of underdevelopment in the periphery.

---

[3] Rostow (1948) describes the years between 1815 and 1847 as perhaps the interval of the fastest development of domestic resources in all of Britain's economic history.

[4] The urban–rural shift in England and Wales went from 37%/63% in 1811 to 65%/35% in 1871, respectively (Law 1967).

[5] In the earlier Dutch period of hegemony, the Dutch cities of Amsterdam and Leiden became important economic sources for the emerging world system (see Rodriguez and Feagin 1986).

[6] To quote Cairncross (1953: 65) regarding the transformation: "Under the influence of a few compelling forces, operating steadily over the greater part of a century, society was gradually transformed in scale and structure, in custom and belief, in the work that had to be done and the livelihood that the work afforded."

4.1.1 "Workshop of the World"

Historians have used the phrase "workshop of the world" to describe Britain's industrial development and export of manufactured products during its period of hegemony (Langer 1969; Wallerstein 1979a, b). In the mid-nineteenth century, manufactured goods composed 93% of British exports (Landes 1977). By this point in time, Britain supplied half of the manufactured goods used in the industrializing countries of France, Germany, and the United States (Wallerstein 1979a, b). British production of two-thirds of the world's coal, half of the iron, five-sevenths of the steel, and about half of the cotton cloth produced commercially also demonstrated the industrial power of Britain in the world-economy in the middle of the nineteenth century (Hobsbawn 1969; Landes 1977).

While the rate of growth of the British labor force was the same as the growth of the total population from 1800 to 1830, and slightly higher from 1830 to 1860, the output per worker and output per unit of capital increased. Affected by increased mechanization, estimated productivity per worker more than doubled from 1800 to 1860, and productivity per unit of capital increased by almost three-fourths (Feinstein 1978).

Overall, British economic change in the early to mid-1800s involved the completion of the transition to the factory system of production that had started in the latter part of the eighteenth century. In structural terms, it was the final stage in the transition to industrial capitalism. With variation by branches of industry, by the mid-nineteenth century large-scale manufacturing greatly replaced handicraft production in small shops. The factories of large-scale production employed up to hundreds of propertyless workers (men, women, and children) to operate machinery for eighteen or more hours a day (Marx 1967).[7]

The factory system diffused rapidly. While the incentive to mechanize sometimes lessened with declining wages, throughout the first half of the nineteenth century there was a steady rise in mechanized production (Hunt 1981). According to Landes (1969), the number of power-looms in England's textile industry increased from 2400 in 1813 to 55,500 in 1829, to 100,000 in 1833, and to 250,000 in 1850.[8] The number of cotton-textile factories fluctuated, but increased in the long term from 2210 factories in 1858, to 2887 in 1861, to 2549 in 1868 (Marx 1967).

"Whoever says Industrial Revolution says cotton." With these words Hobsbawn (1969: 56) emphasizes a central feature of the industrialization in Britain known as the Industrial Revolution that transpired from the late 1700s to the 1840s. As Hobsbawn (1969) explains, cotton led the way in Britain's development of industrial

---

[7] According to an 1860 report of a county magistrate in Nottingham, "Children of nine or ten years are dragged from their squalid beds at two, three, or four o'clock in the morning and compelled to work for a bare subsistence until ten, eleven, or twelve at night, their limbs wearing away, their frames dwindling, their faces whitening, and their humanity absolutely sinking into a stone-like torpor, utterly horrible to contemplate.... (quoted in Marx 1967: 243–244)."

[8] Hobsbawn (1969: 64) cites 85,000 power-looms for 1833 and 224,000 for 1850.

capitalism. Much of the early urban growth, mechanization, and price movement of the Industrial Revolution was associated with this single industry. Cotton towns showed "the earliest and the most remarkable development" of the urban areas in the Industrial Revolution (Mantoux 1961: 358). For example, with the construction in Manchester of spinning mills powered by steam, the city's population grew from 50,000 in 1790 to 95,000 in 1801, counting the suburban population (Mantoux 1961). With increases of over 1000% in spinning productivity and over 100% in weaving productivity, cotton cloth production demonstrated the productive superiority of the factory (Landes 1977). Cotton cloth production also demonstrated how the growth of British industrial capitalism was linked to the development of the world capitalist system. Raw cotton was imported into Britain from such peripheral areas as India, the West Indies, and the southern United States to meet industrial consumption needs that went from about 81 million pounds in 1815 to close to 1084 million in 1860 (Rostow 1978). In the same period, the proportion of cotton cloth produced in Britain and exported to markets in Africa, India, America, and Europe increased from 57 to 62% (Hobsbawn 1962).

Cotton led the way to British industrialization, but it was the railroad that enabled this transformation to succeed and made the dominance of modern industry possible in the economy (see Lilley 1978). As explained by Dobb (1963: 296), railroads provided the advantage for industrial capitalists of being "enormously capital-absorbing." At the height of a British railroad boom in the 1840s, the railroads absorbed about half of the country's total investment (Landes 1977). Railroad construction also stimulated the development of the iron, steel, and coal industries. From 1847 to 1848, when 2000 miles of railroad were built in Britain, a large amount of iron was used to construct rails and chairs in train cars, perhaps as much as one-fourth of the iron produced in that date (Dobb 1963).

A measure of success for capital in the railroad industry was the harnessing of labor to produce surplus value, the source of profit. At the peak of the "railway mania" of 1845–1847, the railroad industry employed 300,000 workers, a number greater than in the cotton industry, according to Dobb (1963: 296).[9] As described by Landes (1977), with the very large number of workers, the railroads became laboratories for new techniques in industrial management.

The explosive development of cotton-textile manufacturing, railroads, and other industries such as iron and coal illustrated Britain's great economic expansion in the nineteenth century and brought about a heightened accumulation of capital. According to Feinstein's (1978) estimations, from 1760 to 1860, roughly the time span covering the Industrial Revolution, the accumulation of total capital (national wealth) including land and overseas assets, advanced according to the levels in Table 4.1.[10]

---

[9] Dobb's (1963: 296) 300,000 figure includes workers "on and off the lines." Bagwell and Mingay (1970: 30) give an estimate of 250,000 workers in railroad building in 1848.

[10] Feinstein's figures of capital accumulation are particularly noteworthy because they are derived from an elaborate comparison of estimates.

Table 4.1 Levels of the stock of total capital, Britain, 1760–1860

	£ million at 1851–1860 prices
1760	1630
1800	2070
1830	2840
1860	4640

Source Feinstein (1978: Table 24)

The advancement of the growth of total capital, which almost tripled during the Industrial Revolution, was mainly based on the rise of industrial capitalism, i.e., on the growth of industry and commerce and the diminution of the agricultural sector. The share of national wealth of industry and commerce grew from 5 to 23% during 1760–1860, while the share of agriculture dropped from 77 to 36% (Feinstein 1978).

A central aspect of the rise of British industrial capitalism was the growth of the propertyless, wage workers—the *proletariat*—in industry. Between 1801 and 1861, the British labor force (total employed population) grew from about 4.8 million to approximately 10.8 million workers (Feinstein 1978). Agricultural employment predominated at the beginning of the century with a proportion of 36% of all workers, but by mid-century industrial employment (in manufacturing, mining, etc.) led with 43% of all workers. The development of the industrial labor force involved the growth of factory workforces. In the large industry of textile manufacturing, 62% of the workers were employed in factories by 1860 (Feinstein 1978).[11]

4.2 Capital Migration

The advance of industrial capitalism in Britain was connected to the migration of British capital migration in the world-system. British capitalists sought four important resources abroad: sources of raw cotton for British textile factories, food imports for an increasingly urban labor force, consumer markets to sell industrial commodities, and peripheral regions with unorganized, working classes to serve as opportunities for high returns on capital investment. In contrast to Dutch colonization in the seventeenth century, in the nineteenth century, British capitalist expansion did not always require military force. British capital loans could be made to regions abroad, leaving to native leaders of the regions the matter of reorganizing production to serve the interests of capital.[12] Regardless of the method of expansion, the spread of a social system that produced profit through exploitation usually meant the repression of workers in areas that came under its control.

---

[11] In 1860, the textile industry still had about 450,000 hand workers (Feinstein 1978).
[12] The foreign loans also were made for the purchase of British industrial goods, which served to support British industrialization (Luxemburg 1968).

During the period of British hegemony, the British accounted for about one-fourth of the world trade and enjoyed more than twice the amount of the world commerce of its two closest competitors, France and Germany (Rostow 1978). Through import and export commerce, and through foreign investments, segments of the British capitalist class linked the functioning of the British domestic economy to areas throughout the world. For example, vegetable oil for making soap and for industrial use was imported from West Africa, raw cotton from the West Indies and the southern United States, and food grains from India (Fieldhouse 1973; Hobsbawn 1962).[13] Cotton textiles were exported to such peripheral areas such as India and South American countries, and railroad materials to such places as Egypt, Greece, and Turkey (Luxemburg 1968). In a similar manner, British capital loans spread throughout the world-economy (Jenks 1927).

Although the British had been in areas of India since 1600, it was in the late eighteenth century (particularly after the Battle of Plassey in 1757) and in the nineteenth century that British rule advanced at a massive scale in the subcontinent (Frank 1979). Indian goods such as cotton, indigo, silk, sugar, and saltpeter were needed by British traders to exchange for spices in the East Indies and for tea in Canton.[14] In addition, the British saw India as a possible source of raw cotton for English cotton factories and as a market for products produced by British industrialization.[15]

To meet these needs, the British East India Company reorganized much of the Indian economy.[16] Communal land use was dissolved, and on lands where for generations villages had tilled as a community, cultivation was converted into a commodity form of a landowner-employee arrangement (Wolpert 1977). To dominate the vast Indian market for cotton products, Manchester cotton manufacturers obtained low tariffs for raw cotton from India, as well as low tariffs for British cotton products imported into India. But high British tariffs were imposed on cotton goods manufactured in India (Harnetty 1972; Wolpert 1977). Unable to compete with the cheaper machine-made cotton products from Britain, which were massively imported in India and distributed throughout by the new railroad system, the Indian textile handicraft industry lost spinners and weavers in a migration to agricultural workforces (Frank 1979; Chandra 1981).[17] Partly disadvantaged by

---

[13] Deane (1979) points out that by the 1840s between 10 and 15% of Britain's population was dependent on foreign wheat.

[14] The British trade with China in opium from India became the source of two major military conflicts—the Opium Wars—in the mid-1800s. Through these conflicts, the British and other Western powers forced the Chinese emperor to grant trading privileges to Western powers, and in 1898 the Chinese handed over Hong Kong to the British for a 99-year lease (Carroll 2007).

[15] Marx (1967) cites the increase of cotton export from India to Britain as follows: in 1846: 34,540,143 lbs. in 1846; 204,141,168 lbs. in 1860; and in 445,947,600 lbs. in 1865.

[16] The British East India Company was created by a Royal charter granted by Queen Elizabeth I in 1600 and was dissolved in 1874 when the government of British India took control of its functions. The Company effectively ruled much of India between 1757 and 1858 (Robins 2012).

[17] According to Wolpert (1977: 411), by the end of the nineteenth century the proportion of India's population dependent directly on agriculture for support had increased to about 90%. Nonetheless,

high British tariffs, from 1815 to 1832 the value of Indian cotton goods exported dropped by more than 90%, from £1.3 million to under £100,000, as the 150,000 population of textile-producing Dacca declined (Hayter 1982).

India never became a major supplier of raw cotton for English cotton factories as British textile manufacturers had hoped. The Indian village culture could not adopt to a system of massive, cotton production. It was the southern United States that rose in the late eighteenth century and early nineteenth century to occupy the role of being the major source of raw cotton for English textile factories. As explained in Sven Beckert's *Empire of Cotton* (2014), a major determinant in the successful arrangement of a system of massive cotton production was securing the labor supply for the very labor-intensive production of raw cotton. Growers in the southern United States solved the labor issue through forced labor, i.e., the importation of African slaves and the continued use of slaves after the African slave trade was ended. Moreover, land was secured for the expansion of cotton production through US policies that eliminated large Native American populations from the US southern region through treaties or military actions. Eventually by the mid-nineteenth century, the US war with Mexico acquired the southern region of Texas, in addition to other lands, as a slave, cotton-producing region in the country.[18] The harnessing of a large labor supply of African slaves, the removal by forced relocation and killing of Native Americans populations, the acquisition of land through a war with Mexico, etc.—all were cogs in the southern United States that enabled the accumulation of capital in the British cotton industry (Beckert 2014).

While the British purchase of cotton from the southern United States did not represent British capital migration for investment, it did represent a transfer of money value that merchants, growers, and investors in agriculture could use to enlarge their capital accumulation. The US cotton trade expanded dramatically as British production of cotton cloth for the world market grew, and as the proportion of slave labor grew "in lockstep" in US cotton-producing areas (Beckert 2014: 103).[19] Cotton exports accounted for 2.2% of all US exports in 1796 and by 1820 it accounted for 32%. During 1815–1860, cotton accounted for more than half of all US exports, making cotton and "the backs of slaves" the foundation for the US rise in the world-economy (Beckert 2014: 119).

---

the number of cotton mills in India rose in the late nineteenth century, reaching 144 mills by 1895 (Sahoo 2015).

[18] Texas became a slave-owning region after its independence from Mexico in 1836. The rise of cotton prices made Texas attractive for illegal white immigrants in the early 1830s who wanted to grow cotton with slaves, which the Mexican government had banned. The result was a war of independence from Mexico by the white immigrants (Burrough et al. 2021).

[19] According to Beckert (2014), the US internal slave trade moved about a million slaves to the Deep South by the first half of the nineteenth century mainly to work in cotton plantations. Marx commented on the connection between European labor and unfree labor in the interregional circuit of the cotton economy as follows: "In fact, the veiled slavery of the wage-workers in Europe needed, for its pedestal, slavery pure and simple in the new world (1967: 759–760).".

4.2 Capital Migration

In *The Accumulation of Capital*, Luxemburg (1968) describes the consequences that the penetration of British, French, and German capital in Egypt had on the country's peasant economy. From the 1840s to the 1870s, the rulers of Egypt (Mehemet Ali, Said Rasha, and Ismail Pasha) undertook a vigorous and expensive program of economic development. Loans worth in the millions were continually obtained from banking houses in England and other places in Europe to buy materials for constructing canal irrigation systems, for buying steam plows (mainly from Britain), for constructing large sugar factories, and for building railroads. While the Egyptian royal families prospered from this economic development, the country's *fellaheen* (peasantry) paid for it. As the price of cotton or sugar increased, the ruling Egyptian families took possession of the fellaheen's lands for their private estates. The fellaheen also had to provide free labor power for economic development. Enlarging the traditional *corvée* practice, 20,000 fellaheen were made available to work in construction projects and later for the rulers' estates. The workers were not paid, and they had to provide for their own subsistence while at work. Taxation on peasant holdings also was greatly increased in this period of development. By the 1870s, the fellaheen in upper Egypt were so heavily taxed that they destroyed their own dwellings and ceased planting crops in order to avoid paying taxes. By the late 1870s, ten thousand peasants starved because they could not afford the irrigation tax on their fields and had killed their cattle in order to avoid paying tax on them (Luxemburg 1968).

Capital migration to Ireland occurred as a transformation of the British occupation in Ireland that began in the second half of the twelfth century. Through various forms of oppression, the English gained control of Ireland's land and human labor, converting the country into "an agricultural district of England" by the modern era (Marx 1967: 702–703).[20] The first decisive expansion of capitalistic priorities into Ireland from England occurred in the seventeenth century with the intensification of the redivision of land by the mainly Anglo-Protestant landlord class. Involving such measures as the conversion of clan duties into rent payments for landlords and the resettlement of clans, the reallocation of land dealt a deathblow to the Irish clan system of land use (Marx and Engels 1972).[21] The restructuring of the Irish rural economy to increase profits for investment in London's capital market helped supply funds for economic projects and government loans throughout much of the world-economy (see Jenks 1927).

Repeal of the Corn Laws in Britain in 1846 furthered the penetration of English capitalistic interests in Ireland. The repeal of the Corn Laws eliminated preferential status of Irish grain in British markets. With this loss of trading advantage, the

---

[20] In an historical review of farming conditions in Ireland during 1600–1920, Cormac Ó Gráda (1990: 168) comments regarding 1800–1850, "the low wages associated with the 'potato standard' underpinned the huge tillage acreage that made Ireland to some extent Britain's 'granary.'"

[21] Ó Gráda (1990: 165) states a different perspective from Marx and Engels (1972): "It has been shown, surely to the satisfaction of everybody by now, that traditional historiography has been misled by farmer-nationalist propaganda and its depiction of the typical landlord as cruel and neglectful."

landowning class in Ireland, which consisted mainly of native Anglo-Protestants and English absentee landlords, reorganized the predominantly rural Irish economy of small holdings into large-scale pasture lands to produce animal products. The landlords drastically reduced the number of small holdings through an enclosure movement, often destroying country huts and forcibly ejecting tenant farmers. In the early 1840s, about one in two holdings in Ireland consisted of farms of one to five acres, but by the early 1850s less than one in six were in this size range (Kennedy 1973).

In the regions of extensive farm consolidations, Irish peasants faced evictions and a greater dependence on wage work, often as migrant labor. With the country's earlier deindustrialization that resulted from trade changes of the Act of Union (1801), towns did not provide an economic alternative to the dispossessed Irish peasants (Hobsbawn 1962). To the contrary, urban centers, e.g., Dublin, Cork, and Kilkenny, added to rural blight as their thousands of unemployed industrial workers migrated to the countryside to look for work (Marx and Engels 1972).[22] With the additional hardship of famine, the Irish people had almost no economic alternatives. Most of the Irish laboring class faced severe poverty and starvation, or emigration for those who could afford to pay for transportation. In the potato famine of 1845–1848, three-quarters of a million Irish perished, and one and a half million emigrated to Britain and America (Kennedy 1973). Given the policies that enhanced British capitalist development in Ireland's agriculture or that limited Irish industrial trade with foreign countries, the Irish working class mainly faced the alternative of emigration to seek economic betterment.

In the United States, British capital investment constituted only a small portion of the capital supply that was amassed during the country's industrialization. By 1870 the amount of British capital invested in the United States reached £200 million, but this total amount was less than the annual average gross capital formation of $1.3 billion reached in the country by the 1870s (Bagwell and Mingay 1970). As Chap. 5 will describe, British capital in the United States was invested primarily in railroad securities and government bonds.

This section has attempted to give a sense of the scope of British capital migration to regions in the capitalist world-system during the British period of hegemony. In the section that follows, I focus on labor migration that was associated with the emergence of British industrial dominance in the world-system.

4.3   Labor Migration and Industrial Development

Many patterns of labor migration were associated with the development of British industrial capitalism beginning in the second half of the eighteenth century. The

---

[22] From 1800 to 1840 Dublin's woolen manufacturing workforce dropped from 4918 to 602; Cork's workforce of 9586 weavers, hosiers, and wool combers in 1800 decreased to 488 by 1834; and Kilkenny's blanket manufacturing labor force dropped from 3000 in 1800 to 925 by 1822 (Marx and Engels 1972: 131–132).

patterns varied by origin and destination, and by industry and gender, and sometimes moved in opposite directions (Cairncross 1953). Moreover, business cycles in capitalist production and commerce affected the ebb and flow of migration patterns. According to fragmentary evidence of net migration flows in counties in England and Wales, mobility between 1781 and 1830 was above that of 1701–1750, but distinctly below that of 1840–1890 (Hunt 1981). This section highlights three major patterns associated with British industrialization in the eighteenth and nineteenth centuries: rural-rural migration, townward migration, and Irish immigration. These migration patterns were integral to the economic development of Britain in this time period and affected the country's rise to hegemony in the capitalist world-system.

4.3.1 British Labor Migration

The growth of Britain as the workshop of the world-economy in the nineteenth century required the expansion of its industrial labor forces. British industrialization passed through the two phases of textile and capital-goods production. Textile industries led the Industrial Revolution from the late 1700s to the 1830s, and capital-goods industries, e.g., coal, iron, railroads, etc., led after the 1830s. The economic expansion of both phases required an expansion of labor power that was partly met through migration. By the late 1700s and the early 1800s, the demand for industrial labor was beginning to bring about the urbanization associated with industrialism, but it was in the 1830s and 1840s, however, that townward migration accelerated. According to Hobsbawn's (1969) description of the impact of industrial labor on British urban growth, in 1750 only London and Edinburgh had more than 50,000 inhabitants, but by 1801 eight cities had reached this population size. By 1851, twenty-nine cities had passed the 50,000 level, with nine of these cities having over 100,000 inhabitants. Natural increase and in-migration were the source of this urban growth (Pollard 1978; Deane 1979; Hunt 1981).

Some analysts have viewed labor migration from the countryside to urban areas as having been the decisive factor behind industrialization (Dobb 1963; Castells 1979). For Castells (1979: 14), a "fundamental fact" in the first phase of the Industrial Revolution was that urbanization proceeded in great part from "[t]he prior decomposition of the agrarian social structures and the emigration of the population towards the already existing urban areas, providing the labour force essential to industrialization." Yet, contrary to Castells' claim, labor migration characterized the two phases of textile and capital-goods industrialization differently. Migration to rural industrial areas remained very dynamic in the textile phase of the late 1700s and early 1800s, while migration to urban industries accelerated with capital-goods production after the 1830s. Yet, rural–urban migration was just one of the migration patterns associated with the rise of British industrialization, and the patterns included the continuation of rural-rural migration, which in some cases occurred with new purpose as the developing British capitalist economy expanded into the countryside.

Rural-rural migration. As Pollard (1978) and Redford (1968) explain, much of the migration of labor in the first phase of industrialization, i.e., between the late 1700s and the 1830s, occurred in the countryside. At the beginning of the textile phase of industrialization, cotton-textile production was mainly a rural industry (Pollard 1978). In emphasizing the continuity of cultural traditions in the making of the English working-class during industrialization, Thompson (1963) has described how even in the 1830s cotton-handloom weavers, who traditionally were rural workers, outnumbered the total labor force of men and women in the spinning and weaving mills of cotton, wool, and silk in Britain.

At the beginning of the growth of the cotton-textile industry in the late 1700s, rural workers in England, Wales, and Scotland migrated more to industrial villages in the countryside than to factories in the towns.[23] The rural migrants that turned settlements (e.g., Middleton, Oldham, Mottram, and Rochdale) into textile villages consisted of farming families, agricultural laborers, and immigrant artisans (Thompson 1963; Burgess, 1980). William Radcliffe, an observer of this rural industrial growth, described the impact of a growing weaver population in the Pennine uplands:

> ... the old loom-shops being insufficient, every lumber-room, even old barns, cart-houses and outbuildings of any descriptions were repaired, windows broke through the bland walls, and all were fitted up for the loom-shops. This source of making room being at length exhausted, new weavers cottages with loom-shops rose up in every direction . . . . (quoted in Thompson 1963: 275)

Not all labor migration in the rural cotton industry was toward handloom shops in weavers' villages. Workers also migrated to cotton mills that were located next to upland waterways, which served as a source of mechanical power. According to Redford (1968), this migration consisted mainly of transients and other unskilled workers recruited from parish workhouses in the country and in the towns. In England and Scotland, a sizable portion of workhouse labor consisted of children. In the English country mills, children, including those obtained through contracts with parents, constituted one-fourth to one-third of the workers.[24]

Similar to textile production, mining was a rural industry at the beginning of the Industrial Revolution. As British capital increased its dominance in the world-system, mining activity expanded to supply coal and metals for factories (and later for railroads) at home and abroad (see Wrigley 1967; Harley 1989). As described by Pollard (1978), the mining trades had traditionally relied on semi-proletarian

---

[23] Referring to this rural industrial concentration in the 1770s and onward, Thompson (1963: 275) states, "It was the loom, and not the cotton-mill, which attracted immigrants in their thousands."
[24] With increasing passage of legislation to regulate factory child-labor (see Thomis 1974), the use of workhouse children decreased early in the nineteenth century. From 1802 to the end of 1811, the total number of these workers in England amounted to 5815 (Redford 1968). After the Factory Act of 1833 gave children an eight-hour workday, child labor was transported mainly to mining and metal trades.

farm workers as part of the labor supply. As the demand for metals increased in the late 1700s, these seasonal migrants became full-time miners, increasing the household and farming work of the wives and children left in the farms. With the intensification of mining to meet the needs of industrial production in the first half of the nineteenth century (Rostow 1978), wives and children were also brought to work in the mines in such places as the Cornish metal districts (Rule 1970). Evidence presented by an 1842 commission on child labor indicated that in some mines men were required to bring their children to work (Rule 1970). By the 1840s, the mining and quarrying labor force in Britain numbered about 200,000 (Deane and Cole 1967).

The movement of labor to rural textile and mining industries (as well as to iron-production and copper-smelting sites) also involved urban–rural migration of workers. In addition to the workhouse children that were obtained from such cities as London, Edinburgh, and Glasgow, owners of rural mills hired agents in the late 1700s to recruit workers from urban centers of the cotton trade, e.g., Manchester (Redford 1968). With the occurrences of unemployment that accompanied the business cycles of industrial capitalism in the 1800s, some of the unemployed in the towns migrated to the countryside to look for work (Pollard 1978; also see Thompson 1963). In some cases, urban industries expanded into the countryside to take advantage of available rural labor. For example, at the beginning of the nineteenth century, boot and shoe manufacturers in Northampton met increases in demand by putting out more work to families in surrounding villages such as Kettering, Raunds Highan Ferrers, and Earls Barton (Church 1970).

Townward Migration. The number of cotton factories established in industrial towns and cities in Britain increased at the turn of the nineteenth century, causing population increases in the settings of new production (Redford 1968). At the same time, cotton-mill production in some remote areas of the countryside began to decline. The increase of townward migration spurred by urban industrialization contrasted with the low level of migration to cities and towns at the beginning of the Industrial Revolution in England and Wales, and in the manufacturing Lowland towns in Scotland (Dickson and Clark 1980).[25]

Estimates of migration rates, based on baptismal and burial records, for six new industrial counties in England and Wales that led in town population growth during early industrialization indicate the eventual rise of migration to industrial urban areas in the 1751–1830 period (Deane and Cole 1967). Among the six new industrial counties of Cheshire, Lancashire, Monmouthshire, Staffordshire, Warwickshire, and West Riding, three counties had positive and three counties had negative migration rates in 1751–1780, two counties had positive and four had

---

[25] Pollard (1978) cites several reasons for the lack of migration to urban industries from beyond the nearby countryside in the first phase of British industrialization: poor means of transportation, fear and ignorance of the new industrial employment, and lack of social capital among rural people to organize migration to distant industrial districts. In the nineteenth century, the reasons included the settlement requirements of the Poor Law for affected workers, and the interest of landlords to keep laborers available in rural areas for harvest time even if it meant making relief payments.

negative migration rates in 1781–1800, but all six counties had positive migration rates in 1801–1830 (Deane and Cole 1967).[26] Of the six new industrial counties, only the iron-ore mining and metal works county of Monmouthshire in Wales maintained a rising pattern of in-migration throughout 1751–1830.

The negative rates for three of the six new industrial counties in 1751–1780 and for four of the counties in 1781–1800 are consistent with the description given above of the migration of urban workers to the countryside in the early part of industrialization. County-parish data of births and deaths, however, do not present a complete picture of migration. For example, these data do not take into account temporary migrants, i.e., the semi-proletarians who divided their work lives between farming and town work and who died at their place of birth. Nor do the data tell anything about intra-county movement. It does not indicate, for example, the extent to which workers in southern Lancashire migrated to the industrial centers of Manchester or Liverpool.

In contrast to the early period of industrialization in the eighteenth and early nineteenth centuries, from the 1830s and 1840s there was a steady country-to-town migration until the end of the British period of hegemony in the early 1870s. Deane (1979) estimates that from 1841 to 1851 over 700,000 people left the countryside and moved into the towns and colliery districts of England and Wales, and from 1851 to 1861 over 600,000 migrated into the towns. The censuses of 1841 and 1851 indicated that migrants accounted for about half of the populations of most industrial cities (Pollard 1978). More than 1.3 million migrants moved into the towns and colliery districts of England and Wales between 1841 and 1861 (Deane 1979). According to Cairncross (1953), with Irish immigration adding to the movement from the countryside, townward migration peaked in the 1840s.

The impact of migration varied among cities and towns. London, Liverpool, and Manchester grew very rapidly in the 1840s, with the latter two achieving their biggest gain ever from migration in this period. By the end of the 1840s, more than three-fourths of the population older than twenty years of age in Manchester were born elsewhere (Hunt 1981). For the industrial towns in the North, e.g., Middlesbrough, Rotherham, and the railroad centers such as Rugby and Doncaster, the 1850s were the period of greatest in-migration. Colliery centers experienced a steady net in-migration of about 100,000 per decade. In large towns, migration accounted for about one-fourth of town population growth in the 1841–1911 period, and for one-sixth of the growth in mining towns (Cairncross 1953).

The figures in Table 4.2 demonstrate the variability of townward migration among eight large industrial cities in northern Britain. Manchester, Liverpool, and Birmingham experienced substantial more in-migration than the other five cities, and the cities varied by decade of their peak in-migration. The functions

---

[26] The estimates are based on baptismal and burial records. Deane and Cole (1967) caution about the use of baptismal and burial figures. Death records were better kept than those of births, and the reliability of parish registers varied by region. It is Deane and Cole's (1967) view however, that, although the estimates of migration are imprecise for individual counties, the figures are useful for describing broad changes in internal migration.

4.3 Labor Migration and Industrial Development

Table 4.2 Average migration per decade, selected cities, 1841–1880

	Average migration net gain per decade for 1841–1880	Decade with the highest migration gain
Liverpool	+ 70,452	1841–1850: + 107,184
Manchester	+ 48,418	1841–1850: + 73,003
Birmingham	+ 29,858	1851–1860: + 46,861
Sheffield	+ 16,484	1861–1870: + 26,647
Leeds	+ 10,709	1861–1870: + 20,734
Nottingham	+ 10,438	1871–1880: + 21,995
Leicester	+ 6,298	1871–1880: + 17,578
Hull	+ 11,921	1871–1880: + 16,839

Source Cairncross (1953)

that British cities performed in the British domestic economy and in the British-dominated world-economy were sources of variation in net migration gained or lost.[27]

Similar to Amsterdam and Leiden in the Dutch period of hegemony, London and Manchester played specialized roles in finance and manufacturing, respectively, in the world-economy during the era of British hegemony. These specialized economic roles attracted labor in-migration, adding to the natural increase of the populations in the two urban areas (Rodriguez and Feagin 1986). Large working populations were needed to produce for world markets. Poor laborers from southern England, Irish and Jewish immigrants, and foreign investors from the Continent and other world regions helped to increase London's metropolitan population from about 1.2 million at the beginning of British hegemony in 1815 to about 4.0 million by the end of hegemony in 1873 (Rodriguez and Feagin 1986; GB Historical GIS 2019).

In Manchester, rural migrants from southern Lancashire who abandoned the handloom for factory work and immigrants who left poverty in Ireland helped increase the metropolitan population from about half a million at the beginning of British hegemony to about 1.5 million at the end of hegemony. Irish immigration in Manchester reached 34,300 by the 1841 census, making the urban center second only to Liverpool in the number of Irish immigrants (Rodriguez and Feagin 1986). About half a million Irish emigrated from Ireland after the Irish potato famines of 1846–1847, and many settled in Manchester. Supported by net migration gains averaging almost 50,000 migrants per decade in the mid-nineteenth

---

[27] In the 32 data entries listed by Cairncross (1953) for the eight cities across four decades, only Leicester registered a negative net migration, a net loss of 5345 in 1851–1860.

century, Manchester played a major role in the British exportation of half of the cotton goods sold in world markets (Rodriguez and Feagin 1986).[28]

The migration to British towns and cities during British industrialization involved mainly short-distance movement from nearby counties or villages (Chaloner 1968; Redford 1968). As E. A. Ravenstein explained to the Royal Statistical Society in 1885, according to the census of 1871 "the bulk of migrants had journeyed but a very little distance," with long-journey migrants probably constating of fewer than one-fourth of all migrants (Ravenstein 1885: 182–183). The same conclusion had been reached earlier concerning population growth in Lancashire and Cheshire. In the late 1850s, a study of the 1801–1851 census returns concluded that migration into the two counties had been principally derived from adjacent counties, with some migration from Ireland and Scotland (Chaloner 1968).

According to Ravenstein's (1885) "laws of migration," the movement to urban areas involved several steps. Rural migrants who left to nearby towns left population gaps in the countryside that were filled by migrants from more remote districts. In his analysis of labor migration in England in 1800–1850, Redford (1968: 186) concluded that migration "was not a simple transference of people from the circumference of a circle to its center, but an exceedingly complex wave-like motion." Even the emigration from the Highlands reached the manufacturing centers in the western Lowlands through stages. The small farmers and cottiers who were driven from the Highlands during the 1780–1830 reorganization to capitalist farming first gathered in villages and then gradually moved to such manufacturing centers as Lanark, Renfrew, Dumbarton, and Ayr (Dickson and Clark 1980; Redford 1968).

Who were the migrants? Based on his analysis of the 1881 census in the United Kingdom, Ravenstein (1885: 196–198), concluded that, "Woman is a greater migrant than man." There is no reason to believe that women had been less significant during the peak of townward migration in the 1840s. The demand for domestic workers in the rapidly growing urban upper-class was a strong attraction for young women from the countryside. Domestic work caused more young women than young men to out-migrate from rural places, causing gender imbalances among young people in villages (Pinchbeck 1971; Hunt 1981). Urban factory work was a second powerful attraction for young migrant women. According to Oakley (1976: 37), by 1835 46% of the 288,700 factory workers in textile production were women, and in "the 1830s and 1840s the typical female factory worker was the wife or daughter of a handloom weaver, himself forced to enter the factory." The only towns that attracted more males than females were the large centers of iron and coal mining and of machine building, e.g., Airdrie in Scotland and Middlesbrough and West Ham in England (Ravenstein 1885).

---

[28] The success of Manchester manufacturers in obtaining low tariffs on cotton products exported to India, and high tariffs on cotton products imported from India, helped English manufacturers to export the majority of their cotton products (Harnetty 1972; Rodriguez and Feagin 1986).

4.3 Labor Migration and Industrial Development

Similar to women, men migrated as individuals or as part of a family. While the men who migrated from rural districts into the growing towns were a mixed lot, "in which cobblers and tailors rubbed shoulders with starving handloom weavers and gawky husbandmen," since the 1830s a large majority came from agriculture (Redford 1968: 66–67). Indeed, agriculture had become a source of townward migration since after 1814, when the end of the Napoleonic Wars brought a drastic drop in produce prices and many lands were left untilled (Redford 1968). During 1851–1871, the agricultural exodus in England was heavily influenced by the railroad industry, which made travel easier and also became a major source of employment. The railroad industry reduced the agricultural labor force by more than 250,000, or 22% (Bagwell and Mingay 1970). Agricultural workers were a large portion of townward migration, but were one of the less mobile occupational groups (Hunt 1981). By comparison, urban skilled workers were the most mobile. With better pay, better education, and better job-market information (provided by trade unions), urban skilled workers migrated over long distances.

Finally, contrary to Marx's assertion that agricultural enclosures "created for the town industries the necessary supply of a 'free' and outlawed proletariat" (1967: 733), with the exception of the Highland clearings, enclosures did not create a massive migration of displaced peasants to urban factories. For the most part, agricultural families dispossessed by enclosures remained in the countryside, many becoming rural migrants. Moreover, in places where enclosed commons were converted into farmlands, the agricultural population actually increased (Chambers 1953). The conclusion now widely accepted is that, with few exceptions, it was mainly surplus population that migrated from the countryside to the towns during the height of industrialization in Britain (Chambers 1953; Pollard 1978).[29]

In some ways, however, Marx was correct in his assessment of the effects of enclosures on the proletarianization of agricultural workers. Enclosures deprived many agricultural families of independent land subsistence and contributed to their dependence on wage labor. By 1831, there were two wage-earning rural families for each family that occupied land (Deane 1979). The fact that dispossessed farm families worked for employers in the countryside made them no less proletarian than working families in the towns. Marx overrated the impact of enclosures on the growth of the town proletariat because he underestimated the resistance of agricultural labor to urban factories. Rural workers viewed factory work as similar to the degrading conditions of workhouses, and this negative perception initially deterred labor migration from the countryside to urban factories (Redford 1968; Pollard 1978; Hunt 1981).[30] Other factors that deterred rural labor migration to

---

[29] According to Redford (1968), between the 1760s and the 1830s not a single county in England, Wales, Scotland, or Ireland reported a decreased population in census returns.

[30] Redford (1968: 24) comments on the negative attitude concerning the factory: "The reluctance of the respectable settled population to enter the factories is... easy to understand.... [T]he workhouse had become a kind of factory, [and] it was perhaps natural that the factory should be regarded as a kind of workhouse."

urban factories included poor transportation, recruitment for railroad construction, and restrictions of the Poor Law on mobility (Pollard 1978).

Emigration from Britain. Substantial emigration characterized Britain during the British period of hegemony. In the six decades from 1820 to 1870, roughly the span of British hegemony, some 1.3 million British emigrated to the United States, in addition to other countries of destinations (US DHS 2006: Table 2). An additional 1.7 million British migrated to the United States in 1870–1899. This migration represented a new pattern in the world-economy, i.e., a sustained large-scale migration of labor from a core state to a less developed country in the world-system. In the nineteenth century, the United States had not achieved core status. To be sure, it was a strong semiperipheral country acquiring social, political, and economic resources that would bring it to the door of core status by the end of the nineteenth century.

4.3.2 Irish Migration to Britain

The increased townward migration in Britain during the second phase of industrialization of capital-goods production involved a massive Irish influx. For centuries, Celtics had come to Britain, but the number of migrants had been relatively small and involved many seasonal workers. Beginning in the 1820s, however, Irish migration to Britain increased sharply, and by the 1860s many Irish migrants settled permanently in the country. Irish migration to Britain represented a new migration pattern in the development of the capitalist world-economy: large-scale migration from a peripheral country to a core state of the world-system. The pattern would grow across the world regions in the twentieth century and into the twenty-first century. It would also grow to include refugees and asylum-seekers from peripheral areas seeking survival and protection in core countries of the world-system.

Irish economic deterioration and famine were at the root of this new Irish migration. According to Hunt (1981), in the 1820s famine, agricultural decline, and the introduction of steamships greatly increased the movement of poor Irish people to Britain. Estimates given of the number of Irish immigrants and their English-born children in 1835 in Lancashire, which was the county of greatest Irish settlement, ranged from fewer than 100,000–145,000 (Redford 1968). The county's largest manufacturing centers of Manchester and Liverpool had the largest concentrations of Irish immigrants. The census of 1841, the first reliable count, showed the number of Irish immigrants in England and Wales to be 291,000 and in Scotland to be 128,000 (Clapham 1933). In the 1851 census, the number of Irish had grown to 520,000 in England and Wales and 207,000 in Scotland.

The 1861 census recorded an even larger number of Irish immigrants in Britain, 805,637, constituting 4% of the British population (Ravenstein 1885; Clapham 1933). In the 1861 census, the number of Irish immigrants reached 106,889 in London, 83,949 in Liverpool, 52,076 in Manchester, and 63,574 in Glasgow. The

Irish percent of the total population ranged from 3.8% in London to 18.9% in Liverpool (Punch 2016).

Many of the Irish enumerated in the 1851 British census were refugees of the great potato famine in Ireland that occurred in 1845–1848. The famine had grave consequences for the poor of Ireland and reduced their number by about 2 million. Three-fourths of a million perished, another three-fourths of a million left for America, and the remaining half a million migrated to Britain (Hunt 1981). The ports of Liverpool, and Glasgow, as well as ports in South Wales, were the main entry points for the massive Irish influx in Britain. According to Redford (1968), in 1846 over 280,000 Irish immigrants arrived in Liverpool, and of these about 123,000 eventually sailed to other countries. In 1847 more than 300,000 Irish immigrants arrived in Liverpool and 130,000 of these later emigrated to the United States.[31]

Textile manufacturing expanded in Ireland with the beginning of the Industrial Revolution in Britain. But by the 1830s, as steam power spread in the British cotton industry, and as English capitalists dumped their cloth in the Irish market, many handloom weavers in Ireland lost their jobs (Redford 1968). With this industrial defeat, which was aided by the removal of protective duties by the Act of Union, Irish economic development went into reverse. Between 1821 and 1841 the number of non-agricultural workers in Ireland's 32 counties decreased from 1.7 million to 1.6 million, and the number of agricultural workers increased from 2.8 million to 3.5 million (Kennedy 1973). But agricultural work did not provide an economic survival for the Irish. With heightened competition among tenants for land to farm, landlords in Ireland over-divided plots and rented them at prices up to four times higher than what was paid in England (Engels 1958). The agricultural depression suffered at the end of the Napoleonic Wars in 1815 and the repeal of the Corn Law in 1846, which had given Irish grain preferential treatment in the English market, motivated landlords to evict tenants and convert agriculture lands into pastures (O'Brien 1921). Between 1849 and 1870, about 400,000 persons were evicted from Irish farmlands (Kennedy 1973).

In Britain, neighborhoods of the unemployed, evicted, and other poor from Ireland demonstrated the wretchedness of the Irish immigrants. In a visit to Irish neighborhoods in London in 1842, Flora Tristán, a French-Peruvian feminist socialist, noted in her journal the extreme poverty of the Irish migrants she observed (Tristán 2009: 240–241):

> Here are men, women, children, with bare feet in the infected mud of this sewer. Some reclined against the walls for lack of seats to sit down, others crouched on the ground. The children lying in the mud like pigs. No, unless you have seen it, it is impossible to imagine such a horrible misery, such a profound evil, such a complete degradation of the human being. There, I saw the children completely naked, the girls, the women raising with bare feet, wearing only a shirt that fell in rags and revealing their bodies almost entirely naked,

---

[31] Fewer than 20% of the arriving Irish were passengers on business; the remainder were paupers (Redford 1968).

the old men crouched on a bit of straw turned into garbage, the young people dressed in rags. (translation mine)

Diseases like typhus, sometimes called the "Irish fever," were constant health dangers for the Irish in their congested environments (Hunt 1981).

Irish immigrants and their British-born children formed the lower stratum of the labor forces in the British towns where they settled. It was mostly in the Scottish cotton-spinning mills, such as in Glasgow and Paisley, that the Irish entered higher levels of industrial employment (Redford 1968; Hunt 1981). In the main, the Irish immigrant workers did the most menial, unpleasant tasks. Their jobs involved "... the most irksome and most disagreeable kinds of coarse Labour, such for instance as attending on masons, bricklayers and plasterers, excavating earth for harbours, docks, canals and roads, carrying heavy goods, loading and unloading vessels" (Thompson 1963: 433).[32]

In the textile factories of England, the Irish were hired mainly in cleaning jobs. They worked in the blowing-rooms, while English workers were employed as spinners (Thompson 1963: 433).[33] Besides working in the mills and in domestic industries, Irish women, mainly wives and daughters, worked mostly as domestic servants—"of the poorer sort" (Hunt 1981: 164)—and as agricultural workers in market-gardens (Redford 1968).

As Chap. 5 will describe, British and Irish migration during Britain's rise to hegemony extended in great numbers beyond Ireland and Britain into other world regions. Emigrants from Britain and Ireland, along with German emigrants, accounted for many of the estimated 13 million migrants who left Europe for other regions between 1841 and 1880 (Armengaud 1978). Enclosures of peasant lands, poverty, famine, artisan displacement by industrial capitalism, social conflict, pogroms—all played a role in stimulating the great transoceanic migration of Europeans, with the greatest numbers moving to North America (Moch 2003). The European migration headed to the United States, which reached 8.3 million migrants in 1881–1900 and 12.4 million in 1901–1920, became a resource for the reproduction and growth of the country's population especially after the US government greatly restricted immigration into the country in the 1920s.

---

[32] Hunt (1981:164–165) states that a minority of Irish immigrants worked as tailors, shoemakers, and carpenters.

[33] This was not the only involvement of the Irish in England's textile industry. Long after machine production had advanced against the handloom, Irish immigrant households operated as weaving industries. According to Engels (1958:157), "Frequently half a dozen of these handloom weavers—some of them married people—live together in a cottage which has one or two workrooms and one large common bedroom."

4.3.3 Indentured-Labor Migration

Away from the European continent, the early nineteenth century saw the rise of the "coolie" trade as a form of indentured-labor migration to plantations and mines especially in European colonies in the Caribbean, Latin America, and Asia (Jung 2006). The new trade commenced in 1834 with the shipping of 41,056 workers from Bengal to Mauritius (Brown 2013). Coolie labor of men, women, and children from India and mainly men from China was a response to the end of the African slave trade and slavery. The coolie trade provided labor to colonial plantations and other areas that previously used African slaves. Chinese and Indian indentured-laborers normally were contracted to work abroad for five to eight years with very low pay and from which deductions were made to pay for the passage debt (Hu-Dehart 1994). Very bad living conditions, brutal mistreatment, and dangerous work kept the workers' mortality rate high and many died before their contracts ended. The bad and dangerous conditions began in the journeys to reach the work destinations. Mortality rates of indentured-laborers in ships were high, and the harshness of the journey through the Pacific Passage drove some workers to commit suicide (Brown 2013). Many indentured-workers were kept by force from returning to their home countries after their contracts expired and continued to work in servitude.

Indentured-labor migration of Chinese and Indian coolies created a new level of state-regulated migration in the world-system, although with minimal state participation. After signing a joint-treaty in 1866 to limit the coolie trade to treaty ports, the British, French, and Chinese governments undertook attempts to reduce the mistreatment of coolies being transported out of harbors the governments controlled (Brown 2013). One attempt was to require traders to pay for the return of coolies to their home countries after their contracts ended. The Chinese government also pressured Portugal to end the notorious coolie trade out of Macau, which ended in 1874, but not before some half a million Chinese workers had been exported under miserable conditions (Meagher 2008).

Core states in the world-system had been involved in distributing forced-peripheral labor interregionally since the Dutch, British, and other European participation in the African slave trade, but the measures undertaken by British and other European governments to reduce the abuse of coolie labor represented a new concern for labor. The concern sprung partly from the admonitions by abolitionists who saw little difference between slavery and the treatment of coolie labor (Jung 2006). With little or no oversight of coolie working conditions in faraway colonies and development projects, colonial employers faced little or no opposition to their abuse of coolie workers. Termination of the system seemed to be the only real way to end the abuse of coolie labor. The US government terminated the importation of coolie labor in 1862, and British involvement in the coolie trade ended in 1916 (Brown 2020).

From a world-systems perspective, the coolie trade added to the role of peripheral countries as sources of mobile, mass labor for exploitation across different world regions. The brutal African slave trade was the beginning of this world labor system under capitalism, and the coolie trade continued this resourcefulness of peripheral areas for capital accumulation. From the seventeenth to the eighteenth centuries, thousands of British and other Europeans had also entered into temporary, indentured-servant contracts to pay for their journey to North America (Bailyn 1986; Galenson 1978). But, with some exceptions, the British and other European indentured servants did not generally face the level of mistreatment and cruelty Chinese and Indian coolies faced in European colonial plantations.

The patterns of migration described in this section played major roles in Britain's rise to world power during its period of hegemony. In the following section, the migration patterns are discussed from the perspectives of class relations, technological development, the economic cycle, and the state.

4.4 Class Struggle and Migration

At first thought, Irish migration to the manufacturing centers of Britain seems to illustrate the proposition in Chap. 1 that labor will migrate to areas where worker struggles have brought about better working conditions. The large British industrial areas of Irish immigration in the nineteenth century were places of intense worker struggles (e.g., Foster 1974; Brown 1981). Many industrial areas where Irish immigrated, e.g., Manchester, Bolton, and Stockport, had been sites where workers waged struggles over work and food conditions and sometimes won (Munger 1981; Brown 1981). Yet, for the most part, Irish immigrant workers did not benefit in a major way from the struggles of the British workers. The industrial working class was segmented in Britain, and, with few exceptions, e.g., Irish textile workers in Glasgow, Irish immigrants, along with poor English and Scottish workers, including women, made up the lowest stratum of the working class in Britain. Economic successes of British worker activism, thus, did not significantly trickle down to this stratum, nor did government regulations to improve working conditions. Regulations of the Factory Acts concerning the working conditions of children, for example, likely had only minimal effect on Irish child workers. While the Factory legislation helped British children who labored in factories that were open to inspections, it did not bring relief to the Irish children who toiled in textile work in cellar sweatshops out of the view of inspectors. This "home industry" method of production must have been significantly profitable for textile entrepreneurs, since it continued to exist for decades after the development of steam-powered factory production.

The proposition that labor migrates to settings where worker struggles have improved working conditions must also be qualified from the perspective of British industrialization before 1830. Thompson (1963) demonstrates in his study of the making of the English working class that there was an extra-economic factor that greatly influenced the resistance of workers to migrate, viz. the hold of community and culture. As Ravenstein (1885) and Redford (1968) indicated, the industrialization in the West Country and northern districts of England did not draw large numbers of workers from the relatively over-populated, rural areas of southern

England. In the main, the migrants to the factory towns came from surrounding areas that were near to or in the cultural and community orbits of the towns. At the same time that factory owners complained of labor shortages in the first half of the 1800s, evicted and unemployed agricultural workers in the southern counties resisted migration to the northern manufacturing and mining districts (Pollard 1978). Even in the face of abject poverty, the southern agricultural population did not migrate to the northern factories in the early 1800s (Redford 1968). No doubt, as explained by Pollard (1978), the settlement effect of the Poor Laws and the lack of effective transportation (e.g., railroads) in the early part of the nineteenth century were barriers to long-distance migration. But the resistance of southern rural workers to factory work was also real. Another factor that should be considered regarding this resistance was that the tendency of immobility, that is, the inclination to remain in one's cultural area and resist dislocation.

Workers in the countryside viewed factory work with great disfavor, especially in the early period of the Industrial Revolution (Redford 1968; Thompson 1963). Prior to the rise of the factory system, labor casually passed between agriculture and manufacturing during slack times in one or the other industry, but the rise of factory work changed the perception of manufacturing work (Redford 1968). As employers turned to transients, "tramps," orphans, and other "transported" persons to form workforces in the new industries of the Industrial Revolution, factories were perceived to be unsuitable workplaces for respectable people. The similarity of factories to poorhouses where paupers toiled added to the negative perception of factory work. Moreover, the cyclical unemployment of business cycles made factory work unreliable (Hobsbawn 1962). The Poor Law transportation of families in 1834–1837 to manufacturing centers in the north reinforced the negative factory image, which included the threat of unemployed displacement. After 4684 persons were transported to northern textile districts, an economic downturn sent many of the transported workers back to their homes unemployed (Redford 1968). The managed migration of the Poor Law was repelled by the forced migration of the Poor Law. Given their disquietude with factory work, many agricultural southern workers saw emigration to North America, some with the hope of obtaining farmland, as more promising (Pollard 1978).

From the perspective of owners and employers, labor immigration can be a means to arrest advances of worker activism. Redford (1968) posits that the migration of workers under the new Poor Law of 1834 must be studied in relation to the emergence of the Grand National Consolidated Trades Union in 1834 and the hostility of employers to this and other labor organizations. Quoting from the letters of mill owners who supported Poor Law migration, Redford (1968) illustrates how these capitalists desired migrant labor to quell union activism. In some cases, the presence of Poor Law migrants served to bring down the wages of local cotton-textile workers. Moreover, until the 1860s Irish immigrants were frequently used as strikebreakers in the textile mills of Lancashire and Scotland (Hunt 1981). One capitalist, Lord Londonderry, attempted to put down a miners' strike in Durham by importing Irish workers from his Irish estates. It should be pointed out, however, that Irish migrants "were almost as prominent leading strikes as breaking them"

(Hunt 1981: 168). From the perspective of the use of the Irish as strikebreakers, undoubtedly some British workers viewed them unfavorably.

The usual explanation for British and Irish labor migration to the United States in the nineteenth century is that economic opportunities brought by the country's industrial growth and westward expansion motivated the migration (Hansen 1961; Bailyn 1986). Economic historians emphasize labor shortages for the recruitment of immigrant labor from Europe (Habakkuk 1967; Bailyn 1986), and not the desire of employers to repress native labor activism.[34]

Undoubtedly, immigrant workers helped to reduce labor shortages, but US employers also likely used immigrant workers to combat the activism of native workers. The hiring of Irish immigrant women and children in the 1850s by textile manufacturers in Boston eventually replaced the native "Yankee" young women that had made up the factory's earlier workforce. A study by the Massachusetts Bureau of Labor Statistics concluded that the replacement occurred because the supply of Yankee females had become inadequate for the growing industry (Gitelman 1967); yet there may have been another reason. According to Foner (1975a: 108–109), since the early 1830s "the factory girls were among the most courageous fighters of the period...." In New Hampshire and in Massachusetts, the Yankee "young ladies" went on strike when factory owners cut their wages. A 12.5% wage cut in 1836 resulted in a strike of 1,500 Lowell factory women. The young women were determined to battle the "iniquities of the monied aristocracy" and planned "to have their own way even if they died for it" (Foner 1975a: 109).

It was in the interest of employers to promote labor immigration to the extent that it contributed to an over-supply of labor to keep wages down or to counter worker activism. But increasing the supply of immigrant workers also increased the potential for worker struggles as concentrations of labor facilitated collective activism.[35] Moreover, employers were not always successful in increasing the immigrant labor force in industries with a strong presence of native workers. For example, Redford (1968) views the opposition of English laborers as a reason why Irish immigrant workers never exceed 10% of the workforce in railroad construction in England in the 1830s.

4.5 Technological Development

As pointed out in Chap. 1, Wallerstein (1979a) views the enhancement of technology to be a major trend in the development of the capitalist world-system.

---

[34] Habakkuk (1967: 96) views labor shortage as the reason that US industrialists developed labor-saving technology extensively in the nineteenth century: "[T]he supply of machines was more elastic than the supply of labour."

[35] "As the number of co-operating labourers increases, so too does their resistance to the domination of capital, and with it, the necessity for capital to overcome this resistance by counter-pressure" (Marx 1967: 331).

4.5 Technological Development

The growth of technology is integral to the structural consolidation of the world-system. In industrialization, technological development makes possible a large part of the profit "that makes the system worth the while of those who are on the top of it" (Wallerstein, 1979a: 62). Over time, technological innovations that accompanied industrial development spread from core countries to peripheral and semiperipheral regions of the world-economy. But the spread of technology in the world-system traveled through political designs, especially in colonial arrangements. The actions of British manufacturers to counter the textile industry developing in India in the nineteenth century demonstrates a political aspect of the spread of technology in colonial conditions. As mentioned above, to profit in the Indian textile market British cotton capitalists obtained taxes favorable for their trade from the British government and the British-controlled Indian government. The British cotton manufacturers obtained low taxes for the importation of raw cotton from India and for the importation of British cotton products into India, but obtained high tariffs for Indian cotton products imported into Britain. This, along with heavy importation of English cloth, countered the industrialization of India's native textile industry until the 1850s when Indian investors introduced modern cotton mills in Bombay (Mumbai) and later in other Indian areas. Although they faced restrictive colonial taxes, Indian investors expanded the modern cotton-manufacturing industry in India to 144 cotton mills by 1895 (Sahoo 2015).

Chapter 1 associated the migration of unskilled workers with areas where technological innovations lead to the deskilling of the labor process. Simply stated, machines simplify the work process and thus create jobs for unskilled workers, as skilled workers are displaced. British internal migration during the surge of factories in the post-1830s phase of industrialization illustrated this logic. British rural workers (males and females) migrated as individuals or in family units to work in nearby factory districts (Hunt 1981; Ravenstein 1885). Factory owners particularly sought the labor power of women and children (Kuczynski 1967: 63–64) as an unskilled source of labor power.[36] As indicated above in the description of Poor Law migration, government policy helped agricultural families migrate to factory towns.

Irish immigrants, many of whom came from peasant backgrounds, were another labor source that generally lacked craft skills and thus were ready-made for work in capitalist factories. But except for the Glasgow area, Irish immigrants in Britain were not heavily employed as machine operators in the factories during the country's industrialization.

Instead, the Irish were employed to do cleaning and other menial jobs in the British factories. Thus, Irish unskilled workers migrated to areas where the labor process had been simplified, but in the main they did not obtain the jobs of machine operatives created by mechanization. This situation was an early development of

---

[36] According to Marx's observation (1967: 396), "Previously the workman sold his own labour power.... Now he sells wife and child. He has become a slave dealer."

a working-class division present in advanced industrial societies that are conceptualized as labor-market segmentation (see Edwards et al. 1975). In the growth of industrial economies, under conditions of sustained immigration higher quality jobs in core countries are performed by native workers, while the inferior sectors of the labor market become the source of employment for racial minority workers or for immigrant workers who come from peripheral or semiperipheral countries. (Piore 1979). This segmentation is reinforced especially when foreign workers lack legal immigration status.

The development of events in the mechanization of the boot and shoe industry in England in the areas of Northampton and Stafford in the 1850s demonstrated another way that technological development affected unskilled labor migration. When manufacturers in Northampton and Stafford announced in early 1859 that they were going to use machines for the shoe-making processes previously done by skilled (male) workers, the Northamptonshire Boot and Shoe Mutual Protection Society directed the shoemakers of the two counties to go on strike and to search for work in other areas. Using a strike fund to help support their families at home, several hundred shoemakers left (Church 1970). To relieve the strike funds, the shoemakers' union later directed the tramping strikers to send for their families, who traditionally had done the unskilled outwork of the trade. Thus, not only did unskilled workers (women and children) related to skilled labor through families ties not enter the new factories, they migrated away from the new technology. The strike was settled in mid-1859 after the manufacturers agreed to higher piece rates. This example illustrates the organic unity in families that sometimes occurs between different occupational levels in the family.

Industrialization in the boot and shoe industry in Northampton and Stafford also demonstrated that skilled workers will emigrate from areas where technological innovation leads to the deskilling of work. The tramping of the shoemakers in search of work in other counties was an example of this out-migration of skilled labor. Yet, after the settlement of the strike the shoemakers returned to work in the partially mechanized production (Church 1970). Redford's (1968) analysis of labor migration in industrializing England describes similar examples of craftworkers migrating to areas of factory production. For instance, the cotton mills in several districts of Lancashire had operatives who had formerly been village weavers. In other cases, such as in the demise of the woolen industry in the West Country, unemployed craftworkers turned to agricultural work. In London, displaced craftsmen found work in the docks, and in Lanarkshire "starving handloom weavers" were hired as strikebreakers in a mining strike in 1837 (Redford 1968: 58).

In some cases, emigration from Britain was a collective strategy of the craftworkers' struggles in the new capitalist industrial order. Emigration and the threat of emigration became weapons of skilled labor (Redford 1968). Although laws had been enacted in the eighteenth century to prohibit the emigration of craftworkers, as early as 1773 weavers in Paisley who were being tried for unlawful organizing threatened to emigrate as a group to America (Redford 1968). From the late 1700s to the early 1820s, the struggle of craftworkers for the right to emigrate was as important as their struggle for the right to unionize. In both cases, the restrictive laws were repealed in 1824–1825.

With the failure of British trade unions to stop the "godless machine," union-assisted emigration increased in the 1830s through the 1840s. Trade unionists gave several reasons for encouraging the emigration of craftworkers. The primary reason was that emigration would produce higher wages by reducing the labor supply (Carrothers 1966). Another reason was that US prosperity provided emigrants an opportunity to earn more from their work or to own land. A third view was that British emigration to the United States in large enough numbers would equalize the wage levels of the two countries, improving the conditions of British workers (Shepperson 1957). In the 1830s, about fifty trade organizations were involved in helping skilled and unskilled workers migrate to Australia, Canada, and the United States. By the 1840s, the number increased and included the trade unions of glassmakers, bookbinders, compositors, iron molders, and potters (Redford 1968). In the late 1840s, in the midst of turbulent unionizing, the potters' union purchased land in rural southern Wisconsin and sent families from Britain to start a town christened Pottersville (Shepperson 1957). Union-assisted emigration declined drastically in the 1850s with the failure of emigration schemes to achieve the desired goals and with opposition to organized emigration from unions abroad. While trade union emigration involved only a few thousand workers, British employers considered it a threat to their labor supply (Redford 1968).

4.6 Economic Cycles

Chapter 1 gave a twofold logic for the relationship between economic cycles and labor migration: immigrant workers expect to benefit from the prosperity of a growing economy, and employers expect to benefit from the presence of immigrant labor as a means to increase the labor supply and keep wages down during rising prosperity. Several factors, however, may affect the employer predisposition for foreign-born labor.

By the time of British hegemony in the world-system, the British capitalist class was segmented between large and small employers. The increase in capital formation from £1.6 million in 1760 to £4.6 million in 1860 involved the growth of large capitalists, who by the latter date employed large workforces in their factories, railroads, and other large enterprises. Small employers included small shop owners and small farmers who relied on small work crews. This differentiation of employers suggests that they had different needs for immigrant labor.

Undoubtedly, during the rise of British industrial capitalism large and small capitalists favored an increase the labor supply in order to retard the advance of wages. But the attraction of Irish immigrants as a source of labor must have been greater among small employers than large employers. As stated above, except for production in the Scottish Lowlands, in Britain large employers filled factory operative positions with native workers. The Irish workers that were hired in the factories were confined mainly to low-status jobs, e.g., cleaning and working in the blowing-rooms. On the other hand, during the second (post-1830s) phase of the Industrial Revolution, as native rural labor left for the factories or abroad, Irish immigrant workers became increasingly important for small employers, e.g., construction and dock employers and small farmers. With increasing emigration of British and Irish workers overseas during the 1840s through the 1860s, the labor needs of small employers must have surely increased.

The stress of agricultural employers from the loss of workers to town industries and from the diminution of Irish migrant labor is reflected in an August 2, 1852, article, "The Scarcity of Labour," in *The Economist*:

> ... in past times when the inhabitants of towns had less employment and lower wages, they annually furnished to harvest fields large numbers of labourers, who annually availed themselves of that opportunity of acquiring a little fund for extra and special purposes. *Now*, and especially in the present year, employment of every kind is so abundant in the towns, and is so well paid, that the harvest field no longer offers the same temptation .... Another very plain reason which has led to a great scarcity of labourers at this season, is the cessation, to a large extent, of the visits of Irish reapers who were wont in former years to repair to this country for harvest work. (italics in the original)

Noting that in the first six months of 1852 the number of emigrants from the United Kingdom had been 182,986, the article emphasized that emigration was occurring "at the rate of *one thousand persons* per day!" (italics in the original).

The article's mentioning of the scarcity of town workers for employment in harvest fields suggests the greater importance of immigrant labor for the agricultural sector, in comparison to the urban-industrial sector. In the second phase of the Industrial Revolution, while town industries depended on rural workers for migrant labor, the agricultural sector became increasingly dependent on the Irish immigrant labor. Rural emigration of native workers elevated this dependency. At the time of the great scarcity of laborers for the 1852 harvest, the concentration of town workers created such a labor strength that manufacturers threatened to import foreign workers (Marx 1967).

For several reasons, large employers did not give great importance to Irish immigrant labor during times of rising economic prosperity, when wages were expected to rise. Firstly, in some cases the new factory jobs were filled with skilled workers that had been displaced from their craft industries by mechanization. As described above, shoemakers in Northamptonshire and Stafford turned to factory work after the decline of their craft industry. In the industrial districts of Lancashire, factory work attracted unemployed craftworkers. Secondly, an attempt by employers to use Irish immigrants as machine operatives in the factories undoubtedly would have raised resistance from native workers. The Industrial Revolution involved some of the most radical outbursts of the English working class (Stearns 1972). For the laboring class, according to Hobsbawn (1962: 254), "struggle was its very essence."

Thirdly, employers saw a more attractive source of labor power—women and children, the "immigrants" from the household mode of production. Fourthly, employers must have realized that a large-scale recruitment of Irish immigrants into the ranks of the industrial proletariat increased the possibility of worker revolts. In *The Making of the English Working Class*, Thompson (1963) describes connections between Irish radicals and dissident and insurrectionary movements in England, e.g., Luddism and Jacobinism. Surely, factory owners must have considered the potential effects of a large infusion of Irish militant ebullience into an already tumultuous working class.[37]

Of these four reasons why large employers did not seek to rely heavily on cheaper Irish immigrant labor, the first reason is worthy of further elaboration. By revolutionizing the productivity of labor, and hence effecting the displacement of skilled labor, the machine helped to produce (and reproduce) the industrial reserve army—the population of unemployed and partially employed workers needed for expansion of production and for maintaining a pool of labor to keep wages down. For the large manufacturers, only two conditions would have made Irish immigrant workers an attractive source of labor: a rapid expansion in production that would have consumed all the available labor supply, or a massive out-migration of native labor that included women and children.

The enhancement of productivity in the factories through mechanization was not repeated in the harvest fields of nineteenth-century Britain. For British farmers, immigrant labor remained an important resource. The drain of native workers to the cities in prosperous times no doubt made Irish immigrant labor more desirable for rural employers. To hold workers in the countryside, landowners in some districts formed associations (e.g., the Labourers' Friend Society) to award prizes to country workers with long employment periods (Porter 1995).

While it may be expected that anti-immigrant action may increase substantially in times of economic decline when jobs become scarce, no major increase of such action is recorded for the British era of hegemony. Partly because they were foreigners from a colonized region and partly because of the British perception of the Irish as an inferior people, with a few exceptions, Irish workers in England did not occupy an equal status with British workers in the industrial labor forces. British workers occupied the most desirable jobs, characterized by higher pay and greater stability, while Irish workers filled the dirty, low-paying, unstable jobs, e.g., dock loading and migratory farm work (Hunt 1981). A consequence of this working-class segmentation was that it reduced the job competition between British and Irish workers, and, hence, likely decreased the possibility for hostility over jobs between the two worker populations during economic downturns.

In the many instances of economic depression and crisis that the British working class experienced during the development of industrial capitalism (see Marx 1967), the primary targets of working-class collective action (riots, demonstrations, etc.) were economic and political elements of the new capitalist industrial order, and

---

[37] According to Thompson (1963: 442–443), the Irish in England were considered to have "a disposition to challenge authority, to resort to the threat of 'physical force,' and to refuse to be intimidated by the inhibitions of constitutionalism."

usually not Irish immigrants. As studies of worker collective action demonstrate (e.g., Munger 1981; Brown 1981), principal concerns of British working-class protest were food prices, repeal of the Corn Laws, enactment of a minimum wage, parliamentary reform, wages, and the shortening of the workday. This is not to suggest that British workers never acted against Irish immigrant labor, for they did. But with some exceptions, Irish workers were not seen as a cause of economic downturns to the extent that widespread social action was taken for their removal.[38]

Conflict existed between British and Irish workers. There were frequent confrontations between Irish and British workers in railroad construction in northern England and in Scotland, two areas where Irish and British workers at times held similar job (Handley 1970; Treble 1973). In many cases, Irish laborers were driven off the lines by English and Scottish workers who believed that the Irish cheapened wages. But as Handley (1970) explains, this antagonism was ongoing, i.e., not particularly motivated by economic decline, and strongly influenced by a British prejudice that regarded the Irish as papist savages. This prejudice amounted to a level of racialization, no doubt related to the British colonial relation with Ireland (Hickman 1995). To be sure, native workers did not always seek to drive the Irish out. At least in one case, English workers on the Caledonian line gave Irish workers on the nearby Nithsdale line a choice to either demand an increase in wages or to leave their jobs (Handley 1970).

A second factor helps to explain why widespread sentiments against Irish immigrants did not develop beyond the common prejudice in times of economic decline in Britain when jobs became scarce. Irish immigrants did not become an economic issue from the standpoint that they were perceived as usurping social welfare resources. While Irish pauperism was considered a problem in England by 1815 (Redford 1968), in the main areas where the Irish settled, i.e., in Lancashire, Glasgow, and London, there were no governmental efforts to provide food, shelter, or medical care to poor immigrants. A third factor also must be considered. British workers could cope with economic distress by becoming immigrants themselves. They could emigrate to North America or to other places where craftwork was still in demand or where land was available for farming.

4.7 The State

In the period of British hegemony, the British state became involved in supporting labor migration in Britain. For brief periods, the British government assisted

---

[38] Clarke and Dickson (1982) report one case of Irish repatriation from Britain in the early 1800s. According to Clarke and Dickson (1982), Lowland Scots in the area of Paisley blamed the Irish for their economic plight, and deportations were enforced by the local Relief Committees in 1827 and 1842. But as Clarke and Dickson (1982) explain, it is difficult to determine to what extent the deportations were also a consequence of cultural and religious sectionalism.

workers to migrate to areas of industrial development in the country. To a considerable extent, this represented a new role of the state in capitalist society. Chapter 2 described how in medieval England Henry III and Edward III issued proclamations to promote the immigration of Flemish cloth workers, and Chap. 3 described how the Amsterdam municipal government helped provide housing and other inducements to skilled workers fleeing the Spanish sacking of the southern Netherlands. These actions were certainly precursory of the role of the state in industrial development, but they merely offered an invitation or support for foreign workers that were already migrating into the country. That is, the actions did not amount to policies for organizing and carrying out the transportation of the foreign workers into England or Holland.

In comparison, the British government organized the migration of southern rural families in England to northern industrial districts during the 1833–1837 economic upswing (Redford 1968). In this time period, Poor Law agents recruited and transported 4,684 migrants from the south of England to industrial mills in the north. Close to half of the migrants came from Suffolk, and the remainder were mostly from the counties stretching from Norfolk to Wilts Several factors in the 1833–1837 upswing prompted employers to seek state-assisted migration. These factors included the need to control rising wages by increasing the labor supply, the need for more hands to sustain the growth of large-scale production, and the need to replace child labor curtailed by the Factory Act of 1833. High rates of poverty, unemployment, worker riots, and machine-breaking among agricultural workers in the southern counties also motivated the Poor Law Commissioners to promote labor migration from the south to the north of England. The out-migration of surplus labor, preferably to colonies, was seen as the chief remedy for economic depression in southern England (Redford 1968).

British state involvement with labor migration in Britain during the British era of hegemony was short-lived, but it was significant in at least three ways. It was an early effort by the state to obtain migrant labor for industrial capitalism[39]; it demonstrated how capital was able to influence the state to assist in the recruitment of labor; and it was precursory action of state policies to facilitate large-scale labor immigration in the following stage of advanced capitalism.

The attempts of the British government to regulate the coolie trade out of ports it controlled in China and India introduced a new theme—humanitarian concern—in the area of governance of international migration. The British government along with the Chinese and other European governments acted to protect coolie migrants against mistreatment. Coolie labor had coercive and harsh similarities with slavery, e.g., kidnappings, chaining, floggings, and confinement, and British government officials, including officials of the British East India Company, acted to reduce some of the abuses in China and India. In 1842, emigration agents were appointed

---

[39] As Chap. 6 will discuss, since the beginning of the capitalist world-economy states have facilitated the mobility of capital and labor, but the British case in the present discussion was an early effort to directly support capitalist development in the era of the Industrial Revolution.

in India to inspect coolie recruiting conditions and an agent was also appointed in Mauritius to inspect coolie conditions. In 1844, measures were taken to inspect if coolies being shipped to Jamaica, British Guiana, and Trinidad understood their contracts (Brown 2013). The British joined the Chinese in the efforts to shut down the Portuguese coolie trade out of Macau, where the recruitment of coolie workers was known to be extraordinarily coercive and abusive. To the extent that abolitionists helped to reform and finally end the coolie labor system through protests, letter-writing campaigns, and other actions, the termination of Chinese and Indian coolie labor was a legacy of the abolitionist struggle to end the African slave trade.

4.8   Conclusion

This chapter has tried to show the importance of migration for industrialization in Britain's rise to hegemony in the world-economy in the nineteenth century. As stated above, in the global structure of capitalism, the migration also had consequences for other areas in the world-system. Through British hegemonic control in the world-system, industrial development in Britain, which was supported by migration, relegated other world areas, especially British colonies such as Ireland, India, and Egypt, to a dependent commercial-agricultural status. British industrial domination in the world-system slowed or restricted industrialization in these areas. Ireland and India, for example, lost industrial power, or were retarded in gaining it, as they were made dependent on British industrial products. In such peripheral areas, rural labor would remain attached to the agricultural economy (usually with greater intensity) to produce food and raw material products to trade with Britain. This happened in India and to a considerable extent in Egypt.

In Ireland, large-scale rural emigration to Britain was partly a consequence of the subordinating core-periphery order in the world-system. Losing the industrial war to Britain early, Ireland became increasingly incorporated into the British-dominated world-system through the commercialization of its heavily agricultural economy. Rural labor in Ireland became redundant as large landowners enclosed their lands for agricultural commercial development. Dispossessed from their farming subsistence, poor Irish workers emigrated abroad for economic survival by the hundreds of thousands. In Britain and in other regions such as the United States, poor Irish migrants usually took undesirable jobs.

The success of British industrial capitalism also brought about emigration in the British working class. Whether they were driven by conditions at home (e.g., enclosures, deskilling of trade, and unemployment) or attracted by opportunities abroad (to farm land, practice artisan work, or gain higher wages), British workers emigrated abroad by the hundreds of thousands, particularly to developing semiperipheral areas such as in North America, Australia, and New Zealand.

Large-scale emigration of British and other Europeans to the United States in the nineteenth century had a dialectical nature. Firstly, the immigration streams involved workers from opposite poles of the world-system, such as British workers who migrated from a dominant core society and Irish workers from a subordinated peripheral area. Secondly, immigrants had opposite goals. Some migrants, such as British craftworkers, emigrated to escape the proletarian status of working for capitalism by acquiring land ownership or establishing a business in the United States, and others, such as Irish peasants, emigrated to find wage work in US capitalistic industries. But collectively immigrants constituted a social force that supported the economic development of the United States, eventually into the next hegemonic power in the world-system.

References

Armengaud, Andre. 1978. Population in Europe 1700–1914. In *The Fontana Economic History of Europe: The Industrial Revolution*, vol. 3, ed. Carlo M. Cipolla, 22–76. Glasgow: William Collins Sons & Co.

Arrighi, Giovanni. 2010. *The Long Twentieth Century: Money, Power and the Origins of Our Times*. New York: Verso.

Bagwell, Philip S., and G.E. Mingay. 1970. *Britain and America: A Study of Economic Change, 1850–1939*. New York: Praeger.

Bailyn, Bernard. 1986. *Voyages to the West: A Passage in the Peopling of America on the Eve of the Revolution*. New York: Random House.

Beckert, Sven. 2014. *Empire of Cotton: A Global History*. New York: Vintage Books.

Boxer, C.R. 1957. *The Dutch in Brazil, 1624–1654*. Oxford: The Clarendom Press.

Brown, Brian R. 1981. Industrialism Capitalism, Conflict, and Working-Class Contention in Lancashire, 1842. In *Class Conflict and Collective Action*, ed. Louise A. Tilly and Cherles Tilly, 111–142. Beverly Hills: Sage.

Brown, Kevin. 2013. *Passage to the World: The Emigrant Experience 1807–1940*. Barnsley, UK: Seaforth Publishing.

Brown, Kevin. 2020. The Coolie Trade, 1838–1916: The Migration of Indentured Labor from India and China. *Portuguese Literary and Cultural Studies*, 30–46.

Burgess, Keith. 1980. Scotland and the First British Empire, 1707–1770s: The Confirmation of Client Status. In *Scottish Capitalism*, ed. Tony Dickson, 89–136. London: Lawrence and Wishart.

Burrough, Bryan, Chris Tomlinson, and Jason Stanford. 2021. *Forget the Alamo: The Rise and Fall of an American Myth*. New York: Penguin Press.

Cairncross, A.K. 1953. *Home and Foreign Investment 1870–1913*. Cambridge: Cambridge University Press.

Carroll, John. 2007. *A Concise History of Hong Kong*. New York: Rowman & Littlefield.

Carrothers, W.A. 1966. *Emigration from the British Isles*. New York: Augustus M. Kelley.

Castells, Manuel. 1979. *The Urban Question: A Marxist Approach*. Cambridge: MIT Press.

Chaloner, W. H. 1968. Preface to the Second Edition. In *Labour Migration in England, 1800–1850*, ed. Arthur Redford, vii–xii. New York: Augustus M. Kelley.

Chambers, J.D. 1953. Enclosure and Labour Supply in the Industrial Revolution. *The Economic History Review* 5 (3): 319–343.

Chandra, Bipan. 1981. Karl Marx, His Theories of Asian Societies, and Colonial Rule. *Review* V (Summer): 13–91.

Church, R. A. 1970. Labour Supply and Innovation 1800–1860: The Boot and Shoe Industry. *Business History* 12 (January): 25–45.

Clapham, J. H. 1933. Irish immigration into Great Britain in the Nineteenth Century. *Bulletin of the International Committee of Historical Sciences* V (July): 596–604.

Clark, Tony, and Tony Dickson. 1982. Class and Class Consciousness in Early Industrial Capitalism: Paisley 1770–1850. In *Capital and Class in Scotland*, ed. by Tony Dickson, 8–60. Edinburgh: J. Donald.

Deane, P. 1979. *The First Industrial Revolution*, 2nd ed. Cambridge: Cambridge University Press.
Deane, P., and W.A. Cole. 1967. *British Economic Growth 1688–1959: Trends and Structure*. Cambridge: Cambridge University Press.
Dickson, Tony, and Tony Clarke. 1980. The Making of a Class Society: Commercialization and Working-Class Resistance 1780–1830. In *Scottish Capitalism*, ed. Tony Dickson, 137–180. London: Lawrence and Wishart.
Dobb, Maurice. 1963. *Studies in the Development of Capitalism*. New York: International Publishers.
Edwards, Richard C., Michael Reich, and David M. Gordon (eds.). 1975. *Labor Market Segmentation*. Lexington, MA: D. C. Health.
Engels, Friedrich. 1958. *The Condition of the Working Class in England* trans by W. D. Henderson, and W. H. Chaloner. Stanford: Stanford University Press.
Feinstein, C. H. 1978. Capital Formation in Great Britain. In *The Cambridge Economic History of Europe*, VII: *Capital, Labour, and Enterprise*, Part I, ed. by Peter Mathias, and M. M. Postan, 28–96. Cambridge: Cambridge University Press.
Fieldhouse, D.K. 1973. *Economics and Empire 1830–1914*. Ithaca, New York: Cornell University Press.
Foner, Philip S. 1975. *History of the Labor Movement in the United States*, vol. 1. New York: International Publishers.
Foster, John. 1974. *Class Struggle and the Industrial Revolution: Early Industrial Capitalism in Three English Towns*. London: Weidenfeld and Nicolson.
Frank, Andre Gunder. 1969. *Latin America: Underdevelopment or Revolution*. New York: Monthly Review Press.
Frank, Andre Gunder. 1979. *Dependent Accumulation and Underdevelopment*. New York: Monthly Review Press.
Galenson, David W. 1978. British Servants and the Colonial Indenture System in the Eighteenth Century. *The Journal of Southern History* 44 (1): 41–66.
Gallagher, John, and Ronald Robinson. 1953. The Imperialism of Free Trade. *Economic History Review* 6 (1): 1–15.
GB Historical GIS. "Population Statistics, Total Population," *A Vision of Britain through Time*. London: University of Portsmouth. Accessed 29 Sept 2019. http://www.visionofbritain.org.uk/unit/10097836/cube/TOT_POP.
Gitelman, H. M. 1967. The Waltham System and the Coming of the Irish. *Labor History* 8 (Fall): 227–253.
Gráda, Cormac Ó. 1990. Irish Agricultural History: Recent Research Work in Progress. *The Agricultural History Review* 38 (2): 165–174.
Habakkuk, H.J. 1967. *American and British Technology in the Nineteenth Century*. Cambridge: Cambridge University Press.
Handley, James E. 1970. *The Navvy in Scotland*. Cork: Cork University Press.
Hansen, M. 1961. *The Atlantic Migration 1607–1860*. New York: Harper & Row.
Harley, C. Knick. 1989. Coal Exports and British Shipping, 1850–1913. *Explorations in Economic History* 26 (3): 311–338.
Harnetty, Peter. 1972. *Imperialism and Free Trade: Lancashire and India in the Mid-Nineteenth Century*. Vancouver: University of British Columbia Press.
Hayter, Teresa. 1982. *Creation of World Poverty*. London: Pluto Press.
Hickman, Mary. 1995. The Irish in Britain: Racism, Incorporation and Identity. *Irish Studies Review* 3 (10): 16–19.
Hobsbawn, E.J. 1962. *The Age of Revolution 1789–1848*. New York: New American Library.
Hobsbawn, E.J. 1969. *Industry and Empire*. Baltimore: Penguin Books.
Hu-Dehart, Evelyn. 1994. Chinese Coolie Labor in Cuba in the Nineteenth Century: Free Labor of Neoslavery. *Contributions in Black Studies* 12: 38–54.
Hunt, E.H. 1981. *British Labour History, 1815–1914*. Atlantic Highlands, NJ: Humanities Press.
Jenks, L.H. 1927. *The Migrations of British Capital to 1875*. New York: Alfred A. Knopf.

References

Jung, Moon Ho. 2006. *Coolies and Cane: Race, Labor, and Sugar in the Age of Emancipation.* Baltimore: Johns Hopkins University Press.

Kennedy, Robert, Jr. 1973. *The Irish: Emigration Marriage, and Fertility.* Berkeley: University of California Press.

Kuczynski, J. 1967. *The Rise of the Working Class* trans. by C. T. A. Ray. New York: McGraw-Hill.

Landes, David S. 1969. *The Unbound Prometheus.* Cambridge: Cambridge University Press.

Landes, David S. 1965. Technological Change and Development in Western Europe, 1750–1914. In *The Cambridge Economic History of Europe,* Vol. VI, *The Industrial Revolutions and After: Incomes, Population and Technological Change (I),* ed. by H. J. Habakkuk, and M. Postan, 274–456. Cambridge: Cambridge University Press.

Landes, David S. 1977. The Industrial Revolution. Encyclopaedia Britannica. In *Macropaedia,* Vol. 6, 15th ed., 229–242.

Langer, William L. 1969. *Political and Social Upheaval, 1832–1852.* New York: Harper & Row.

Law, C.M. 1967. The Growth of Urban Population in England and Wales, 1801–1911. *Transactions of the Institute of British Geographers* 41: 125–143.

Lilley, Samuel. 1978. Technological Progress and Industrial Revolution 1700–1914. In *The Fontana Economic History of Europe,* vol. 3, *The Industrial Revolution,* ed. by Carlo M. Cipolla, 187–254. Glasgow: Collins.

Luxemburg, Rosa. 1968. *The Accumulation of Capital.* New York: Monthly Review Press.

Magdoff, Harry. 1978. *Imperialism: From the Colonial Age to the Present.* New York: Monthly Review Press.

Mantoux, Paul. 1961. *The Industrial Revolution in then Eighteenth Century.* New York: Harper & Row.

Marx, Karl. 1967. *Capital,* vol. I. New York: International Publishers.

Marx, Karl, and Frederick Engels. 1972. *Ireland and the Irish Question.* New York: International Publishers.

Meagher, Arnold J. 2008. *The Coolie Trade: The Traffic in Chinese Laborers to Latin America 1847–1874.* Bloomington, IN: Xlibris Publishing.

Moch, Leslie Page. 2003. *Moving Europeans: Migration in Western Europe since 1650.* Bloomington: Indiana University Press.

Munger, Frank. 1981. Contentious Gatherings in Lancashire, England, 1750–1830. In *Class Conflict and Collective Action,* ed. Louise A. Tilly and Charles Tilly, 73–110. Beverly Hills: Sage.

O'Brien, George. 1921. *The Economic History of Ireland from the Union to the Famine.* London: Longmans, Green and Co.

Oakley, Ann. 1976. *Woman's Work: The Housewife, Past and Present.* New York: Vintage Books.

Pinchbeck, Ivy. 1971. *Women Workers and the Industrial Revolution.* New York: Augustus M. Kelley.

Piore, Michael. 1979. *Birds of Passage: Migrant Labor and Industrial Societies.* Cambridge: Cambridge University Press.

Pollard, Sidney. 1978. Labour in Great Britain. *The Cambridge Economic History of Europe.* Vol. VII, *The Industrial Economies: Capital, Labor, and Enterprise (I),* ed. by Peter Mathias, and M. M. Postan, 97–179. Cambridge: Cambridge University Press.

Porter, Roy. 1995. *London: A Social History.* Cambridge: Harvard University Press.

Punch, Kieron. 2016. Tallying the Irish in Britain over the Past Two Centuries. *The Wildgeese, Exploring the heritage of the Irish Worldwide.* Accessed 10 June 2022. https://thewildgeese.irish/profiles/blogs/irish-in-britain-census-statistics#comments.

Ravenstein, E. G. 1885. The Laws of Migration. *Journal of the Statistical Society,* XLVIII, Part II (June): 167–235.

Redford, Arthur. 1968. *Labor Migration in England, 1800–1850.* New York: Augustus M. Kelly Publishers.

Robins, Nick. 2012. *The Corporation that Changed the World: How the East India Company Shaped the Modern Multinational.* London: Pluto Press.

Rodriguez, Nestor, and Joe R. Feagin. 1986. Urban Specialization in the World-System: An analysis of Historical Cases. *Urban Affairs Quarterly* 22: 187–220.

Rostow, W.W. 1948. *British Economy of the Nineteenth Century.* Oxford: Clarendon Press.

Rostow, W.W. 1978. *The World Economy: History & Prospect.* Austin: University of Texas Press.

Rule, J.G. 1970. Some Social Aspects of the Cornish Industrial Revolution. In *Industry and Society in the South-West*, ed. Roger Burt, 71–106. Exeter: University of Exeter.

Sahoo, Rajib Lochan. 2015. Indian Cotton Mills and the British Economic Policy, 1854–1894. *Proceedings of the Indian History Congress* 76: 356–367.

Shepperson, W.S. 1957. *British Emigration to North America.* Minneapolis: University of Minnesota Press.

Stearns, P.M., ed. 1972. *The Impact of the Industrial Revolution: Protest and Alienation.* Englewood Cliffs, NJ: Prentice-Hall.

Thomis, Malcolm I. 1974. *The Town Labourer and The Industrial Revolution.* London: B. T. Batsford.

Thompson, E.P. 1963. *The Making of the English Working Class.* New York: Random House.

Treble, J. H. 1973. Irish Navvies in the North of England, 1830–50. *Transport History* 6 (3): 227–247.

Tristán, Flora. 2009. *Paseos en Londres.* Miami, FL: Ed Cid Editor.

US Department of Homeland Security (DHS). 2006. *2005 Yearbook of Immigration Statistics.* Washington, D.C. Accessed March 16, 2021. https://www.dhs.gov/sites/default/files/publications/Yearbook_Immigration_Statistics_2005.pdf.

US Department of Homeland Security (DHS). 2010. *2009 Yearbook of Immigration Statistics.* Washington, D.C. Accessed 25 Nov 2020. https://www.dhs.gov/sites/default/files/publications/Yearbook_Immigration_Statistics_2009.pdf

Wallerstein, Immanuel. 1979. *The Capitalist World-Economy.* London: Cambridge University Press.

Wallerstein, Immanuel. 1979. Underdevelopment and Phase-B: Effect of the Seventeenth-Century Stagnation on Core and Periphery of the European World-Economy. In *The World-System of Capitalism: Past and Present*, ed. Walter L. Goldfrank, 73–84. Beverly Hills: Sage Publications.

Wolpert, S. A. 1977. British Imperial Power (1858–1920). In *Encyclopaedia Britannica,* 15th ed., Macropaedia, vol. 9, 408–418.

Wrigley, E.A. 1967. The Supply of Raw Materials in the Industrial Revolution. In *The Causes of the Industrial Revolution in England*, ed. R.M. Hartwell, 97–120. London: Methuen & Co.

Monopoly Capital, US Hegemony, and Migration

The United States achieved "unquestioned hegemony" in the world-system following the end of World War II during 1945–1970 (Wallerstein 2006: 77). US standing in the world-system rose to hegemonic status as war devastation reduced the industrial capacity of European core states and Japan, and as the United States emerged from the war as a political and military world power (Wallerstein 1982). The political rivals that the United States faced in the period of hegemony were mainly the Soviet bloc, China, and their allies who pursued a socialist path. Heightened monopolization by corporations, greater internationalization of capital, and US state support for capital at home and abroad were among the developments that characterized the setting of US hegemony. In the United States, urban migration supplied labor power for the spatial restructuring of corporate capital in metropolitan areas. For the first nineteen years of US hegemony, a US–Mexico agreement annually imported thousands of temporary Mexican farmworkers (*braceros*) to work in the US agricultural sector. Puerto Rican migrants also arrived, mainly in the area of New York City, after the United States took possession of Puerto Rico as a colony, and especially after US companies expanded in the island's economy.

Arrighi (2010) compares the economic mode that elevated the United States as a global economic and political power in the twentieth century with the mode that sustained British dominance in the world-economy in the nineteenth century as corporate capitalism versus free-trade imperialism. While the British mode increased intercapitalist competition, US corporate capitalism reduced competition to decrease the instability and uncertainty of the market. Corporate capitalism reduced instability and uncertainty by undertaking "vertical integration" in the bureaucratic, commercial organization of the different tasks involved from production to transportation to marketing. In this way corporations could achieve greater control of prices and quantities to lessen the effects of market fluctuations. Moreover, while the British mode linked the home economy with markets in foreign regions that were occupied and controlled by the British, the US mode used a method of selective internalization into the US economy through foreign industrial investment. With some exceptions, this mode enabled US capitalist firms to establish operations abroad without undertaking direct political control or a lengthy occupation of a foreign region. After World War II, and especially during the Cold War with the Soviet Union, the US government became a direct supporter and planner in expanding US capital abroad (Arrighi 2010).

US capital invested heavily in Western Europe after World War II, bringing the region closer to the US economic and political spheres. Through the Marshall Plan to rebuild war-torn areas not under Soviet control and through rearmament of the region, the United States infused billions of dollars in Western European economies. This interaction with Western Europe helped elevate the US economy into a period of unprecedented wealth, with the US government playing a key role in monetary planning. By 1961, US banks controlled half of the Eurodollar market. US leadership in the world-system declined however during 1968–1973 when the United States experienced military, financial, and ideological crises (Arrighi 2010).

Increased managed and autonomous migration from the semiperiphery and periphery to the core became a prominent feature of the world-system as core areas moved into the stage of advanced capitalism after World War II.[1] At this stage, the core areas developed new needs for the labor power of migrant men and women from peripheral and semiperipheral countries, whether the migrants were authorized or not (Castles and Kosack 1973; Sassen-Koob 1984; Rodriguez 2004). The Irish temporary and permanent migrations into Britain during the late eighteenth and nineteenth centuries were a precursor to this development, but usually without the legal dimensions of visas and border controls. Large-scale unauthorized Mexican immigration in the United States, which accelerated in the 1940s, represented an autonomous experience of migration that at one level contradicted the world division by nation-state borders, but at another level complemented the service-support infrastructure for professional and technical workforces in the country.

Undocumented Mexican migrants had crossed the US border without visas for decades earlier than the 1940s, but the sizes of the unauthorized migration patterns that paralleled the importation of Mexican braceros for agricultural work were much larger, and the patterns had a seasonal character of temporary migration (Massey et al. 1987). The unauthorized migration of Mexicans, and later of Central Americans, developed into major patterns affecting US immigration and border policies for the remainder of the twentieth century and into the twenty-first century.

Before proceeding with the analysis of the chapter, it is important to acknowledge the nineteenth-century prelude to the rise of US hegemony in the twentieth century. European capital and labor migration into the United States in the nineteenth century constituted valuable resources for the economic development of the

---

[1] By autonomous migration I refer to the movement across inter-state borders without visas, i.e., without assistance of the state. Historically a large "migration industry" of formal and informal operators has helped migrants carry out their autonomous international migration (see Hernández-León 2005; Gammeltoft-Hansen and Sørensen 2012).

country. This was especially true given that the US government restricted immigration from the 1880s to the 1920s, creating a drastic immigration low at the start of US hegemony in 1945. The fertility of previous generations enlarged by immigration would have to make up for the low immigration numbers at the takeoff of US hegemony.

The discussion below is divided into six sections. In Sect. 5.1, I describe capital and labor resources that arrived in the United States in the nineteenth century and played a role in supplying the country for economic development. Section 5.2 focuses on the development in the United States of a monopoly corporate structure and urban restructuring into metropolitan and suburban areas that undergirded corporate development in the United States. In the Section 5.3 I describe US capital circulation in the world-system especially to Latin America. Section 5.4 describes labor migration associated with the rise of US hegemony, and the Sect. 5.5 analyzes migration patterns from the perspectives used in the previous two chapters of class relations, technological development, economic cycles, and state actions regarding migration. In Sect. 5.6, the discussion addresses the significance of migration for economic development in the United States during its period of hegemony.

5.1 Nineteenth-Century Prelude

Periods of hegemony in the world-system do not emerge overnight. They are the end result of social and demographic changes that accumulate over time. The social change includes political, economic, and social-spatial developments, and the demographic change includes the growth of labor forces and migration. As the previous two chapters have shown, international migration played an important role for the Dutch and British to strengthen labor forces for economic growth. Yet the case of US hegemony presents an opposite scenario. The beginning of US hegemony in 1945 occurred at the tail end of very low immigration levels as a result of policies enacted by the US government to restrict immigration. Restrictions were enacted first against Asians, beginning with the exclusion of Chinese immigrants in 1882, and later against immigration in general with the passage of immigration quotas, culminating with the 1924 National-Origins Quota Act.[2]

Annual immigration dropped dramatically after the passage of the 1924 Act. In the 10 years preceding the beginning of US hegemony in 1945 the annual average of new immigrants was 47,917, which was only 5.8% of the annual average of 820,239 new immigrants in the first 10 years of the twentieth century (US DHS 2011: Table 1). That is, due to the 1924 Act, but also partly due to the Great

---

[2] The 1924 Act based the quotas on the sizes of national-origin populations already in the United States. This generally gave larger quotas to countries in western Europe that had long sent immigrants to the United States and smaller quotas to countries in southern and eastern Europe that had sent fewer immigrants to the United States. Mexico was left out of the quota system, thanks to agricultural interests.

Table 5.1 US private foreign assets and investments and state foreign credits and claims, 1945–1965 ($Billion)

	1945	1950	1955	1960	1965
Private assets and investments	$14.7	$19.0	$29.1	$49.4	$81.1
State credits and claims	$2.1	$12.5	$14.2	$18.5	$25.1

Source US Census Bureau (1968: table 1200)

Depression of the 1930s, immigration levels dropped by more than 90%. The US period of hegemony commenced after about a decade and a half of severe immigration decline. This major drop in immigration seemingly contradicts the central thesis of this book of the importance of migration for capitalist development, and especially for the development of hegemony in the world-system.

The answer to this paradox lies in the nineteenth-century prelude to US industrialization in the twentieth century. Transfers of capital and labor from Britain and other countries to the United States helped to shore up US economic development in the nineteenth century.[3] To be sure, the growth of US capital was dynamic. In 1840–1900, the US capital stock increased by 23.4 times, while the population increased 4.4 times, the labor force 5.1 times, and land in production 5.7 times (Davis and Gallman 1978). While British-owned capital constituted a small portion of the total US capital supply, the canal and railroad projects it helped finance were closely associated with labor migration. For example, the Erie Canal, which was financed through the selling of over $7 million of New York state bonds in London, was built largely by Irish immigrant workers (Jenks 1927; Greenleaf 1970). Later in the century, railroad companies, e.g., New York & Erie and Baltimore & Ohio, also depended heavily on British capital and Irish and British immigrant labor (Jenks 1927; Shepperson 1957; Erickson 1957).

According to the figures in Table 5.1, the number of US immigrants in the nineteenth-century decades with more than a million immigrants, i.e., 1840–1899, amounted to 18,008,151. The first three decades of the twentieth century brought another 18,845,278 immigrants for a grand total of 36,853,429 during 1840–1929. Europe accounted for 85% of US immigration from 1840 to 1929. The four largest percentages of European immigrants came from Germany (18%), Italy (15%), Ireland (14%), and Britain (13%). While Russia accounted for 11% and Asia for 3%, together they accounted for 4.4 million immigrants in the 1840–1929 period. Women formed 40% or more of the European immigrant groups arriving in the United States (Moch 2003).[4]

---

[3] This includes the transatlantic African slave trade that brought many workers to the United States. The trade was officially abolished on January 1, 1808, although "legal abolition rarely meant an actual end of the trade (Curtin 1969: 231)".

[4] Using data from a 1929 compilation of international flow data of 42 sending areas and 39 receiving areas, Donato and Gabaccia (2015) give the women percentages for all nineteenth-century international flows as 30.8% among emigrants and 32.9% among immigrants.

The high volume of European emigration to the United States in the nineteenth and early twentieth centuries made Europe an important population resource for the United States when immigration in the country dropped to very low levels in the 1930s to the mid-1940s. Immigrants arriving in the late nineteenth century often had high fertility levels and their fertility remained high especially if they settled in rural areas (Bogue 1959; Guest 1982). The US-born second-immigrant generations and their children would help provide human resources for economic development in the country when US immigration was held to drastically low numbers.

Relative to later years, the total fertility rate remained high in the late nineteenth and early twentieth centuries, with white women averaging a total fertility rate of 4.24 in 1880 and 3.17 in 1920 (Haines 2008: table 1).[5] The accumulation of generations of US-born descendants of immigrants, combined with relatively high total fertility rates, helped increase the US labor force by 30% from 1930 to 1945, reaching 65,140,000 civilian and military employees by the later date (US Census Bureau 1950: table 209).

5.2 Monopoly Development and US Hegemony

US hegemony was a period of intense development for the capitalist world-system, more intense than in the previous two periods of hegemony. A monopolistic corporate sector in the United States aided in this development.[6] In some manufacturing industries, two or three corporations would account for over one-half of the industry's net capital assets. For example, in 1947 just three corporations owned 92.1% of net capital assets in the linoleum industry, 100.0% in the aluminum industry, 88.5% in the copper smelting and refining industry, 66.6% in the agricultural machinery industry, 68.7% in the motor vehicles industry, and 64.0% in the meat products industry (Federal Trade Commission 1964). Another indicator of monopoly capital was the large proportion of the labor force employed by a small proportion of corporations. In 1947, 4.2% of 240,881 manufacturing enterprises employed 59.4% of the manufacturing labor force of 14,294,300 workers, while 65.5% of the enterprises employed only 7.2% of the labor force (The Conference Board 1956).

The growth of monopoly capital continued even in the declining years of US hegemony. By the 1960s, 50 firms owned 36% of all the manufacturing assets among 420,000 manufacturing corporations, and the top 200 firms accounted for 56% (Feagin 1982). In 1966–1967, the 200 largest US corporations acquired 100

---

[5] The total fertility rate refers to the average number of children born to a woman if she were to experience the current age-specific fertility rates through her lifetime over the course of her reproductive life.

[6] In the United States, the consolidation of businesses into large monopoly corporations was initially rigorously pursued in the 1898 to 1902 period, partly as a reaction to a previous economic recession (see Gordon et al. 1982, pp. 106–112).

companies, which had a total asset value of $7.8 billion (Sweezy and Magdoff 1972). The development of monopoly capital in agriculture was just as impressive, as capital from such diverse sources as land companies, railroads, and oil corporations merged into agricultural corporations that controlled over one million acres over several states (see Galarza 1977).

Large agricultural corporations derived a disproportionate share of benefits from governmental programs. In 1967, 60% of farmers received 13.3% of government payments, while the richest 5% of farmers, mostly corporations, received 42.4% of government payments (Bonnen 1972).

It is important to note that the effects of monopoly capital went beyond controlling activities in different industrial sectors. As Manuel Castells (1980) explains, in the pursuit of economic power monopoly capital reaches into society to influence consumerism, mobilize resources to affect the political system and the mass media, and promote greater state intervention to support capitalism.

During the era of US hegemony, US industrial production accounted for a large portion of production in the world-economy. In 1948, the United States had 56% of the world's mining and manufacturing production, while all of western Europe had only 30% (The Conference Board 1956). By 1953, the United States was producing 63% more crude steel (a basic element of industrial development) than all of western Europe. In 1954, the United States had an export trade surplus of $15.1 billion, while its closest competitor, Britain, had an export trade deficit of $7.8 billion (The Conference Board 1956).

US manufacturing growth during US hegemony involved only a moderate increase in labor power. From 1950 to 1966, worker-hours worked in the US manufacturing industry increased by 19% (from 23.7 billion to 28.2 billion), while by comparison in West Germany the increase was 43% (Mandel 1978). The moderate rise in the use of labor power in the US manufacturing sector was partly related to increasing automation. In pursuit of technological innovation to increase productivity, by the 1960s research and development expenditures in the United States were growing 2.0–2.5 times faster than investments (Inozemtsev 1974).

The relationship between US capital and the state grew in the period of US hegemony. Actions undertaken by the state to help US capital meet challenges at home included economic planning, greater socialization of the risk cost associated with productive development (e.g., through research and construction of infrastructure), crisis management, and ideological manipulation (Mandel 1978).[7] Mandel cites the rise in state expenditure as a proportion of the US GNP, to support the argument of the increase of state intervention on behalf of capital. From 1940 to 1965, state expenditure as a proportion of the US GNP more than doubled from 12.4 to 30.0% (Mandel 1978).

---

[7] In Mandel's words (1978: 484), "State capital thus acts as a prop for private capital [...]".

5.2.1 Restructuring in the United States

Corporate capital accumulation in the United States in the stage of monopoly capitalism advanced the urban processes of metropolitanization and suburbanization. Metropolitanization involved the accelerated concentration of population and economic activities associated with the concentration of capital and drew partly from the migration that resulted from the entrance of finance capital into the agricultural sector (Castells 1976). Suburbanization involved the "selective decentralization and spatial sprawl of population and activities within the metropolitan areas" (Castells 1976: 4). In this process, business and major administrative activities remained in the urban core, while manufacturing plants and retail shopping centers relocated in the suburbs. With the additional relocation of the higher social-status population in the suburbs, non-Whites and other poor working-class groups, including immigrant workers, remained in the central city to work in low-skill and low-paying jobs of the "competitive sector" (as opposed to the monopoly corporate sector).[8]

According to Gordon (1977), the decentralization of corporate enterprises to areas beyond large cities in the twentieth century was a consequence of workers' struggles in central cities. In the mid-1800s, location in central districts of large cities had given manufacturing firms easy access to the labor supply and to rail and water outlets, but by the 1880s corporations in the central cities became increasingly subject to worker strikes (Gordon 1977). Late in the 1890s, manufacturing started moving out of the central city to regain stability and security. By the 1920s, as large corporations consolidated control in their industries, they separated their administrative departments from the production process. Corporate managers located their offices in central business districts where they could more efficiently administer business, and factories were moved to the suburbs (Gordon 1977).

The urban restructuring of monopoly capital increased the demand for a service labor force to support the corporate office workforces in central cities (Sassen-Koob 1984). The service workers included office building cleaners, restaurant and coffee shop workers, etc., and these workers often came from the immigrant ranks. Sometimes immigrant service workers worked off-the-books in small establishments or in subcontracted firms that overlooked unauthorized immigrant status. Service immigrant workers also appeared in the industrial suburbs, such as in the form of "taco ladies" who drove food trucks to sell sandwiches to the workers.

It was in the political and military spheres that some of the most visible signs of the decline of US hegemony appeared. National liberation and revolutionary movements gained momentum across world regions in the 1960s and created significant challenges to US hegemony in Latin America, Southeast Asia, and in other peripheral areas. The US withdrawal from the Vietnam War in 1975 without a victory was a sign of the decline of US hegemony, according to Wallerstein (1979a). In

---

[8] Sociologist Gideon Sjoberg (1999) refers to the large-scale organizational form of monopoly capital as "bureaucratic capitalism".

the economic sphere, the loss of the competitive edge of US products in the markets of other core countries, the dollar and gold crisis, and Nixon's retreat from a free-trade policy, all reflected the decline of US hegemony as well (Wallerstein 1979a, 1982).[9] The end of US hegemony did not mean an end to US world power; it meant a new approach to deal with world affairs. After hegemony, the United States depended more on diplomacy and coalitions with allies to gain international support for political and military ventures in the world-system.

5.3   Circulation of US Capital to the Periphery

Circulation of US capital to peripheral regions of the world-economy increased during the period of US hegemony. Given that many of the regions had already been brought into the orbit of capital investment in earlier times, it seems more appropriate to speak in terms of capital circulation than in terms of capital migration. As in the Dutch and British periods of hegemony, economic investment of US capital abroad, sometimes propped by US political power, was also a crucial part of the rise of US hegemony. During the era of US hegemony, US government financial assistance and private investments abroad increased by almost six times, from $16.8 billion in 1945 to $111.9 billion in 1966 (US Census Bureau 1968: table 1200). By 1960, US capital constituted 59.1% of the total capitalist foreign investment in the world (Mandel 1978). The former hegemon, Britain, was the second largest source of foreign investment, but with less than half of the US percentage.

During US hegemony, Latin America remained an attractive area for US direct investments. From 1943 to 1966, US direct investments in Latin American countries increased from $2.7 billion to $9.9 billion (The Conference Board 1956; US Census Bureau 1968: table 1202).[10] By the late 1960s, Latin America was only behind Canada and Western Europe as the area of major attraction for US capital. But US capital did not have the power and influence in Canada and in Western Europe that it enjoyed in Latin American countries. Indeed, in many of these countries US capital in the form of multinationals ruled industrial sectors with almost a free hand (see Barnet and Muller 1974). In many cases, US corporations were already firmly established in Latin America countries by the beginning of US hegemony. For example, by 1928 US firms had invested $1.5 billion in Cuba (mainly in the sugar industry) and the monopolies of Standard Oil of New Jersey, International Telephone and Telegraph, and United Fruit Company had numerous subsidiaries and affiliates throughout Latin America (Winkler 1971).

---

[9] For Wallerstein (1982), this decline was part of the secular decline of the capitalist world-system that had begun with the rise of revolutionary and liberation movements in different world regions since the mid-1910s.

[10] The *Survey of Current Business* of September 1973 (table 7), gives a figure of US direct investments in Latin America of $10.8 billion for 1965 (US Department of Commerce 1973).

The Latin American region proved to be profitable for US capital investment. For example, between 1947 and 1960, private investment transfers from the United States to Brazil totaled $1.8 billion, and the flow of investment returns from Brazil to the United States totaled $3.5 billion (Frank 1970). US private investment flow to the seven largest Latin American countries (Argentina, Brazil, Chile, Peru, Venezuela, Colombia, Mexico) in 1950–1961 totaled $3.0 billion and the return profits and interests totaled $6.9 billion, of which $2.1 billion was a net capital return, apart from the Latin American servicing of US loans.

As Table 5.1 demonstrates, during the period of US hegemony, US government foreign financial assistance increased as private foreign assets and investments grew.

Actual US foreign financial assistance was greater in 1945–1965 than shown in Table 5.1 if indirect loans and grants made by the US government through world financial institutions are considered. These institutions include the Asian Development Bank and the Inter-American Development Bank. From 1945 to 1967, five world financial institutions funded by the US government provided $1.4 billion in foreign financial assistance (US Census Bureau 1968: table 1209).

From 1945 to 1967, the US government also spent $37.6 billion in foreign military aid (US Census Bureau 1968: table 1209).[11] Most of the military aid consisted of grants for military supplies and services. As mentioned in Chap. 4 on British hegemony, it is not always necessary for core powers to impose their military forces in peripheral areas at great financial expense. Core powers can support local rulers and elites in peripheral countries to maintain work conditions favorable for capital accumulation and to suppress reform movements.[12]

5.4 US Capital Expansion into Mexican Agriculture

In this section, I examine the relationship between US capital penetration into commercial agricultural in Mexico, the development of the US–Mexico bracero program of temporary imported labor, and the parallel rise of unauthorized labor migration into the United States. The concern is not to search for a direct cause-and-effect relationship, but to understand how US capital penetration advanced the commercialization of Mexican agriculture, which displaced rural workers and made migration a survival strategy for many of these workers. Mexican urban industrialization after 1940 stimulated a mass migration of impoverished rural families to Mexican cities (Balán et al. 1973; Unikel 1968). But for many rural workers

---

[11] This figure does not include amounts spent by the Central Intelligence Agency (CIA) in covert foreign involvement. The CIA keeps its budget secret.

[12] The US-led overthrow of the democratic government of Guatemala in 1954 remains a classic example in this regard (Immerman 1982). Many other examples exist of US military and political involvement to support repressive regimes in Latin America and other world regions (see Hayter 1981; Menjívar and Rodríguez 2005).

(and later urban workers as well) migration to the United States as braceros or undocumented workers became another survival strategy.

After the end of Lazaro Cardenas' nationalistic presidency in 1940, the Mexican government pursued an export-oriented agrarian policy that slowed land distribution to peasants, brought 690,000 hectares of land into production through irrigation, and gave control of irrigation districts to large agricultural capitalists (NACLA 1976). The benefits of these agrarian developments were shared by US corporate farmers who during World War II started operations in Mexico's northwest region. With increasing commercialization of Mexico's agricultural production, by 1957 60% of Mexican agricultural products were destined for export, and 2% of the farmers accounted for 70% of the export sales values. In the 1960s, the exportation of vegetables to the United States accelerated, from a sales value of $20 million in 1962 to over $100 million in 1969 (NACLA 1976).[13]

The US-related commercialization of agriculture in Mexico drew labor power from the population of landless workers, which grew by 74% between 1940 and 1960 (NACLA 1976). By 1960 the number of landless agricultural laborers was over 3 million. At least half a million migrant farm workers were in Mexico's northwest region where powerful large landowners had ties to US agribusiness (NACLA 1976). In the 1940–1950 period, big landowners in the northwest region increased their possessions through political maneuvering and reduced the communal lands (*ejidos*) distributed by the government to peasants. In the northwestern state of Sonora, the workable land contained in ejidos fell from 40 to 17% (Russell 1977).

From 1940 and through the 1960s, ejidos became an important source of migratory farm labor. By the 1960s, in some areas of Mexico's northwest region, 40% of migrant farm workers came from ejidos (NACLA 1976). With government policies favoring the development of large-scale commercial farming, ejido peasants were left with little financial assistance to buy farming equipment and build irrigation systems. In some ejidos, farmers were only able to make $50 a month in the 1960s (NACLA 1976). Because of this poverty, many ejido farmers rented their lands to large landowners and joined migratory labor forces. By the mid-1960s, with advancing mechanization in commercial farming, about 2 million farm workers in Mexico faced severe unemployment (NACLA 1975).

Many ejido farmers who were pressured off their lands by US–related commercial farming migrated to the United States, either as braceros or as undocumented workers (NACLA 1975; Galarza 1977). Coordinating with agricultural capital, the US government pressured Mexico in the 1947–1954 period to open additional

---

[13] US and Mexican agricultural officials and experts shared ideas and approaches for agricultural production and reform in the 1930s and 1940s (Olsson 2017). Opening headquarters of operations near Mexico City in 1943, the Rockefeller Foundation undertook a program of agricultural technical innovation in collaboration with Mexican officials that resulted in the advancement of agricultural production known as the green revolution. The knowledge gained in the green revolution in Mexico was shared with other peripheral countries (Olsson 2017).

bracero recruitment centers in northern Mexico, where a plentiful supply of workers existed. The Mexican government refused at first, probably because it did not want to upset the supply of labor in Mexico's northern agriculture, but it eventually opened seven centers close to the US border (Garcia y Griego 1980). Many ejido farmers who were not recruited as braceros joined the growing concentration of workers in the border area, from which many workers migrated without visas to the United States (NACLA 1975).

Since the 1910–1920 revolutionary period, migration from agricultural regions to industrializing urban areas characterized most of the internal migration in Mexico (Weaver and Downing 1976). This migration accelerated after 1940 when the six Mexican states that border the United States, and four others in the northern zone, underwent high rates of urbanization (Balán et al. 1973). Led by US investors, foreign capital investments in Mexico supported the development of manufacturing industries, which spurred urbanization (Twomey 2001). Foreign investment in manufacturing expanded rapidly during 1940–1945 and doubled by 1952 to reach a total of $728 million of foreign capital stock (Aviel and Aviel 1982). US foreign direct investment in Mexican manufacturing reached $391 million in 1960. By the mid-1970s, US foreign direct investment in manufacturing reached three-fourths of the $3.0 billion US investment in Mexico (Aviel and Aviel 1982).

But even with their high growth rates, the industrializing centers in Mexico could not provide enough jobs for the urban workforces and the arriving rural migrants. With the help of foreign capital, the Mexican government attempted to increase production, and thus employment, through a policy of Import Substitution Industrialization assisted by price controls on staple foods, but this worked against small formers (Hernández-León 2008). The foreign capital investment in the Mexican economy that supported industrial growth also brought technological innovations that diminished the capacity of industry to absorb labor (Russell 1977; Barnet and Muller 1974; NACLA 1975). High population growth rates in the countryside led to more urban migration and the subdividing of ejidos to mini-plots, which further stimulated out-migration in search of work to sustain families (Hernández-León 2008). With growing unemployed or underemployed worker populations, industrial urban areas thus became a source of migrant labor as well. The propertyless migrant population of rural and urban persons in Mexico increased from 3.5 million in the 1940s to 7.5 million in the 1960s (NACLA 1976).

5.5   Labor Migration and US Hegemony

This section describes two patterns of labor migration mentioned above that transpired in the United States during the US period of hegemony. One pattern concerned internal labor migration to metropolitan areas. The migration of African Americans and Mexican Americans was part of this pattern but usually with consequences different from the experiences of White migrants. The second pattern concerned the importation of temporary Mexican braceros mainly into the country's agricultural sector and the parallel migration of Mexican unauthorized migrants into the United States. Neither of the two patterns was novel in the history of the world-system. The concentration of capital in towns and cities has brought about the accumulation of migrant labor since the dawn of capitalism, and foreign labor has crossed sociopolitical borders since the medieval emergence of capitalism. But what was novel in the two patterns for the United States was their volume and intensity, and actions undertaken by the state to support the two migration patterns.

5.5.1 Internal Migration

The metropolitan form that Castells (1976) associated with the concentration of monopoly capital contained 53% of the US population of 133 million in 1940. Table 5.2 demonstrates the parallel growth of the US and metropolitan populations from 1940 to 1970, which covers the US period of hegemony from the mid-1940s to the late 1960s and early 1970s. Across the decades from 1940 to 1970, the metropolitan population accounted for a larger share of the total US population, from about half of the population in 1940 to more than two-thirds by 1970. At every census year, the growth rate of the metropolitan population was larger than the growth rate of the total population in the country. The metropolitan areas of capital concentration thus had a greater population dynamic than the general population of the country.

US metropolitan areas with strong connections to economic development in the world-system had particularly dynamic economies and population growth and attracted domestic and foreign migrants. These metropolitan areas contained centers of finance capital and manufacturing that were connected to markets across world regions. The financial centers of Amsterdam, London, and New York City, and the manufacturing centers of Leiden, Manchester, and Houston, illustrate the specialized role some metropolitan areas played in the world-system across the eras of Dutch, British, and US hegemony, respectively (Rodriguez and Feagin 1986).

Table 5.2 US and Metropolitan populations, 1940–1970

	US population (million)	Metropolitan population (million)	Metropolitan percent of US population
1940	132.6	69.3	52.6
1950	152.3	84.5	56.1
1960	180.7	112.9	63.0
1970	204.9	139.4	68.6

Source US Census Bureau (1977: tables 2, 14)

5.5 Labor Migration and US Hegemony

Migration was a significant source for metropolitan growth. From the 1940s through the 1950s, the net migration in metropolitan areas and the percentages that the net migration constituted of the total metropolitan increase were as follows: 1940s-7.2 million (44%) and 1950s- 8.1 million (35%). But in the 1960s, the contribution of net migration to metropolitan growth dropped to 5.3 million, accounting for only 26% of the metropolitan growth in the decade (US Census Bureau 1974: 124). In the 1940s, about 30% of total urban growth was due to rural–urban migration (Bogue 1959: 39). Rural-farm areas experienced a net migration loss of 8.6 million persons for the decade, while the metropolitan areas that reached a population of 100,000 or more by 1950 gained 6.4 million persons through migration (Bogue 1959). A large part of this metropolitan growth occurred in suburban rings.

The 1950–1960 decade was "*a period of unprecedented suburbanization*" (Bogue 1959: 29, italics in the original). Central city populations in metropolitan areas in the decade increased by 10.3% to reach 57.8 million, while the suburban and other outlying populations in the metropolitan areas increased by 47.6% to reach 54.5 million (US Census Bureau 1968: table 17). In the decade of the 1950s, manufacturing, warehousing, and transportation facilities were increasingly located in industrial suburbs. The suburban population growth accounted for 75.1% of total metropolitan population increase in the 1950s, and for 77.5% in the 1960s (Berry and Kasarda 1977). The swelling of suburban populations also included large housing tracts of white-collar workers who commuted to office jobs in the central cities.

Castells' (1976) claim of the decentralization of manufacturing activity within metropolitan structures is supported by employment analysis of the time interval of the US period of hegemony. Between 1947 and 1967, central cities had a net loss of 293,307 manufacturing jobs, representing a 4% decline, while suburban rings gained 3,902,326 manufacturing jobs, representing a 94% increase (Berry and Kasarda 1977). From about the beginning of US hegemony to its end by 1970, the suburban share of metropolitan manufacturing jobs went from 36 to 53%. We can also see the decentralization from the standpoint of blue-collar/white-collar distribution. An analysis of 101 longitudinally comparable metropolitan areas found that in the decade of the 1960s, central cities lost 828,257 blue-collar employees but gained 485,447 white-collar employees, while suburbs gained 1,119,134 blue-collar workers and 2,059,123 white-collar workers (Berry and Kasarda 1977).

Despite the significance of migration for metropolitan growth, natural increase (births minus deaths) almost always outweighed the significance of net migration for metropolitan population growth. In the 1960s, only four of the 100 standard metropolitan areas in the county experienced greater gain from net migration than from natural increase (US Census Bureau 1968: table 18).[14] During the decade, 40% of the net migration into metropolitan areas came from inside the country,

---

[14] Three of the four metropolitan areas were in California and the fourth in Florida.

and 60% came from outside the country (US Census Bureau 1974: 124), as immigration from abroad gained momentum in a secular rise that spanned into the twenty-first century.[15]

Bogue (1959) described the "residentially mobile" population in the United States in the period 1940 to 1958 as follows.[16] The migrants were disproportionately in their late teens, twenties, and early thirties. They were persons with less than 7 years of schooling or who completed high school, or who had college experience. The rates of migration among persons in the labor force were higher among the unemployed than among the employed. Among females, professionals and service workers usually had higher than average migration rates than in other occupations, and among males, professionals, operatives, and farm laborers had higher rates of residential mobility (Bogue 1959).

These characteristics also generally described internal migrants in the 1960s. According to the US Census Bureau (1968: table 37; 1974: 133–140), among adults, persons 20–29 years old were the most migratory. The under-educated and persons with college experience had higher than average migration rates. In the labor force, the unemployed migrated more than the employed, and the occupations of professional, managerial, sales workers, and laborers (farm and non-farm) led in migration rates. Two-thirds of migrant couples moved because of job-related reasons. Partly because of the migration of couples, the numbers of male and female internal migrants were similar in the decade (US Census Bureau 1968: table 37; 1974: 138–139).

The contribution of internal migration to the growth of metropolitan populations was not shared equally in all regions of the country. In the 1940s, metropolitan areas in the Atlantic Metropolitan Belt, the Gulf Coast, and the Pacific Southwest experienced the largest numbers of net migrants (Bogue 1959). The migrants to the metropolitan centers in these regions were part of the larger migration patterns westward, northward, and southward to old as well as new commercial and industrial centers (Bogue 1959). During 1950–1970, the western region of the United States continued to experience large in-migration patterns, but migratory gains declined in the Northeast (Heer 1975), when companies were leaving the Northeast for southern and southwestern destinations. In the South, net migration continued to contribute substantially to metropolitan growth. Non-metropolitan areas in the South contribute migrants to southern cities, as well as to northern and western urban areas (US Census Bureau 1974: 124–125). In the 1960s, Middle Appalachia had the highest rates of out-migration, as the region underwent a decline in mining, with little alternative employment (US Census Bureau 1974: 126).

---

[15] A new US immigration policy in 1965 replaced immigrant quotas with a family and employer preference system, which stimulated the rise of immigration.

[16] Residentially mobile referred to persons who changed residence from one county to another or from one state to another.

5.5 Labor Migration and US Hegemony

Table 5.3 Population distribution of African Americans in US regions, 1940 and 1966

	1940 (%)	1966 (%)
Northeast	11	17
North Central	11	20
South	77	55
West	1	8

Source US Census Bureau (1968: table 19)

5.5.2 Racial Minority Migration

Internal migration to metropolitan areas during the period of US hegemony involved the minority populations of African Americans and Mexican Americans, the two largest racial minorities in the country during US hegemony. By the end of the period of US hegemony, these two populations occupied definite places in the metropolitan urban structures that formed the social-structural environment of monopoly capital. Both groups had rural-work origins, but by the end of US hegemony the two groups were substantially integrated in lower-status occupations of urban labor markets. Puerto Ricans were a third racial minority group involved in the migration to metropolitan areas during the US period of hegemony. As US citizens, Puerto Ricans represented a force of internal migration, but as a people from a Caribbean colony, i.e., an external possession of the United States, they were often seen as foreigners on the US mainland.

African American migration during the period of US hegemony consists of two conjoining movements: out-migration from the South and rural–urban migration. African American out-migration from the South ensued after the Civil War, but it reached a large-scale level around the time of World War I. The out-migration slowed during the Great Depression, but regained intensity during World War II (Pinkney 1975).[17] Table 5.3 shows the change of the regional distribution of the African American population from 1940 to 1966 due to migration and natural increase.

Whereas in 1900, 90% of African Americans lived in the South, by 1966 only slightly more than one-half of the African American population remained in the South (Pinkney 1975). A total of 3.7 million African Americans left the South between 1940 and 1963 (National Advisory Commission on Civil Disorders 1968).

Much of the African American out-migration from the South headed to urban areas in other regions. This migration helped reverse the rural/urban distribution of African Americans. In 1900, prior to the exodus from the South, 77% of African Americans lived in rural areas; but by 1960, 73% of African Americans lived in

---

[17] Charles Tilly (1979:189) describes the patterns of African American out-migration that emerged from the South as "a broad straight line from Tallahassee to Boston, another heavy line from New Orleans to Chicago, and a spindly one from Houston to Los Angeles... [with] lines leading to cities along the way".

urban areas (Pinkney 1975). For African Americans, urban life meant living in metropolitan areas. By 1968, 69% of the African American population of 22.0 million lived in metropolitan areas, predominantly in central cities (US Census Bureau 1969: table 17).[18]

Blocked by a host of financial and racial restrictions, fewer than a fourth of African Americans in metropolitan areas in 1960 settled in the suburbs, while most metropolitan Whites settled in suburban rings and other areas outside central cities (US Census Bureau 1968: table 17). Inside low-income communities in central cities, African Americans faced labor markets with vanishing opportunities as jobs increasingly receded toward the rims of the central cities, or toward industrial and commercial suburban areas (Wilson 1996).

Out-migration from the South enabled many African Americans to distance themselves from some of the harshest conditions of racism and racial oppression, but for many African Americans the migration brought low-paying, manual work in the metropolitan areas of other regions. In 1970, while White men and women workers were concentrated in the occupations of professional/technical, clerical, craftwork, and operative, African American men and women were concentrated in the occupations of clerical, service, operative, and laborer (US Census Bureau 1973a: table 81). This structural inequality contributed to the overall economic subordination of African Americans, whose median family income in 1970 of $6067 was only 60% of the White family annual income of $9961 (US Census Bureau 1973a: table 83).

While they shared structural, racial subordination, African Americans and Mexican Americans had significant differences in their US experiences. African Americans were brought into the society as slave workers, and Mexican Americans became part of society as a conquered people and as immigrants, because of the US-Mexico war of 1846–1848. In addition, African Americans developed large-scale migration patterns out of the South to large urban areas in the Northeast, North Central and the West, while Mexican Americans underwent urbanization mainly in the Southwest where they originated. Two significant exceptions to the Mexican American concentration in the Southwest were settlement in the Midwest and the participation in farm-labor migratory streams that commenced in southern Texas and circulated throughout the country (Valdéz 2000).

By 1930, the Mexican-origin population in the United States reached 1.5 million, and small numbers of Mexicans trickled from rural to urban areas (Romo 1975). US-born Mexican Americans migrating to the cities in the Southwest were joined by Mexican immigrants fleeing poverty in Mexico, where peasants worked for 20–30 cents per day (Cardoso 1980).[19] The Mexican American trickle to the cities gained momentum after the Great Depression. By the end of the 1940s, when the Mexican population numbered about 2.3 million in the Southwest (Galarza

---

[18] Census data is usually subject to a margin of undercount. General population figures have an undercount of about 2%. For the African American and Mexican American minority groups, the undercount is usually higher.

[19] In Lawrence Cardoso's words, "Migration was the only liberation" (1980: 5).

et al. 1970), and about 100,000 in the Midwest (Cardenas 1978), approximately two-thirds of the Mexican-origin population in the Southwest lived in urban areas (Tienda 1983). Many Mexican Americans lived in the 29 metropolitan areas in the Southwest. By the end of the 1950s, 79% of Mexican Americans in the Southwest were urban dwellers (Grebler et al. 1970), and this proportion rose to 85% by the end of the 1960s (US Census Bureau 1970a: table 3). Ten standard metropolitan statistical areas had Mexican-origin populations of over 100,000 by 1970 (US Census Bureau 1970b: table 13).

Similar to the employment conditions of urban African Americans, the jobs that Mexican Americans and new Mexican immigrants occupied in metropolitan areas such as Los Angeles and San Antonio in the Southwest, and Chicago in the Midwest, were concentrated in manual occupations. By the late 1960s, most Mexican-origin workers in urban areas were in the three occupational categories of operatives, service workers, and laborers (US Census Bureau 1970b: table 8). The economic conditions of Mexican Americans in metropolitan areas varied according to region. In the Chicago metropolitan area, for example, Mexican men and women workers had a median annual income in 1970 of $6578 and $3318, respectively, while in the San Antonio metropolitan area the median incomes of Mexican men and women workers were $4151 and $1723, respectively (US Census Bureau 1973b: table 15). In some metropolitan labor markets, Mexican American annual incomes in 1970 were less than half of the national median income of $9590 (US Census Bureau 1973b: table 83).

Puerto Ricans composed the second largest Latin American-origin population in the United States after Mexican-origin people during the US period of hegemony. The 1960 census counted 892,513 Puerto Ricans in the country, which was much smaller than the 3.3 million Spanish-surname population of mainly Mexican Americans in the Southwest (US Census Bureau 1965a, b). But the socioeconomic and political relationship of Puerto Ricans to the United States was in some ways more complicated than the Mexican American experience.[20] While both populations had US citizenship status, the Puerto Ricans through a 1917 US congressional act the Mexicans through a 1848 treaty with Mexico, the Puerto Rican island homeland remained a colony of the United States. As a colony, the island experienced the economic forces from the United States that historically created advantages for investors from core states and disadvantages for working populations in peripheral countries. Understanding this contradictory colonial experience that creates wealth for the colonizer and poverty and restrictions for many colonial workers helps to understand why Puerto Ricans arrived as migrants in the United States in the twentieth century.

---

[20] Accurate sizes are not available of racial minority populations for the years before the US census improved its enumeration of these populations in the late twentieth century. Some of these populations lived in fluid housing arrangements or did not use English as their primary language, making the work of the census challenging. In 2020, Puerto Ricans in the country numbered 6.0 million and Mexican-origin persons numbered 37.2 million (Pew Research Center 2022).

Puerto Ricans owned most of the Puerto Rican farmland when the United States acquired the island from Spain in 1899. But after the United States took possession of the island, new policies affecting control of the land forced Puerto Rican farmers to sell their land to US companies. US investors took control of 60% of sugar production, and a monopoly of tobacco production and shipping lines, by 1930 (Feagin and Feagin 1993). A land reform policy in the 1940s, however, made the Puerto Rican government the largest landowner in the island by the end of the 1950s, which saw sugar production declined for three decades.

As foreign-controlled companies grew in Puerto Rican, more and more Puerto Ricans became the low-wage workforces for international investors, including the foreign owners of large monopoly corporations on the island. An economic boom followed on the island when a Puerto Rican governor implemented a development program called Operation Bootstrap in the late 1940s to attract US corporations to the island. The incentives attracted 1700 factories, creating over 140,000 manufacturing jobs, and a sharp rise in construction work by 1975 (Feagin and Feagin 1993). While capital investment and per capital income grew, still the growth was not enough to offset the public tax burden to pay for the infrastructure of the new industrial growth, especially as US companies were given 10-year tax exemptions. Moreover, US corporations brought technology to the island for production that reduced the need for labor (History Task Force 1979). Many Puerto Ricans adopted the strategy of migration to the United States for economic survival.

Puerto Rican migration to the United Stated remained relatively low in the four decades after the United States took possession of Puerto Rico, averaging a few hundred to a few thousand per year, but in the 1940s the number of migrants emigrating to the United States rose to 15,100 per year and to 25,300 per year by the 1960s (Vázquez Calzada 1979). The net migration of Puerto Ricans to the United States reached 834,000 migrants in the "great migration" of 1940–1969 (Feagin and Feagin 1993). As with most migrant streams, the movement of Puerto Ricans was not unidirectional, but a series of back and forth flows as different categories of migrants (unemployed, seasonal, temporary, permanent) crossed to the mainland or returned to Puerto Rico according to different economic and social motivations. In the last decade of the great movement of Puerto Ricans to the US mainland, i.e., between 1960 and 1970, 586,636 migrants left the island and 283,424 migrants and their children returned (Vázquez Calzada 1979).

Almost three-fourths of Puerto Rican migrants to the United States in 1960 settled in New York state, and almost two-thirds in 1970 (Vázquez Calzada 1979). The primary destination was New York City. Arriving Puerto Rican workers in New York City complemented the generations of European immigrant workers that had settled in the city before Congress shut the immigration valve through the 1924 National-Origins Quota Act. As US citizens, Puerto Ricans, thus, entered New York City as a timely infusion of new labor that was no longer available in large numbers from Europe. But the Puerto Ricans did not arrive under conditions of their choosing. They arrived at the time the city was entering the phase of monopoly capitalism.

In New York City, Puerto Ricans became concentrated in blue-collar occupations more than Whites and Blacks (Rodríguez 1979). This concentration decreased by the 1970s as more Puerto Ricans entered service occupations, and as some Puerto Rican women entered clerical work. Across all occupations in New York City, Puerto Ricans were paid less than Whites and Blacks, and Puerto Rican women were paid less than Puerto Rican men. As Rodríguez (1979) has described, the Puerto Rican labor force in the city felt some of the largest impacts as monopoly capitalism affected the economy of the New York area in the late 1960s and 1970s. Having the largest proportion of blue-collar jobs, Puerto Ricans were more affected by automation than Whites and Blacks. The sending of industrial plants and factories to the suburbs by monopoly capital also caused job displacement among Puerto Ricans, who were for the most part out of reach of suburban jobs. Moreover, suburbanization of industries reduced the tax base of the city, which in turn reduced revenues to pay for city services needed by unemployed city residents, including Puerto Ricans. Unemployment of blue-collar workers grew as manufacturing firms left the city for non-union areas in the southern United States or for foreign countries that had large low-wage populations. These dislocations, combined with other restrictions caused by racism, left Puerto Rican workers in precarious conditions (Rodríguez 1979). Facing these adversities, thousands of Puerto Ricans annually chose to return to the island, at the same time that thousands chose to leave the island for the United States.

The inferior economic conditions of African Americans, Mexican Americans, and Puerto Ricans in the metropolitan settings of monopoly capital illustrated the racial and class contradictions of the immense wealth accumulated by hegemonic US capital in the world-system. In many central cities, the towering office buildings of global capital were situated near the poor, inner-city neighborhoods of racial minority workers. Black and Latino central city neighborhoods often resembled the inferior conditions of working-class communities in peripheral countries, so much so that some scholars turned to theories of internal colonialism to explain the US minority experience of racial oppression and exploitation (Carmichael and Hamilton 1967; Blauner 1972).

5.5.3 Mexican Bracero and Immigrant Labor

In 1942, the governments of the United States, Mexico, and the British West Indies agreed on a program to import thousands of foreign workers into the United States for temporary work mainly in agriculture. The Emergency Farm Labor Supply program was set up to annually provide agricultural labor that supposedly was needed to replace the US labor that left to fight in the military or work in war industries (Hahamovitch 2001). For some US government skeptics, however, the real reason was that US farmers had a penchant for temporary foreign workers, in spite of the plentiful supply of domestic labor. The labor importation program finalized between the US and Mexican governments became known as the Bracero

Program, and the imported Mexican laborers became known as "braceros" after the Spanish word "brazos" for arms. Braceros were imported to work mainly in agriculture, with small numbers placed in railroad construction crews. The bracero program represented a strategy of state support for capital that had been growing since the late nineteenth century in other world regions (Hahamovitch 2001). It was the strategy of employers in one country temporarily hiring workers from another country through intergovernment agreements to do work that was unattractive to domestic workers because of the dirty and dangerous nature of the work and the low pay employers provided.

Originally organized as measure to procure labor during World War II, the bracero program lasted 22 years, illustrating its significance far beyond the end of the war. From the perspective of the world-system, the bracero program represented evolving structural relations between core and peripheral societies. From the perspective specifically of US economic development during US hegemony, the program represented the increasing importance of Mexican migrant labor for the US economy.

Several features of the bracero program demonstrate that it was a new means of obtaining labor in the stage of monopoly capitalism. The bracero program was based on an intergovernmental agreement and heavily subsidized and administered by agencies of the US government, and to some extent the Mexican government.[21] As the Mexican government demanded to be clarified on paper, the "employer" of braceros was the US government (Craig 1971). The long-term span of the program and the total 4.8 million braceros contracted were unprecedented undertakings of the state in formalizing a migratory labor system for capital's interests. Secondly, the bracero program was distinct from earlier movements of foreign labor to this country because it only allowed the importation of workers (males) and not their families.[22] In the view of the American Farm Bureau Federation, which represented agricultural capital, "Mexican workers [braceros] unaccompanied by wives and families... can fill our seasonal peaks and return home... without creating difficult social problems" (quoted in Galarza 1977: 32). According to Burawoy (1976), this type of migrant labor system effectively separated the use of labor power from the cost of the production and reproduction of the labor power. In other words, advanced capitalist societies used the labor power of young foreign workers, while the sending peripheral countries of these migrant workers paid the cost

---

[21] Private recruiting agencies contracted Mexican migrant workers in the early twentieth century (Reisler 1976), and the US government arranged the importation of temporary Mexican contract workers in 1907 and in 1917–1921 (Garcia y Griego 1980). But none of these antecedents had the characteristics of the massive bracero program initiated in 1942.

[22] The bracero program created hardships for the wives and families of the workers who left for the United States. For interviews of Mexican women who went through this bracero-related experience, see Lindberg (2018). In the late 1940s and 1950s, the US government implemented small programs for the use of temporary foreign workers in the US East Coast and in US territories (Briggs 2004). Some of these programs possibly used women workers.

5.5 Labor Migration and US Hegemony

of producing this labor supply, i.e., the cost of nutrition, health care, schooling, etc.

Finally, the regimentation of braceros by the state and by the growers made these workers an almost ideal form of labor power. Being under the custody of US growers and railroad crew supervisors, braceros could be applied to work with greater efficiency than domestic labor, which had freedom of movement.[23] The rigid supervision minimized the development of activism among braceros.[24] One grower described bracero workers by saying "[W]e used to own slaves, now we rent them from the government" (quoted in Moquin and Van Doren 1971: 334). This level of almost total control of the workforce approached the working conditions of the sottoposti in the era of late medieval capitalism described in Chap. 2.

Agricultural and railroad corporations blamed a labor shortage due to the war for their demand for Mexican contract workers (Galarza 1977). This was partly true given that war industries paid higher wages than agricultural work and thus attracted some native workers away from the fields. But farming corporations had requested Mexican contract workers even before the US entered into the wars with Germany and Japan (Craig 1971). For corporate growers, a labor shortage did not necessarily mean an actual shortage of workers. It also could mean having to use higher-wage, native workers, a condition called by some growers "a fate worse than death" (Galarza 1977: 250). According to Reisler (1976: 82), "a labor shortage existed whenever [the growers] were unable to hire sufficient workers to harvest crops at the utmost speed and at the most efficacious moment for the lowest possible wages."

With the institutionalization of the bracero program in 1952 through Public Law 78, the Department of Labor became the prime contractor for braceros, giving the US government a greater share of the program's financial costs (Galarza 1977). The costs included the maintenance of US inspectors in Mexico, the maintenance of a contracting center in the United States, and the transportation of braceros. From 1952 to 1959, the Department of Labor spent $17.7 million on the program (Galarza 1964).

A total of 4.9 million braceros were contracted between 1942 and the end of the program in 1964 (Barrera 1979). As Table 5.4 indicates, the annual number of braceros contracted to work in the United States rose sharply in 1949 and reached almost half a million by the mid-1950s. The actual number of braceros working each year could be greater than the number contracted, since contract extensions and renewals are not included in the annual counts. On the other hand, some of

---

[23] The absence of US citizenship among braceros was a critical variable in this regard. In 1927, a California agricultural official comparing Mexicans to Puerto Rican workers, who are US citizens, characterized the critical difference as follows, "The Mexicans can be deported if they become county charges, but the others are here to stay and they are less efficient." (cited in García-Colón 2017: 143).

[24] Even under constant supervision bracero crews occasionally undertook work stoppages when they felt their treatment was unfair.

Table 5.4 Braceros contracted to work in the United States, 1942–1964

Year	Braceros contracted	Year	Braceros contracted
1942	4203	1954	310,476
1943	52,098	1955	390,846
1944	62,170	1956	444,581
1945	49,454	1957	450,422
1946	32,043	1958	418,885
1947	19,632	1959	447,535
1948	33,288	1960	427,240
1949	143,455	1961	294,149
1950	76,519	1962	282,566
1951	211,098	1963	195,450
1952	187,894	1964	181,738
1953	198,424		

Source Barrera (1979: 117)

the reported 4.9 million braceros were repeat migrants who participated in the program for several years, making the actual number of migrants smaller.

Initially, braceros were recruited in three centers located in Mexico City and two other interior cities. But under pressure from the United States, the Mexican government opened additional centers close to the US border during 1947–1954 (Garcia y Griego 1980). Braceros came from all parts of Mexico and included small farmers, ejido peasants, day laborers, sharecroppers, indigenous workers from southern Mexico, and taxi drivers, porters, and elevator operators from cities. The first timers were usually younger than 40 (Galarza 1977).

Except for 69,000 braceros that worked on railroads during World War II, the use of braceros was fairly limited to a small agricultural corporate sector located mainly in Texas, California, Arizona, New Mexico, and Arkansas (Craig 1971; Garcia y Griego 1980). For example, the almost 450,000 braceros contracted in 1959 were employed in less than 2% of all US farms (Craig 1971). While in the late 1950s, braceros constituted about one-fourth of the seasonal hired labor force in US agriculture, in the months that they were heavily imported they constituted over 90% of the workforces picking specific crops in certain areas of the country (Galarza 1964). This specialized use of bracero labor power in corporate farming fulfilled the 1947 recommendation of a special governor's committee in California that braceros should be used as "shock troops," i.e., "a flexible group which can be readily moved from operation to operation and from place to place...." (quoted in Galarza 1964: 55).

For agricultural capital, the bracero migratory labor system enabled important accomplishments by the time of the system's termination in 1964. By maintaining wages constant at levels that discouraged native workers, growers who contracted braceros were able to reduce operating costs by as much as one-half in some cases. For example, in beet farming, growers who used braceros reduced harvest

5.5 Labor Migration and US Hegemony

cost from $32 an acre to $13 (Galarza 1977). The increasing use of braceros, who became two-thirds of non-local harvesters in California in 1959 (Garcia y Griego 1980), undoubtedly also enabled corporate farmers to divert more capital to mechanization to reduce the need for labor. In the decade of the 1950s, the number of farmworkers underwent the greatest reduction—41%—of any ten-year period in US history (Craig 1971). With increasing productivity and new lands in cultivation, the farm dollar volume in the Fresno area (the recognized capital of agribusiness) increased from $44 million in 1940 to $381 million by 1960 (Galarza 1964). Mexican foreign migrant labor was at the base of this enormous capital accumulation, and for making agriculture the main US exporter.

The bracero program has been viewed as causing a surge of undocumented migration in the 1940s (Samora 1971). Mexican workers who sought to be recruited into the program and were not simply migrated on their own. Many other Mexican workers bypassed the recruitment centers and migrated to the United States on their own without visas. As the numbers of recruited braceros increased in the 1940s, the annual number of apprehended undocumented migrants at the US border rose from 11,300 in 1942 to 468,300 by 1950 (US DHS 2019: table 33).[25] In the early 1940s, Texas farmers probably hired more undocumented Mexicans than farmers in other states because, since the Mexican government prevented braceros from working in Texas, which the Mexican government perceived to be an anti-Mexican state (Garcia y Griego 1980). By 1954, the number of apprehended undocumented Mexicans through Operation Wetback exceed one million.[26]

Ironically, several years prior to Operation Wetback, US Border Patrol officers were involved in converting undocumented Mexican migrants into braceros. These were times when bracero negotiations between the United States and Mexico broke down, and the United States resorted to recruiting braceros on the US side of the border. During 1947–1950, almost a quarter of a million apprehended undocumented Mexican migrants were legalized and contracted as braceros (Garcia y Griego 1980). To recruit undocumented migrants into bracero workforces, the US Border Patrol opened entry points in several US border towns to invite undocumented migrants to cross over and be converted to braceros on the US side of the border. Sometimes Mexican police attempted to keep the migrants from crossing to the US side (Galarza 1964).

The defeat of Public Law 78 in Congress in 1964 did not end the seasonal migration of Mexican workers to work in US farms and in other workplaces. Instead, the end of the bracero program converted the legal flow of braceros into

---

[25] According to sociologist Mario Barrera (1979: 122), "The bracero program acted as a magnet drawing Mexican workers into the northern part of Mexico. When many were not accepted as braceros, they crossed the border anyway".

[26] The over one million apprehended Mexican migrants in 1954 represented the results of "Operation Wetback." The operation involved roundups of undocumented migrants in Mexican-origin communities by 800 Border Patrol officers and US military units (Garcia y Griego 1980).

even larger streams of unauthorized Mexican workers.[27] The post-bracero undocumented migration became a windfall resource for agricultural employers as the Mexican farm-labor supply grew, and as growers no longer had to comply with governmental regulations regarding the employment of foreign Mexican workers. Agribusiness had hired undocumented Mexican workers throughout the bracero program. In many corporate farms, undocumented Mexican migrants had worked alongside braceros (Galarza 1977). The president of the wealthy and powerful Imperial Valley Farmers Association in California commented on the extensive use of undocumented Mexican migrants in commercial farming during the bracero program: "Every farmer from Brownsville to San Diego uses these people" (quoted in Galarza 1964: 60). US farmers were protected against federal penalties for hiring undocumented migrant workers through a special bill passed in Congress in 1952.[28]

In addition to increasing the volume of unauthorized migrants from Mexico, the termination of the bracero program also promoted a shift in the nature of working-class Mexican migration to the United States. In contrast to the migration of individual men to rural areas in the bracero program, the undocumented migrant streams increasingly included families headed to urban areas (Cornelius et al. 1982; Browning and Rodriguez 1985). To be sure, Mexican immigrants had long been attracted by US urban labor markets, but the surge of unauthorized immigration after the bracero program ended accelerated the Mexican migration to urban areas. By 1970, 88% of all Mexican foreign-born in the country lived in urban areas (US Census Bureau 1970b: table 4).[29] Metropolitan areas throughout the Southwest and in the Midwest, and later in other regions, became principal destination points for undocumented Mexican migration. In the metropolitan areas such as Los Angeles, Chicago, and Houston, undocumented migrants often formed informal labor pools for daily hire given their lack of legal status. Their labor power supported economies and the professional and technical workforces of monopoly capital through such industries as construction, landscaping, personal and business services, and food-related industries. Without legal status, undocumented Mexican migrants remained a vulnerable, exploitable sector in the segmented metropolitan labor markets where they labored.

---

[27] In 1964, when the bracero program ended, fewer than 100,000 undocumented Mexican migrants were apprehended, but by the early 1970s the number reached half a million (US 2010S 2010: table 33).

[28] The congressional bill was known as the Texas Proviso, since the Texas congressional delegation introduced the bill to protect employers, especially farmers, who hired undocumented workers from facing charges of harboring unauthorized migrants. Basically, the message of the bill was that, while it was against the law to be undocumented, it was not against the law to hire the undocumented.

[29] Mexican foreign-born constituted 18% of the 4.5 million Mexican-origin population in the country in 1970.

5.5.4 Jamaican Temporary Workers

A year after the start of the Bracero Program, the US government began the recruitment of temporary workers from the British West Indies (BWI) in a plan to use this seasonal labor for the years 1943–1947. Much smaller than the contemporaneous bracero program of Mexican workers, the BWI program imported temporary migrant labor from the Caribbean primarily to work on US farms on the East Coast (Hahamovitch 2001). As with the bracero program, the justification for the BWI labor importation program was that the wars with Germany and Japan had created a labor shortage for US farmers. Men and women from Barbados were the first workers to arrive under the BWI program, but Jamaican men soon followed and in larger numbers.[30] Similar to the bracero program, the US government became the official contractor of the imported Caribbean workers, which were distributed to eligible farms. Six to seven thousand Jamaican workers concentrated annually in harvest work in apple and sugar-cane farms on the East Coast, with smaller numbers of workers from Barbados, Dominica, St. Lucia, and St. Vincent (Griffith 1986).

While the bracero program of Mexican workers was terminated in 1964, the importation of Jamaican and other Caribbean workers for agricultural work in the United States continued beyond the planned termination date of 1947 and into the present. The US government continued the importation of BWI labor first by allowing employers to contract directly with the workers and later by creating a temporary agricultural worker visa, the H-2 visa,[31] through the Immigration and Nationality Act of 1952. Historically US government officials attempted to reduce the number of imported Jamaican workers by promoting domestic workers as suitable for agricultural work or by offering to import workers from Puerto Rico, but East Coast farmers steadfastly refused alternative sources of labor (Griffith 1986). Through fights in the courts and lobbying efforts in Congress, East Coast farmers have managed to keep the seasonal Jamaican workforce of temporary workers. Nonetheless, the temporary importation of Jamaican workers has not mushroomed since its inception in 1943 in the way the bracero program did into several hundreds of thousands annually before it was terminated. By 2020, the number of imported Jamaican "temporary workers and family members" stood at 12,182, down from 19,198 in 2019 (US DHS 2022: table 28, 2020: table 28).

Similar to many braceros who were imported from Mexico, Jamaican and other BWI workers are seen as attractive labor by US farmers because they come from a foreign peasant background spent in low-income or poverty conditions. As foreigners, imported workers can be deported from the United States. As peasants they have a semiproletarian status in which they work spans of four to six months for capital and still keep their peasant social and economic resources for survival

---

[30] Only men were recruited in the Jamaican program.
[31] The H-2 visa was later changed to H2A for agricultural work and H2B for non-agricultural work.

during spells of non-wage work. For US employers this helps to lessen the pressure from workers for higher wages or collective bargaining because only part of the workers' total income comes from wage labor and wage labor is only part of their work life. For the workers, peasant status also means having a peasant household where other family members such as spouses and children can work in household agriculture when the H2A worker is away working in the United States, which helps maintain household production. The household labor arrangement also increases stability and security of the peasant family household. If temporary work in the United States is reduced or suspended, such as because of a crop failure due to a natural disaster, the family household can endure until H2A work in the United States returns.

An increase in stability and security may not necessarily mean upward social mobility because the wages of H2A work are simply not high enough to elevate working families into a higher-class status. H2A wages increase survivability and material status but do not necessarily transform the class of imported temporary workers. For this reason, many of the Jamaican H2A workers stay in the program of temporary labor importation for years.

5.6 Analysis

In the four sections that follow, I use conditions of internal migration in the United States and labor migration from Mexico during US hegemony to discuss the four perspectives presented in Chap. 1: (a) class relations between capital and labor, (b) technological change, (c) the economic cycle, and (d) the state. The section attempts to demonstrate the role of the migration patterns within capitalist development during US hegemony in the world-system.

5.7 Class Relations

Internal migration in Britain during the period of British hegemony served capital to displace artisan workers, by the time of US hegemony, however, negotiations and collective bargain became the mode for solving tensions between industrial capital and labor (Cleaver 1979). In the auto plants of Detroit, in the steel mills of Pittsburg and Chicago, and in other industrial areas, capital met labor's demands with negotiation and collective bargaining, and usually not by replacing industrial workers with internal migrants or foreign workers, with the exception of agricultural production. Nevertheless, internal migration enabled monopoly capital in the United States to restructure spatially in metropolitan areas. Especially beginning in the 1940s, working families migrated to central cities and suburban rings to take jobs in the corporate centers of administration and production in large urban areas.

Yet, the internal migration to metropolitan areas did not have equal outcomes for Whites and racial minority workers. Whites accessed better work and living conditions in the suburbs, as the majorities of African Americans and Mexican

Americans settled in less prosperous labor markets in central cities. On the surface, this differentiation appeared as a function of a disparity in human capital, given that Whites had significantly higher educational levels than the racial minorities. But lower educational levels for African Americans and Mexican Americans were mainly a function of generations of racial exclusion from educational systems equal in quality to those that Whites accessed (Feagin 2006; Telles and Ortiz 2008). The disadvantaged conditions of Black and Latino metropolitan working classes that concentrated mainly in central cities had been produced by White-controlled society through a history of institutional exclusion.

Racial differentiation of working populations in metropolitan areas represented a repeat of capital's use of segmented labor forces to organize work. In the previous two periods of hegemony, this was illustrated by European colonial uses of African slaves in the Americas and by the use of Irish immigrants to do the undesirable jobs during Britain's Industrial Revolution.[32] While internal migration to urban areas outside the South did not bring social equality for African Americans, it did produce some degree of economic improvement relative to Whites. By the end of US hegemony in the late 1960s, African American families living outside the South had larger family incomes as a percentage of White incomes than in the South. The percentages that African American median family income represented of White income, by region, were Northeast—65%, North Central—77%, West—74%, and South—54% (Perlo 1975). Mexican American incomes also varied by region. As described above, Mexican Americans working in northern and western metropolitan areas gained higher salaries and wages than those who remained in southern metropolitan areas. In the final analysis, during US hegemony internal labor migration kept racial minorities in segmented labor forces with unequal opportunities compared with Whites, but it also brought some racial minorities a degree of economic mobility compared to the racial minorities who remained in southern metropolitan areas.

The use of Mexican migrant labor by capital in the agricultural sector during the era of US hegemony was a different story from what happened in the metropolitan areas. Agricultural employers claimed they need braceros because of a labor shortage create by World War II, but continual union organizing attempts among farm workers undoubtedly affected the employers' demand for foreign workers. In California, bracero workers were imported into settings that had experienced unionization attempts that at times created crises for agricultural capital. Historically, the agricultural sector remained among the least organized industry in the country (Galarza 1964). The powerlessness of farm workers was partly related to their migratory nature (which made it difficult to unionize), and to state policies that favored agricultural employers in matters of farm-labor employment, including the use of foreign workers. Seasonal migration to the United States gave

---

[32] The relationship between capital accumulation and racial minority group status among workers has led to concepts of "racial capitalism" (Robinson 2000; also see Cox 1959; Du Bois 1989). Social prejudice was so strong against the Irish in Britain and in the United States in the nineteenth century as to depict them as racially different from other Whites (Mac an Ghaill 2000).

braceros better working opportunities, but only relative to poor economic conditions in Mexico. Constrained by contract regulations, braceros did not even have the freedom to select their employers (Galarza 1964).[33]

By the time of the implementation of the bracero program in 1942, California agriculture had a history of labor strife that went back to at least the 1880s (Meister and Loftis 1977). The labor movement advanced in agriculture in 1915 when the newly formed Agricultural Workers Organization of the Industrial Workers of the World sent organizers among migrant workers in several states to better working conditions (Foner 1975b). By 1933, communists and other radicals organized a strike in California by more than 10,000 cannery and agricultural workers for almost four weeks. The strike threatened the state's cotton crop valued at over $50 million (Chacon 1980). With the formation of several unions of Mexican immigrant workers, California growers experienced over 140 strikes in the 1930s (Reisler 1976).

During the 1940s and 1950s, when the US government launched a series of efforts to counter the US labor movement,[34] the National Farm Labor Union (NFLU) organized and conducted strikes in areas of California's agribusiness. A leader of the NFLU described the reaction of agribusiness to this activism as follows: "By the end of 1952 it had become clear... that the corporate farmers against whom most of the action had been directed had organized a formidable deterrent to unionization, the 'bracero' system...." (Galarza 1977: xi). The US bracero agreement with Mexico did not permit braceros to be used as strikebreakers. But US growers did not always follow the agreement.[35]

An examination of the labor market impact of the bracero program in the seven states where most of the braceros worked found that it had reduced domestic farmworker employment and reduced farm wages (Morgan and Gardner 1982). The wage loss to non-bracero farm workers amounted to $139 million per year (in 1977 dollars). Through the program, US farmers hired 120,000 more workers at 15–20 cents less per hour than would have been hired without the program.[36]

In addition to serving agricultural employers, in the larger economy undocumented Mexican migrants also served corporate capital directly until the Immigration Reform and Control Act (IRCA) of 1986 outlawed the hiring of undocumented migrant labor. Undocumented migrant labor is associated with the low-paying occupations of the informal secondary labor market sector more than with the

---

[33] For a discussion on "unfreedom" among migrant workers in managed migration see Polanco (2019).
[34] The efforts included the Labor-Management Relations Act, the Communist Control Act, and Congressional committee investigations. McCarthyism and the Red Scare of the 1950s served as the background for some of these measures.
[35] In one strike by farm workers in California in 1947, more than 100 braceros were kept working for weeks with the help of federal and local law enforcement agents. The braceros were removed only after transients and undocumented workers were hired to continue the work (Galarza 1977).
[36] Given the financial benefit the bracero program provided for farmers, braceros were seen as a substitute for mechanization (Levine 2004).

5.7 Class Relations

formal primary sector. But there were moments during US hegemony when corporate capital in urban areas directly hired undocumented migrant workers, such as in times of economic transitions in the economy. Shortly after the end of US hegemony, for example, automobile parts suppliers in the Los Angeles metropolitan area experienced an economic depression and turned to undocumented migrant labor as a transitional strategy to restructure the automobile parts industry (Morales 1983). Facing international competition and economic decline, automobile parts assemblers and suppliers turned to undocumented labor to have labor flexibility as working conditions, including wages, declined, and as thousands of higher-paid workers lost their jobs during the economic downturn of the industry.

Undocumented migrant labor offered employers a means to deal with difficult economic times in an easier manner than with domestic labor. Normally, undocumented migrant labor was not protected by union contracts, and, having unauthorized status, undocumented workers could not completely defend their jobs because they were vulnerable to deportation. Not all corporate employers, however, were attracted to undocumented labor for its vulnerability and lack of power during the pre-IRCA years. For some corporate employers, a principal attraction was the self-regulation of undocumented workers. Undocumented migrant workers use a host of informal social networks of friends, kin, and compatriots to secure employment (Flores-Yeffal 2013), and sometimes undocumented workers use their informal networks to increase efficiency in their workplaces. This mutual support among workers reduced the management concerns of employers (Browning and Rodriguez 1985; Waldinger and Lichter 2003).[37]

After the implementation of IRCA, undocumented Mexican labor continued to serve corporate capital, but mainly in an indirect mode. Many undocumented migrants found jobs with contractors who provided business services to corporations. These services included cleaning office buildings, cleaning parking lots, maintaining landscapes in commercial properties, working in food services for corporate office workers, etc. Thousands of undocumented migrants also found work in providing informal personal services to middle-class and upper middle-class households. Still other undocumented migrants found jobs in a second tier of the secondary sector of the labor market—in ethnic workplaces such as ethnic restaurants, bakeries, and car repair shops in immigrant neighborhoods (Light 2006). While many undocumented migrants did not work in the workplaces of corporate capital, they worked in formal and informal enterprises that supported, directly or indirectly, the professional and technical workforces of corporate capital.

By the end of the era of US hegemony, African Americans and Mexican Americans dependent on the inferior employment conditions of the competitive sector

---

[37] The informal network benefits of undocumented migrant workers include recruiting more workers when needed, coordinating and covering for each other when a worker needs to return home, playing double work roles when a worker falls ill, etc. This coordination comes from informal group solidarity, but also from the concern that a co-worker does not lose her or his job due to a personal or family emergency.

in central cities were experiencing unemployment rates about twice as high as that of White workers and a sub-employment rate of over 20% (Feagin 1978).

5.8 Technological Development

By the time of US hegemony, the relationship between migration and the degradation of skilled work, which characterized the Industrial Revolution in Britain, was practically non-existent in the United States. Artisanship had largely disappeared in US production for the mass market by the 1960s. By 1965, only 13% of the US labor force was classified as craft and kindred workers (US Census Bureau 1968: table 324).

A new technological development that grew during the period of US hegemony was automation and mechanization to replace or reduce the labor needed for production. By the 1960s, technological development was significant enough to concerns social scientists that it would enhance the social stratification of African Americans as automation and mechanization would reduce the demand for unskilled and semi-skilled labor (Broom and Glenn 1965). From this perspective, Black migrants from the South would find diminished job markets in northern industrial districts, even if Black education and job skills increased. Indeed, all manual labor would be affected by the growing technological development.

In the 1960s, as US hegemony was drawing to an end, and as the high-tech industry of Silicon Valley was taking shape, the relationship that developed between migration and automation and high-tech development was not the displacement of labor, but the use of labor for low-skill support for the emerging high-tech workforce. The migrant labor in the budding Silicon Valley in the 1960s included immigrant workers doing low-skill work, especially women who did cleaning and other service jobs in high-tech computer and software firms and in academic institutions (Matthews 2003). Undocumented migrants also worked in food industries catering to high-tech workforces.

Another movement that brought decreasing opportunities in northern job markets was the migration of manufacturing firms away from unionized and higher-wage labor in northern industrial areas to southern labor markets with lower wages and fewer labor unions, and with open-shop laws. Northern industries migrated from urban areas with more than half a century of class struggle by organized labor to areas in the south that had a pro-business climate and right-to-work laws. To gain jobs, southern local governments often enticed northern manufacturers through tax abatements and construction of commercial infrastructure at taxpayers' expense. Rather than taking the costly path of automation and remaining in northern urban centers of organized labor, many manufacturing firms such as in textile, apparel, and furniture production decided to migrate to friendlier business environments in the southern United States (Gordon 1977; Newman 1983).

Plant closings and corporate relocations in northern regions of the country had greater impacts on minority workers than on White workers. A study of Illinois for the years 1975–1978 found that the percentage of Black, Hispanic, Asian and other

5.8 Technological Development

minority workers who lost their jobs because of plant closings and relocations was greater than the percentage the groups represented in the general population. When firms relocated from central cities to suburbs, the employment decline for minorities was also greater for racial minorities than for Whites (Squires 1984).[38]

With the help of the Mexican government, some US manufacturing firms applied a new spatial technology to increase capital accumulation in the 1960s. The technology was the "twin plants" approach to production through the Border Industrialization Program (BIP) in Mexico. The Mexican government created the program in 1965 to attract foreign manufacturers to Mexican border towns. BIP gave foreign manufacturers, mostly from the United States, duty-free importation of manufacturing materials and machinery for production of export products (Ericson 1970). In the twin-plant approach, US manufacturers kept administrative and storage facilities on the US side of the border, and factories on the Mexican side.

The key benefit of the *maquiladora* program (as it came to be known) for foreign manufacturers was having access to the low-wage labor of Mexico. Workers in the *maquilas* came from Mexican border towns and from interior areas of Mexico (Davila and Saenz 1990). The often harsh and repetitive working conditions of the maquila assembly plants, which hired many young women (Fernández Kelly 1983; Peña 1997), were reminiscent of the working conditions of young women in the British factories of the Industrial Revolution. By 1970, some 160 maquiladoras, mainly US-owned, were participating in BIP, paying the Mexican workforces daily wages of US$1.40 to $3.20 (Ericson 1970). Even at the high point of $3.20 per day, the wages paid by the maquilas to Mexican workers were 88% less than the average daily wages of US manufacturing workers in 1970, whose earnings averaged $3.36 per hour (US Census Bureau 1971: table 353).

While mechanization opened a path to manufacturing work for unskilled labor in the Industrial Revolution, during the US period of hegemony the advance of mechanization drastically reduce the amount of unskilled labor in some industries. The agricultural sector was a prime example of this technological development. New tractors and combine harvesters played a major role in raising US agricultural productivity to unprecedented heights during 1940–1970 (Moore and Simon 1999). Agricultural productivity rose as the number of farmworkers declined dramatically, and as the presence of machines increased in the agricultural fields. In cotton farming, which was highly labor-intensive, the cotton harvest done by combine pickers rose from 8% in 1950 to 96% in the late 1960s (Runsten and LeVeen 1981; Ganzel 2007). Each combine machine replaced about 80 manual harvest workers, and equipped with lights they could operate into the night hours.

---

[38] According to the study, minorities accounted for 20% of employment in firms that closed down compared to 14% of the statewide labor force. Firms relocating from central cities to suburbs accounted for almost 20% of job loss for minorities, but less than 10% of job loss for Whites (Squires 1984). On the other hand, minorities gain jobs when they are hired for jobs from which White workers retire.

5.9 The Economic Cycle

As proposed in earlier chapters, workers are attracted to areas undergoing an economic upturn with the hopes of finding jobs and obtaining material benefits of prosperity. During an economic upturn, employers find immigrant workers attractive because these workers add to the labor supply, which can retard wage increases in some industries, and fill jobs that native workers shun or abandon for better paying ones. In addition, some employers find migrant workers desirable in business upturns because as outsiders these workers may impede labor solidarity.

The post-World War II period of US hegemony involved a slow but steady upturn in the country's Gross Domestic Product. Four brief recessions occurred by 1960, but they were considered mild, as unemployment stayed below 8% of the labor force (US Bureau of Labor Statistics 2021). By the 1960s, some economists believed that serious economic depressions and recessions were extinct phenomena in the "New Economics" of government stabilization policies (Gordon 1969).

For migrants to cities and metropolitan areas, migration was a means to seek opportunity in the centers of economic growth. But not all migrants shared a similar opportunity structure. African American migrants responded more sharply to changes and regional variations in economic opportunity than did White migrants, but African Americans were more often looking for work, while Whites looked for specific jobs (Tilly 1979). As the Irish who migrated to industrial England in the nineteenth century, the racial minorities who migrated to US urban centers mostly found lower-status jobs. By the 1940s, with the new labor relations based on collective bargaining, manufacturing corporations had little need of migrant labor to retard wage increases or break union strikes.

Agricultural production was a major exception to the collective bargaining accord of labor relations. Corporate growers used bracero labor and undocumented Mexican migrants to pay lower wages and oppose unionization in the fields (Galarza 1964; 1977). The use of Mexican migrant labor must be factored into the rise of realized gross income in US agricultural production from $8.4 billion in 1940 to $18.4 billion in 1967 (US Census Bureau 1969: table 914). In the same time period, the percentage of gross income spent on hired waged labor dropped by half, from 30% in 1940 to 16% in 1967. Bracero labor was a benefit for the agricultural industry, but there is no indication that the use of this labor was associated with business cycles, since the labor was regulated by a treaty with Mexico.

Many other immigrants besides Mexicans came to the United States during the US period of hegemony. From 1941 to 1967, 2.4 million persons from outside the Western Hemisphere were admitted as quota immigrants, and from 1948 to 1967 738,336 persons were admitted as displaced persons and refugees (US Census Bureau 1969: table 123; 1968: table 130). The newcomers from outside the Western Hemisphere consisted of different groups (German ethnics, orphans, brides, etc.), and professional, technical, and other office workers usually composed the largest numbers. In his analysis of post-World War II immigration to the United States, demographer Ernest Rubin concluded as follows: "It is perhaps the

5.9 The Economic Cycle

most artificial type of immigration to the United States that has come since the founding of the country. The fraction of immigration that is responsive to cyclical movements in the American economy is scarcely discernable" (Rubin 1958: 144). According to Rubin (1958), after the end of World War II, the basis of immigration policy shifted from economic considerations to political ones.

Economic downturns can pressure foreign workers to return to the home country for different reasons. One reason is that foreign workers may decide to survive an economic recession in their home country, where resources are familiar and visa status is not an issue (Wheatley 2017; Greene 2017). The driver of return migration can be the slowdown of industries, or the weakening of domestic labor during a recession, making foreign workers less attractive to employers as an alternative labor supply. A second reason is that foreign workers may come to be viewed as usurpers of scarce jobs that domestic workers need, and thus the government will act to deport foreign labor that lacks authorization (Hoffman 1974; Acuña 1981).

The deportation of over 400,000 Mexican immigrants in the decade prior to the rise of US hegemony illustrates the second reason. With increasing widespread unemployment in the Great Depression, the US government focused on undocumented Mexican immigrants to lessen the economic crisis of the country. Several bills were introduced in Congress to further reduce immigration quotas during the depression, and one bill sought unsuccessfully to impose quotas for Mexicans, whom agricultural lobbyists had successfully kept out of the quota system (Acuña 1981; Rodríguez and Hagan 2016).

US government officials took a "send-the-Mexican-back-to-Mexico" approach to address the growing unemployment problem of the depression (Acuña 1981). Federal officials estimated that undocumented immigrants were holding 400,000 jobs that US citizens needed (Hoffman 1976). The massive removal program began in 1931, and over 458,000 immigrants with their US-born children were repatriated to Mexico voluntarily or through deportation. Local authorities in the Southwest and the Midwest aided in the Mexican removal. Public welfare officials were favorable to the idea of deporting Mexicans in order to lower the strain on public relief resources. By one calculation concerning Los Angeles County in California, it cost the county $77,249.29 to repatriate one trainload of Mexicans, but it saved $347,468.41 in relief costs (McWilliams 1968). While some business groups worried about the loss of Mexican labor (Acuña 1981), corporate farmers likely felt that their labor supply was secure, given the thousands of unemployed farmers from economically depressed and drought-stricken US farm areas who were looking for work (Galarza 1977).

Operation Wetback, undertaken by the US government during US hegemony, was another massive US expulsion of Mexican migrant labor. US government agencies assisted by military units apprehended and returned to Mexico over one million undocumented Mexicans in 1954 (García 1980).[39] The large-scale roundup of undocumented Mexicans received wide public support, including from Mexican American leaders who viewed undocumented Mexican immigrants as contributing to the social problems of Mexican Americans (Allsup 1982). In terms of the economic cycle in the background, Operation Wetback occurred during a two-year rise in the unemployment rate of non-agricultural industry, from a rate of 3.4 in 1953 to 6.7 in 1954 (US Department of Commerce 1976), but the country did not undergo a sharp recession. Sales and profits of the largest 500 corporations, which formed the backbone of the national economy, steadily climbed in the 1950s (Seltzer 1978).[40]

An argument can be offered that Operation Wetback was launched during a period of general prosperity because of the need to maintain the integrity of the US border with Mexico. But the widespread hiring of undocumented Mexican workers—for which employers received protection from Congress through the Texas Proviso—did not indicate that the integrity of the border was an overriding concern. Moreover, in times when bracero negotiations broke down between the US and Mexican governments, the Border Patrol welcomed undocumented Mexican migrants to convert them into braceros on the US side of the border.

Public anti-immigrant sentiments fueled by newspaper depictions of undocumented Mexicans as "dangerous, malicious, and subversive" must have influenced the decision to undertake Operation Wetback (Acuña 1981:156). The apprehension of over 20,000 undocumented Mexican migrants in industrial jobs in large cities during the operation indicated that undocumented Mexican labor had developed a public visibility outside rural areas or traditional ethnic districts (Samora 1971). The context of large urban labor markets placed undocumented Mexicans more out in the open than in agricultural fields, making them easier targets for scapegoating and restrictionist demands. The widespread support for Operation Wetback demonstrated that in the policy spaces of the public sphere, non-economic factors such as anti-immigrant sentiments could affect the expulsion of migrant labor beyond the effects of economic cycles.

5.10 The State

More than was done by the Dutch and British governments in the previous two periods of hegemony, the US government played a major role in assisting the

---

[39] US border enforcement had been growing since the mid-1940s when the Mexican government complained that lax US border enforcement was causing Mexico to lose workers to the United States (Lytle Hernández 2010).

[40] From Mandel's (1978) long-wave perspective, the 1950s were part of a boom period in a long wave of economic prosperity from 1940/45 to 1966 that entered a downturn in the late 1960s. The 1950s contributed to a 5.2% annual growth in industrial output during 1940–1967. This rate of industrial production growth had been surpassed only in the industrial takeoffs of the mid-1800s and the early 1900s (Mandel 1978).

migration of capital and labor in the US period of hegemony. One reason for the difference was simply that US government had much greater resources to allot in society and across world regions, including the Marshall plan to help rebuild Europe after World War II. After achieving decisive victories at the end of World War II, the United States gained superpower status and ascended to hegemony in the world-system. The government enjoyed the economic capacity to undertake major development projects abroad and in US society. Using power and resources, the government supported US capitalist expansion abroad, the restructuring of labor forces in US urban centers, the acquisition of foreign labor for US agriculture, and the social incorporation of undocumented migrants in the country.

One way the United States supported US capitalist expansion was by countering opposition abroad to US capitalist interests and by containing the spread of communist influence (real or imagined) in regions of the world-economy. Often the search for profits and the fight against communism were one and the same (Magdoff 1978). Countering opposition abroad involved supporting foreign authoritarian governments, and at times supporting the overthrow of foreign governments (Menjívar and Rodríguez 2005). These actions included supporting a coup of the elected government in Syria in 1949 when the government was slow to support US business interests in the country (Wilford 2013), supporting the removal of the democratically elected government of Iran to install a pro-Western government leader in 1953 (Kinzer 2003), and organizing the overthrow of the democratic government of Guatemala in 1954 when the government passed policies to help poor workers and peasants, which the United States viewed as working against US business interests in that country (Schlesinger and Kinzer 1983).

The United States government was no less supportive of capitalist development in the home front. As monopoly capital took shape in the metropolitan areas of US society, the US government supported urban redevelopment and housing construction projects for new business enterprises and working-class settlements. Federal urban renewal grants gave cities massive federal funds to rebuilt downtowns for businesses as out-migration to the suburbs by mainly Whites had left blighted areas in central cities. Federal legislation enacted in 1949, 1954, and later paid for much of the redevelopment construction. The Federal Housing Administration provided loans to help Whites, but not Blacks, buy houses in the suburbs, since the agency maintained a policy of segregation (Capps 2015). Thus, the federal government helped large corporations of monopoly capital restructure in metropolitan areas by funding improvements in central cities for businesses and supporting housing for suburban workforces, which grew significantly from internal migration.

It was in the bracero program where the US government directly participated in organizing labor migration to US industries. On the insistence of the Mexican government, the US government became the official employer of the temporary migrants, who by the late 1950s numbered 450,000 per year. The farmers' association of the American Farm Bureau performed many of the administrative functions in the program, as did the few railroad companies that also hired braceros. To be sure, given that braceros were restricted mainly to agricultural work, the government's involvement did not signify a new guest-worker policy for US employers as occurred in Western Europe after the war. The bracero program was derived from the strong influence of the agricultural lobby in Congress. Moreover, agricultural capital assured government officials that Mexican migrant workers were a temporary workforce that would return to Mexico after the harvests, or that could be deported at any time (Rodríguez and Hagan 2016). Nonetheless, the bracero program did serve as a model for H-2 programs that followed in which private firms took on the management of imported temporary workers (Hernández-León et al. 2022).

While the United States did not take a hard turn to a guest-worker program of foreign workers during its period of hegemony, the same was not true of countries in western Europe. After World War II, several, western European governments launched programs during 1945 to 1974 to recruit foreign workers for postwar rebuilding and to sustain a postwar boom. US capital investment in western European industries partly affected the need for foreign labor. The postwar programs brought a new labor migration system in western European countries in terms of the sizes of the recruited workforces, the widespread use of foreign labor, and the span of areas from which foreign workers were recruited (Castles and Kosack 1973).[41] In addition to guest workers, workers from former colonies, refugees, and clandestine migrants joined the migrant streams to the labor markets of western Europe.

The German Federal Republic had the most organized government recruitment program, reaching a total foreign population in the country of 4.0 million by the 1970s (Castels 1986). Germany recruited men and women guest workers in Mediterranean countries, in Spain, Greece, Turkey, Morocco, Portugal, Tunisia, and Yugoslavia. In the 1970s, the "oil-crisis" recession, the tendency of temporary guest workers to develop a permanent presence, and the growth of the foreign-worker population in western European countries partly through family reunification led countries to end guest-worker recruitment (Castles 1986). Some countries had already ended their recruitment a few years earlier.

While the US government did not develop a major official guest-worker program besides the bracero program, the country did have a large-scale immigration of undocumented Mexican workers, many of whom migrated temporarily for seasonal work. After the end of the bracero program in 1964, the number of undocumented migrants apprehended at the US southwestern border increased from 110,371 in 1965 to 1,097,739 in 1976 (USDHS 2019: table 33).

Many undocumented migrants were apprehended multiple times in a year, but the more than one million count in 1976 meant that many thousands were migrating into the country. This amounted to a revolving-door enforcement practice especially when enforcement was increased in the interior of the country. Researchers estimated the size of the undocumented foreign-born population in the United States to be between 2.5 and 3.5 million by the 1980 census (Bouvier

---

[41] A few, prewar guest worker programs had existed in some areas of western Europe, but these early programs did not have the size and intensity of the postwar programs (Castles 1986).

and Gardner 1986). After years of congressional deliberations on how to respond to growing undocumented immigration from Mexico, the US government chose not to repeat the repatriation campaigns of the Great Depreciation and Operation Wetback, nor to enact a guest-worker program for temporary workers as was done in western Europe. Instead, in 1986 the government offered amnesty and legalization through IRCA to undocumented migrants who had been in the country for at least five years, and for at least 90 days in the previous year for agricultural workers (González Baker 1990). To close the labor market for undocumented migrants, the new policy also brought penalties against employers who hired undocumented workers. Across the country, 2.7 million undocumented migrants, mainly Mexicans, received amnesty and legalization.

5.11 Conclusion

Capital and labor migration contributed significantly to the development of US hegemony. But as I have attempted to demonstrate, it did so in a manner that was different than in the previous two periods of hegemony. In contrast to the Dutch and British periods of hegemony, in which capital migrated to create new zones of capital penetration, especially in colonial areas, in the US period of hegemony US capital mainly circulated to regions that were already participating in the world-economy, although at different levels and lengths of time. The Soviet Union, mainland China, and their allies were major exceptions to this world circulation of US capital. Regarding labor migration, the principal pattern of migration sustaining US economic development during hegemony was internal urban migration. This migration involved more than movement to cities and towns, as occurred in England during the Industrial Revolution. The labor migration to urban areas was mainly to metropolitan centers. It was a population movement connected to the spatial restructuring of monopoly capital in metropolitan central cities and suburban rings. By the late 1960s, almost three-fourths of the US population resided in urban areas, and nearly 70% of urban dwellers lived in metropolitan areas. Other core, semiperipheral, and peripheral areas of the world-economy experienced similar trends of urbanization in this period.

Within the internal migration to metropolitan areas, African Americans, Mexican Americans, and other racial minority groups settled predominantly in central cities where they took jobs mainly in manual occupations. The internal migration of racial minorities to central cities in metropolitan areas was a repeat of migration conditions in the Dutch and British periods of hegemony in which racially different, or perceived racially different, groups were used to segment labor forces in areas of production in the world-system. Non-White or ethnically different groups were used to do the hardest work for the lowest pay, or for no pay at all. The examples include the use of enslaved African workers and coerced indigenous peoples in Dutch plantations and other European-controlled work sites of harsh and often dangerous labor in the Caribbean and Latin American region, and Irish men and women employed in low-status jobs during British industrialization.

While the United States did not follow the path of western Europe in developing a postwar guest-worker program for different industries, it did develop with Mexico a temporary labor importation program for agricultural work that by the late 1950s was importing more than 400,000 braceros per year. The bracero program was a fine-tuning of labor migration by agricultural capital and the state. It was a human version of the "just-in-time" production system adopted by some manufacturers later in the twentieth century. This system increased manufacturing efficiency and reduced waste and inventory costs by receiving materials for production just as they are needed by the production schedule (Sayer 1986). In a similar manner, the braceros were imported just as they were needed for the harvest and then sent back to Mexico (although braceros were such a good bargain that some farmers kept them longer). Yet, Mexican migrants eventually broke with the bracero model when it was terminated and developed large patterns of autonomous, undocumented migration into the country. This new pattern of large-scale autonomous migration brought about settlement conditions that the proponents of the bracero program never intended, i.e., an amnesty and legalization program through which millions of Mexicans became permanent residents and eventually many also became citizens.

From the world-system perspective, the temporary use of peripheral labor in core countries represented an additional advantage to be gained from peripheral and semiperipheral areas, apart from the advantage of using these areas as investment regions to exploit raw materials and other products. The additional advantage for core countries was using less-developed and subordinated regions as labor reserves from which to draw temporary labor as needed. By the late twentieth century, this structural benefit drawn by core countries from the periphery and semiperiphery would include high-skill professional and technical labor.

The bracero program stimulated a parallel clandestine migration of thousands and eventually millions of undocumented Mexican workers that spread widely across US labor-intensive industries. In contrast to the importation of individual bracero workers, undocumented Mexican migration included women, children, and whole families, and the destination points were often the labor markets of large urban centers. The autonomous migration of undocumented migrants from Mexico, and later from other countries, acted against the state designs of regulated, temporary worker importations. Autonomous migration in family units transferred the cost of the reproduction of the foreign-born labor power to the US side of the border. Among individual undocumented migrants, the strategy was to work in the United States to remit money back home to improve their families' quality of life. The survival strategy of autonomous migration indicated that working-class communities in peripheral and semiperipheral countries had elevate their struggles for survival to the spatial level of the world-system by migrating across nation-state borders without authorization.

References

Acuña, Rodolfo. 1981. *Occupied America: A History of Chicanos*. New York: Harper & Row.
Allsup, Carl. 1982. *The American G. I. Forum*. Austin: University of Texas Press.
Arrighi, Giovanni. 2010. *The Long Twentieth Century: Money, Power and the Origins of Our Times*. New York: Verso.
Aviel, David, and JoAnn B. Aviel. 1982. American Investments in Mexico. *Management International Review* 22 (1): 83–96.
Balán, Jorge, Harley L. Browning, and Elizabeth Jelin. 1973. *Men in Developing Society: Geographic and Social Mobility in Monterrey, Mexico*. Austin: University of Texas Press.
Barnet, Richard J., and Ronald E. Muller. 1974. *Global Reach: The Power of the Multinational Corporations*. New York: Simon and Schuster.
Barrera, Mario. 1979. *Race and Class in the Southwest: A Theory of Racial Inequality*. Notre Dame: University Press.
Berry, Brian J. L., and John D. Kasarda. 1977. *Contemporary Urban Ecology*. New York: Macmillian.
Blauner, Robert. 1972. *Racial Oppression in America*. New York: Harper & Row.
Bogue, D.J. 1959. *The Population of the United States*. Glencoe, Illinois: The Free Press.
Bonnen, J. 1972. The Effect of Taxes and Government Spending on Inequality. In *The Capitalist System*, ed. Richard C. Edwards, Michael Reich, and Thomas E. Weisskopf, 235–243. Englewood Cliffs, N. J.: Prentice-Hall.
Bouvier, Leon F., and Robert W. Gardner. 1986. Immigration to the U.S.: The Unfinished Story. *Population Bulletin* 41 (4): 3–50.
Briggs, Vernon M., Jr. 2004. Guestworker Programs Lessons from the Past and Warnings for the Future. Cornell University IRL School, DigitalCommons@ILR. Accessed May 30, 2020. https://digitalcommons.ilr.cornell.edu/cgi/viewcontent.cgi?article=1021&context=briggstestimonies.
Broom, Leonard, and Norval Glenn. 1965. *Transformation of the Negro American*. New York: Harper & Row.
Browning, Harley L., and Nestor Rodriguez. 1985. The Migration of Mexican Indocumentados as a Settlement Process: Implications for Work. In *Hispanics in the U.S. Economy*, edited by George Borjas and Marta Tienda, 277–292. New York: Academic Press.
Burawoy, M. 1976. The Functions and Reproduction of Migrant Labor: Comparative Material from Southern Africa and the United States. *American Journal of Sociology* 81: 1050–1087.
Capps, Kriston. 2015. How the Federal Government Built White Suburbia. CityLab, September 2. Accessed May 15, 2020. https://www.citylab.com/equity/2015/09/how-the-federal-government-built-white-suburbia/403321/
Cardenas, Gilbert. 1978. Los Desarraigados: Chicanos in the Midwestern Region of the United States. *Aztlan* 7 (2): 153–186.
Cardoso, Lawrence A. 1980. *Mexican Emigration to the United States 1897–1931*. Tucson: University of Arizona Press.
Carmichael, Stokely, and Charles Hamilton. 1967. *Black Power: The Politics of Liberation in America*. New York: Random House.
Castells, Manuel. 1976. The Wild City. *Kapitalistate* 4–5 (Summer): 2–30.
Castells, Manuel. 1980. *The Economic Crises and American Society*. Princeton: Princeton University Press.
Castles, Stephen. 1986. The Guest-Worker in Western Europe—An Obituary. *International Migration Review* 20 (4): 761–778.
Castles, Stephen, and Godula Kosack. 1973. *Immigrant Workers and Class Structure in Western Europe*. London: Oxford University Press.
Chacon, Ramos D. 1980. The 1933 San Joaquin Valley Cotton Strike: Strikebreaking activities in California Agriculture. In *Work, Family, Sex Roles, Language*, ed. Mario Barrera, Albert Camarillo, and Francisco Hernandez, 33–70. Berkeley: Tonatiuh-Quinto Sol International.

Cleaver, Harry. 1979. *Reading Capital Politically*. Austin: University of Texas Press.
Cornelius, W.A., L.R. Chavez, and J.G. Castro. 1982. *Mexican Immigrants and Southern California: A Summary of Current Knowledge*. San Diego: University of California, Center for U.S.-Mexican Studies.
Cox, Oliver Cromwell. 1959. *Caste, Class, and Race: A Study in Social Dynamics*. New York: Monthly Review Press.
Craig, Richard B. 1971. *The Bracero Program*. Austin: University of Texas Press.
Curtin, Philip D. 1969. *The Atlantic Slave Trade: A Census*. Madison: University of Wisconsin Press.
Davila, Alberto, and Rogelio Saenz. 1990. The effect of maquiladora employment on the montly flow of Mexican undocumented immigration to the US, 1978–1982. *International Migration Review* 24 (1): 96–107.
Davis, Lance E., and Robert E. Gallman. 1978. Capital Formation in the United States during the Nineteenth Century. *The Cambridge Economic History of Europe*. VII: Peter Mathis (ed.), *The Industrial Economies: Capital, Labour and Enterprise* (II). Cambridge: Cambridge University Press.
Donato, Katherine M., and Donna Gabaccia. 2015. *Gender and International Migration*. New York: Russell Sage Foundation.
Du Bois, W.E.B. 1989. Negroes and the Crisis of Capitalism in the United States. *Monthly Review* 41 (1): 27–36.
Erickson, Charlotte. 1957. *American Industry and the European Immigrant*. Cambridge: Harvard University Press.
Ericson, Anna-Stina. 1970. An Analysis of Mexico' Border Industrialization Program. *Monthly Labor Review* 95 (5): 33–40.
Fagin, Joe R., and Clairece Booher Feagin. 1993. *Race and Ethnic Relations*, 4th ed. Englewood Cliffs, NJ: Prentice-Hall Inc.
Feagin, Joe R. 1978. *Racial and Ethnic Relations*. Englewood Cliffs, N. J.: Prentice-Hall.
Feagin, Joe R. 1982. *Social Problems: A critical power-conflict perspective*. Englewood Cliffs, N. J.: Prentice-Hall.
Feagin, Joe R. 2006. *Systemic Racism: A Theory of Oppression*. New York: Routledge.
Federal Trade Commission. 1964. The Concentration of Productive Facilities. In *Monopoly Power and Economic Performance*, ed. Edwin Mansfield, 65–73. New York: W. W. Norton.
Flores-Yeffal, Nadia Y. 2013. *Migration Trust-Networks: Social Cohesion in Mexican US-Bound Emigration*. College Station: Texas A&M University Press.
Foner, Philip S. 1975. *History of the Labor Movement in the United States*, vol. 2. New York: International Publishers.
Frank, Andre Gunder. 1970. On the Mechanisms of Imperialism: The Case of Brazil. In *Imperialism and Underdevelopment: A Reader*, ed. Robert I. Rhodes, 89–100. New York: Monthly Review Press.
Galarza, Ernesto. 1964. *Merchants of Labor: The Mexican Bracero Story*. Santa Barbara, California: McNally & Loftin.
Galarza, Ernesto. 1977. *Farm Workers and Agri-business in California, 1947–1960*. Notre Dame: Notre Dame University Press.
Galarza, Ernesto, Herman Gallegos, and Julian Samora. 1970. *Mexican-Americans in the Southwest*. Santa Barbara, CA: McNally & Loftin.
Gammeltoft, Thomas, and Ninna Nyberg Sørensen. 2012. *The Migration Industry and the Commercialization of International Migration*. London: Routledge.
Ganzel, Bill. 2007. India and Pakistan during the Green Revolution: Farming in the 1950s & 60s. Ganzel Group. Accessed March 21, 2021. https://livinghistoryfarm.org/farminginthe50s/crops_16.htmls.
García, Juan Ramon. 1980. *Operation Wetback: The Mass Deportation of Mexican Undocumented Workers in 1954*. Westport, CT: Greenwood Press.

References

Garcia y Griego, Manuel. 1980. The Importation of Mexican Contract Laborers to the United States, 1942–1964. Working Paper in U.S.—Mexican Studies, 11. University of California, San Diego. Program in United States-Mexican Studies.

García-Colón, Ismael. 2017. "We Like Mexican Laborers Better": Citizenship and Immigration Polices in the Formation of Puerto Rican Farm Labor in the United States. *CENTRO Journal* 29 (2): 134–171.

González Baker, Susan. 1990. *The Cautious Welcome: Legalization Programs of the Immigration Reform and Control Act*. Washington, D.C.: Urban Institute.

Gordon, David M. 1977. Class Struggle and the Stages of American Urban Development. In *The Rise of the Sunbelt Cities*, ed. David C. Perry and Alfred J. Watkins, 55–82. Beverly Hills: Sage.

Gordon, David M., Richard Edwards, and Michael Reich. 1982. *Segmented Work, Divided Workers: The Historical Transformation of Labor in the United States*. Cambridge: Cambridge University Press.

Gordon, R. A. 1969. The Stability of the U.S. Economy. In *Is the Business Cycle Obsolete?*, edited by Martin Bronfenbrenner, 3–34. New York: Wiley.

Grebler, Leo, Joan W. Moore, and Ralph C. Guzman. 1970. *The Mexican-American People, The Nation's Second Largest Minority*. New York: The Free Press.

Greene, Joshua. 2017. From Mexico to Hawaii: Tracing the Migration History of One Family in Esperanza, Jalisco. In *Deportation and Return in a Border-Restricted World: Experiences in Mexico, El Salvador, Guatemala, and Honduras*, ed. Bryan Roberts, Cecilia Menjívar, and Néstor. Rodríguez, 47–66. Switzerland: Springer International Publishing.

Greenleaf, Barbara Kaye. 1970. *American Fever: The Story of American Immigration*. New York: Four Winds Press.

Griffith, David. 1986. Peasants in Reserve: Temporary West Indian Labor in the U.S. Farm Labor Market. *International Migration Review* 20 (4): 875–898.

Guest, Avery M. 1982. Fertility Variation among the U.S. Foreign Stock Population in 1900. *International Migration Review* 16 (3): 577–594.

Hahamovitch, Cindy. 2001. In America Life Is Given Away: Jamaican Farmworkers and the Making of Agricultural Immigration Policy. In *The Countryside in the Age of the Modern State: Political Histories of Rural America*, edited by Catherine McNicol Stock and Robert D. Johnston, 134–160. Ithaca: Cornell University Press.

Haines, Michael. 2008. Fertility and Mortality in the United States. EH.net (Economic History Association). Accessed December 3, 2022. https://eh.net/encyclopedia/fertility-and-mortality-in-the-united-states/.

Heer, D.M. 1975. *Society and Population*, 2nd ed. Englewood Cliffs, N. J.: Prentice-Hall.

Hernández-León, Rubén. 2005. The Migration Industry in the Mexico-U.S. Migratory System. *California Center for Population Research, UCLA On-Line Working Paper Series*. Accessed July 30, 2022. https://escholarship.org/uc/item/3hg44330.

Hernández-León, Rubén. 2008. *Metropolitan Migrants: The Migration of Urban Mexicans to the United States*. Berkeley: University of California Press.

Hernández-León, Rubén, Efrén Sandoval Hernández, and Lidia Muñoz Paniagua. 2022. In *Race, Gender, and Contemporary Labor Migration Regimes: 21st Century Coolies?* edited by Leticia Saucedo and Robyn Magalit Rodríguez, (in publication). Northampton, MA: Edward Edgar Publishing.

History Task Force. 1979. *Labor Migration Under Capitalism: The Puerto Rican Experience*. New York: Monthly Review Press.

Hoffman, Abraham. 1974. *Unwanted Mexican Americans in the Great Depression: Repatriation Pressures, 1929–1939*. Tucson: University of Arizona Press.

Immerman, Richard H. 1982. *The CIA in Guatemala: The Foreign Policy of Intervention*. Austin: University of Texas Press.

Inozemtsev, N. 1974. *Contemporary Capitalism: New Developments and Contradictions*. Moscow: Progress Publishers.

Jenks, L.H. 1927. *The Migrations of British Capital to 1875*. New York: Alfred A. Knopf.

Kelly, Fernández, and María Patricia. 1983. Mexican Border Industrialization, Female Labor Force Participation and Migration. In *Women, Men, and the International Division of Labor*, ed. June C. Nash and María Patricia Fernández. Kelly, 205–223. Albany, NY: State University of New York Press.

Kinzer, Stephen. 2003. *All the Shah's Men: An American Coup and the Roots of Middle East Terror*. Hoboken, NJ: Wiley.

Levine, Linda. 2004. Immigration: The Labor Market Effects of a Guest Worker Program for U.S. Farmers. CRS Report for Congress. Washington, D.C. Accessed June 4, 2020. https://digitalcommons.ilr.cornell.edu/cgi/viewcontent.cgi?article=1200&context=key_workplace.

Light, Ivan. 2006. *Deflecting Immigration: Networks, Markets, and Regulation in Los Angeles*. New York: Russell Sage Foundation.

Lindberg, Eleanor. 2018. *Sí, me afectó*: The Women of Bracero Families in Michoacán, 1942–1964. Oberlin College. Senior Symposium. Accessed May 30, 2020. https://digitalcommons.oberlin.edu/seniorsymp/2018/presentations/30.

Lytle Hernández, Kelly. 2010. *Migra! A History of the U.S. Border Patrol*. Berkeley: University of California Press.

Mac an Ghaill, Máirtín. 2000. The Irish in Britain: The Invisibility of Ethnicity and Anti-Irish Racism. *Journal of Ethnic and Migration Studies* 26 (1): 137–147.

Magdoff, Harry. 1978. *Imperialism: From the Colonial Age to the Present*. New York: Monthly Review Press.

Mandel, Ernest. 1978. *Late Capitalism*. London: New Left Books.

Massey, Douglas, Rafael Alarcón, Jorge Durand, and Humberto González. 1987. *Return to Aztalan: The Social Process of International Migration from Western Mexico*. Berkeley: University of California Press.

Matthews, Glenna. 2003. *Silicon Valley, Women, and the California Dream: Gender, Class, and Opportunity in the Twentieth Century*. Stanford: Stanford University Press.

McWilliams, Carey. 1968. *North from Mexico*. New York: Greenwood Press.

Meister, Dick, and Anne Loftis. 1977. *A Long Time Corning: The Struggle to Unionize America's Farm Workers*. New York: MacMillan.

Menjívar, Cecilia, and Néstor Rodríguez. 2005. *When States Kill: Latin America, the U.S., and Technologies of Terror*. Austin: University of Texas Press.

Moch, Leslie Page. 2003. *Moving Europeans: Migration in Western Europe since 1650*. Bloomington: Indiana University Press.

Moore, Stephen, and Julian L. Simon. 1999. The Greatest Century That Ever was: 25 Miraculous Trends in the Past 100 Years. Cato Institute, Policy Analysis No. 364. Washington, D.C.

Moquin, Wayne with Charles Van Doren. 1971. *A Documentary History of the Mexican Americans*. New York: Praeger.

Morales, Rebecca. 1983. Transitional Labor: Undocumented Workers in the Los Angeles Automobile Industry. *International Migration Review* 17: 570–596.

Morgan, Larry C., and Bruce L. Gardner. 1982. Potential for a U.S. Guest-Worker Program in Agriculture: Lessons from the Braceros. In The Gateway: U.S. Immigration Issues and Policies, edited by Barry Chiswick, 361–411. Washington, DC: American Enterprise Institute.

National Advisory Commission on Civil Disorders. 1968. *Report of the National Advisory Commission on Civil Disorders*. New York: Bantam Books.

Newman, Robert J. 1983. Industry Migration and Growth in the South. *The Review of Economics and Statistics* 65 (1): 76–86.

North American Congress of Latin America (NACLA). 1975. *Las Maquiladoras en Mexico, Nueva Lanza Del Imperialismo*. Berkeley, CA.

North American Congress of Latin America (NACLA).1976. Harvest of Anger. *Latin America & Empire Report* 10 (July-August): 18–30.

Olsson, Tore C. 2017. *Agrarian Crossing: Reformers and the Remaking of the US and Mexican Countryside*. Princeton: Princeton University Press.

Peña, Devon G. 1997. *The Terror of the Machine: Technology, Work, Gender, and Ecology on the U.S.-Mexico Border*. Austin: University of Texas Press.

References

Perlo, Victor. 1975. *Economics of Racism U.S.A.* New York: International Publishers.

Pew Research Center. 2022. A Brief Statistical Portrait of U.S. Hispanics. Accessed July 30, 2022. https://www.pewresearch.org/science/2022/06/14/a-brief-statistical-portrait-of-u-s-hispanics/.

Pinkney, Alphonso. 1975. *Black Americans*. Englewood Cliffs, New Jersey: Prentice-Hall.

Polanco, Geralinda. 2019. Migration Regimes and the Production of (Labor) Unfreedom. *Journal of Asian American Studies* 22 (1): 11–30.

Reisler, M. 1976. *By the Sweat of Their Brow*. Westport, CT: Greenwood Press.

Robinson, Cedric J. 2000. *Black Marxism: The Making of the Black Radical Tradition*. Chapel Hill, NC: The University of North Carolina Press.

Rodriguez, Nestor. 2004. "Workers Wanted": Employer Recruitment of Immigrant Workers. *Journal of Work & Occupation* 31 (4): 453–473.

Rodriguez, Nestor, and Joe R. Feagin. 1986. Urban Specialization in the World-System: An analysis of Historical Cases. *Urban Affairs Quarterly* 22: 187–220.

Rodriguez, Nestor, and Jacqueline Hagan. 2016. U.S. Policies to Restrict Immigration. In *Migration in an Era of Restriction and Recession: Sending and Receiving Nations in a Changing Global Environment*, edited by David L. Leal and Nestor Rodriguez, 27–38. Switzerland: Springer International Publishers.

Rodríguez, Clara E. 1979. Economic Factors Affecting Puerto Ricans in New York. In *Labor Migration Under Capitalism: The Puerto Rican Experience*, edited by History Task Force, 197–221. New York: Monthly Review Press.

Romo, Ricardo. 1975. Responses to Mexican Immigration, 1910–1930. *Aztlan* 6 (Summer): 173–196.

Rubin, E. 1958. United States. In *Economics of International Migration*, ed. Brinley Thomas, 133–145. London: Macmillan.

Runsten, David, and Phillip LeVeen. 1981. Mechanization and Mexican Labor in California Agriculture. Monographs in U.S.–Mexican Studies, 6. San Diego, CA: University of California, San Diego, Program in United States–Mexican Studies.

Russell, Philip. 1977. *Mexico in Transition*. Austin: Colorado River Press.

Samora, Julian. 1971. *Los Mojados: The Wetback Story*. Notre Dame: Notre Dame University Press.

Sassen-Koob, Saskia. 1984. The New Labor Demand in Global Cities. In *Cities in Transformation: Class, Capital, and the State*, edited by Michael Peter Smith, 139–171. Beverley Hills: Sage Publications.

Sayer, Andrew. 1986. New Developments in Manufacturing: The Just-in-Time System. *Capital & Class* 10 (3): 43–72.

Schlesinger, Stephen, and Stephen Kinzer. 1983. *Bitter Fruit: The Untold Story of the American Coup in Guatemala*. Garden City, NY: Anchor Books.

Seltzer, Rick. 1978. The Development of the Crisis in the United States. *U. S. Capitalism in Crisis*, edited by the Crisis Reader Editorial Collective, 35–45. New York: Union for Radical Political Economics.

Shepperson, W.S. 1957. *British Emigration to North America*. Minneapolis: University of Minnesota Press.

Sjoberg, Gideon. 1999. Some Observations on Bureaucratic Capitalism: Knowledge about What and Why? In *Sociology for the Twenty-first Century: Continuities and Cutting Edges*, ed. Janet L. Abu-Lughod, 43–64. Chicago: The University of Chicago Press.

Squires, Gregory D. 1984. Capital Mobility Versus Upward Mobility: The Racially Discriminatory Consequences of Plant Closings and Corporate Relocations. In *Sunbelt/Snowbelt: Urban Development and Regional Restructuring*, ed. Larry Sawers and William K. Tabb, 152–162. New York: Oxford University Press.

Sweezy, Paul M. and Harry Magdoff. 1972. *The Dynamics of U.S. Capitalism*. New York: Monthly Review Press.

Telles, Edward E., and Vilma Ortiz. 2008. *Generations of Exclusion: Mexican Americans, Assimilation, and Race*. New York: Russell Sage Foundation.

The Conference Board. 1956. *The Economic Almanac 1956*. National Industrial Conference Board. New York: Thomas Y. Crowell.

Tienda, Marta. 1983. Residential Distribution and Internal Migration Patterns of Chicanos: A Critical Assessment. In *The State of Chicano Research on Family, Labor, and Migration*, ed. Armando Valdez, Albert Camarillo, and Tomas Almaguer, 149–186. Stanford: Center for Chicano Research.

Tilly, Charles. 1979. From the Metropolitan Enigma: Race and Migration to the American City. In *Urban Scene: Myths and Realities*, ed. Joe R. Feagin, 188–207. New York: Random House.

Twomey, Michael J. 2001. "A Century of Foreign Investment in Mexico." First Congress of Mexican Economic History. October. Mexico, D.F. Accessed May 12, 2020. http://www-personal.umd.umich.edu/~mtwomey/econhelp/MexInv.pdf

Unikel, Luis. 1968. "El proceso de urbanización en México: Distribución y crecimiento de la población urbana." *Demografía y Economía* 2 (2): 139-182.

US Bureau of Labor Statistics. 2021. Unemployment Rate, retrieved from Federal Reserve Bank of St. Louis. Accessed August 30, 2021. https://fred.stlouisfed.org/series/UNRATE.

US Census Bureau. 1968. *Statistical Abstract of the United States: 1968*, 89th ed. Washington, D.C.: Government Printing Office.

US Census Bureau. 1969. *Statistical Abstract of the United States: 1969*, 90th ed. Washington, D.C.: Government Printing Office.

US Census Bureau. 1971. *Statistical Abstract of the United States*, 92nd ed. Washington, D.C.: Government Printing Office.

US Census Bureau. 1965a. *1960 Census: Subject Reports, Puerto Ricans in the United States: Social and Economic Data for Persons of Puerto Rican Birth and Parentage. PC(2)-1D*. Accessed July 30, 2022. https://www.census.gov/library/publications/1965a/dec/population-pc-2-1d.html.

US Census Bureau. 1965b. *1960 Census: Subject Reports, Persons of Spanish Surname: Social and Economic Data for White Persons of Spanish Surname in Five Southwest States. PC(2)-1B*. Accessed July 30, 2022. https://www.census.gov/library/publications/1965b/dec/population-pc-2-1b.html.

US Census Bureau. 1970a. *Census of Population: 1970a. Subject Reports, pc (2)-10, Persons of Spanish Surname*. Washington, D. C.: Government Printing Office.

US Census Bureau.1970b. *Census of Population: 1970b. Subject Reports, Final Report pc (2)-1c, Persons of Spanish Origin*. Washington, D. C.: Government Printing Office.

US Census Bureau. 1973a. *Census of Population: 1970, Vol. 1, Characteristics of the Population, Part 1, United States Summary–Section 1*. Washington, D.C.: Government Printing Office.

US Census Bureau. 1973b. *1970 Census of Population, Subject Reports: Persons of Spanish Origin. Report Number PC(2)-1C*. Washington, D.C.: Government Printing Office.

US Census Bureau. 1974. Current Population Reports, Series P-23, No. 49. *Population of the United States, Trends and Prospects: 1950–1990*. Washington, D.C.: Government Printing Office.

US Census Bureau. 1977. Statistical Abstract of the United States:1977, 98th ed. Washington, DC: Government Printing Office.

US Department of Commerce. 1973. *Survey of Current Business 53 (9)*. Washington, D.C.: Government Printing Office.

US Department of Commerce. 1976. *Business Statistics 1975 (May)*, 20th ed. Washington, D.C.: Government Printing Office.

US Department of Homeland Security (DHS). 2011. *2010 Yearbook of Immigration Statistics*. Washington, D.C. Accessed July 26, 2019. https://www.dhs.gov/sites/default/files/publications/Yearbook_Immigration_Statistics_2010.pdf.

US Department of Homeland Security (DHS). 2019. 2018 *Yearbook of Immigration Statistics*. Washington, D.C. Accessed September 24, 2021. https://www.dhs.gov/immigration-statistics/yearbook/2018

US Department of Homeland Security (DHS). 2022. 2020 *Yearbook of Immigration Statistics*. Washington, D.C. Accessed July 30, 2022. https://www.dhs.gov/immigration-statistics/yearbook/2020

Valdés, Dionicio Nodín. 2000. *Barrios Norteños: St. Paul and Midwestern Mexican Communities in the Twentieth Century*. Austin: University of Texas Press.

Vázquez Calzada, José L. 1979. Demographic Aspects of Migration. In *Labor Migration Under Capitalism: The Puerto Rican Experience*, edited by History Task Force, 223–236. New York: Monthly Review Press.

Waldinger, Roger, and Michael I. Lichter. 2003. *How the Other Half Works: Immigration and the Social Organization of Labor*, 2003. Berkeley: University of California Press.

Wallerstein, Immanuel. 1979. *The Capitalist World-Economy*. London: Cambridge University Press.

Wallerstein, Immanuel. 2006. The Curve of American Power. *New Left Review* 40: 77–94.

Wallerstein, Immanuel. 1982. Crisis as Transition. In *Dynamics of Global Crisis*, edited by Samir Amin, Giovanni Arrighi, Andre Gunder Frank, and Immanuel Wallerstein, 11–54. New York: Monthly Review Press.

Weaver, Thomas, and Theodore E. Downing, eds. 1976. *Mexican Migration*. Tucson: Bureau of Ethnic Research, Department of Anthropology, University of Arizona.

Wheatley, Christine. 2017. Driven "Home": Stories of Voluntary and Involuntary Reasons for Returning among Migrants in Jalisco and Oaxaca, Mexico. In *Deportation and Return in a Border Restricted World: Experiences in Mexico, El Salvador, and Honduras*, ed. Bryan Roberts, Cecilia Menjívar, and Néstor. Rodríguez, 67–86. Switzerland: Springer International Publishing.

Wilford, Hugh. 2013. *America's Great Game: The CIA's Secret Arabists and the Shaping of the Modern Middle East*. New York: Basic Books.

Wilson, William Julius. 1996. *When Work Disappears: The World of the New Urban Poor*. New York: Alfred A. Knopf.

Winkler, Max. 1971. *Investments of United States Capital in Latin America*. Port Washington, New York: Kennikat.

Migration and Hegemonic Development 6

I have investigated the relationship between migration and hegemonic development chronologically beginning with the rise of Florentine dominance in wool trading in Catholic Europe in the thirteenth century and followed by the periods of Dutch, British, and US Hegemony. In my analysis, migration appeared as a means and as an outcome of capitalist development.[1] Migration was essential for capitalist development such as when capitalist enterprises needed to expand their labor forces to expand production, or when capitalist employers chose to use migrant labor to struggle against the advances of organized labor. At other times, capitalist development produced social forces of migration such as when agricultural commercialization displaced peasants into migrant streams, or when factory mechanization drove artisans to migrate to seek craftwork in other regions.

The relationships that emerged in the investigation of the association of migration and dominant or hegemonic capitalist development include the following. Firstly, in all the periods investigated, internal and international migration of both capital and labor supported hegemonic development.[2] The international migration of labor was less evident in the thirteenth-century dominance of Florentine merchant-bankers in the wool trade because the workforces of production were much smaller than in the three periods of hegemony that came later. Moreover, in some cases, national boundaries concerned relatively small states, such as the city-state of Florence, and thus crossing a national border had less political meaning than in later times, especially if both sides of the border shared cultural similarities.

Secondly, internal migration was important for the local and national organization of economic activity, and international migration was important as a labor

---

[1] This resembles Anthony Gidden's (1979: 69) concept of the duality of structure where the "structural properties of social systems are both the medium and outcome of the properties that constitute those systems".

[2] I am using "international migration" in a broad sense given that the borders of nations as cultural units did not coincide in the late Middle Ages with the political boundaries in which they existed.

reserve for capital to deal with the limitations of domestic labor. Foreign workers were used to do the work that domestic labor shunned, to augment labor forces, and to weaken labor solidarity. Internal and international migrants in peripheral and semiperipheral areas were also important for hegemonic development, especially as producers of raw materials for finishing processes in the hegemonic state. The labor migration in India and Egypt to produce raw materials for processing in England, as well as migrations in Latin America to work on agricultural lands controlled by US investors, was examples of this relationship. As the circuits of capital accumulation took different sociospatial directions for trade, production, and finance, the associated migration patterns traveled along different geographical paths as well, by freedom of will or coercion.

Thirdly, international migration became a source of internal migration across generational time when the offspring of international migrants became domestic migrants in the destination countries. This migration became an important resource in the setting of US hegemony for the structuration of monopoly capital in a time of very low immigration in the country. The offspring of immigrants who arrived in the late nineteenth and early twentieth centuries helped restructure the urban environments of monopoly capitalism through their internal migration.

Over the 800-year span of the book's analysis, the development of hegemony in the world-system increasingly depended on the migration of capital and labor. Some of this change was due to the economic growth that developed over time. The migration of capital and labor grew as capitalism expanded worldwide bringing more peripheral and semiperipheral areas into the opportunity structures of investment and work, and as populations in world regions grew. Labor migration also grew as core states of the world-system developed relationships with labor from Africa, Asia, and Latin America that differed from populations in the core states in terms of race and ethnicity. The Dutch use of forced indigenous migrant labor in Indonesia to dominate trade in the East Indies, the British use of African slaves in the Caribbean to produce raw materials for factories in England, the US use of Mexican braceros to expand capital accumulation in agribusiness—all demonstrated the special relationships of racial capitalism that evolved between core and peripheral regions based on differences of race and ethnicity. Moreover, this pattern of racialized core-periphery relations expanded into the present.

As the analysis of the book has shown, the migration of capital and labor in the development of dominance in the world-system, including during the prelude stage of Florentine capitalism in the thirteenth and fourteenth centuries, has taken numerous forms. Capital migration has included the movement of financiers and investors to foreign lands and colonies to set up circuits of capital, the transfer of funds to support development projects in the periphery, the remittance of profits gained abroad to home offices, the urban–rural migration of capitalist entrepreneurs to escape the power of craft guilds in towns, the movement of capital in the form of equipment for production, and in the many forms of commodities for finishing processes or for consumer markets. The transfer of human labor power as a commodity through the buying and selling of slaves also must be added to this list of the forms of capital migration.[3]

The forms of labor migration were as varied as the forms of capital migration. In the inception of capitalism in the late Middle Ages in Europe, labor migration mainly involved rural–rural movements. Agriculture was the dominant economy, and most people lived in rural areas in pre-industrial societies. Migration from the countryside to cities and towns was a fraction of the migration between rural areas. Forms of early rural–urban labor migration included peasants who fled serfdom in manorial estates to look for freedom in cities and towns that provided sanctuary. By the time of Dutch hegemony in the seventeenth century, labor migration in some industries reached large numbers for the reasons that populations grew larger and Dutch capitalists undertook large development projects in the countryside that required thousands of workers. The same was true of the country's large fishing industry that covered fisheries far offshore. There was also significant transportation of orphaned children to work in towns in Holland.

War in the southern Netherlands in the late sixteenth and early seventeenth centuries produced the form of refugee migration when craftworkers fled to the northern Netherlands bringing with them new skills and crafts. With their superior naval power, the Dutch acquired colonies in the Americas, Africa, and Asia, but with a few exceptions, the Dutch did not develop emigration to these settings in large enough numbers to develop an imperial world presence as the British would do in their era of hegemony. Nevertheless, the Dutch did establish a sufficient enough presence in their colonies to cause some indigenous populations to undertake refugee migration away from Dutch colonial exploitation.

Several forms of migration, which varied by distance and duration, characterized internal migration in Britain in the setting of British hegemony. According to Ravenstein's (1885) analysis of British censuses in the late nineteenth century, these forms included local migrants, short-journey migrants, stage-migration migrants, long-journey migrants, and temporary migrants. Short-journey migrants accounted for 50–60% of the internal migrants in different British counties, and long-journey migrants accounted for less than 25%. It was, however, in the form of international migration where the British period of hegemony marked a new beginning in migration history.

According to Hobsbawn, "the middle of the nineteenth century marks the beginning of the greatest migration of peoples in history (Hobsbawn 1979: 212)." Hobsbawn's (1979) reference is the "Age of Capital" and the great unsettling and displacement the emergence of industrial capitalism produced in European populations. The Industrial Revolution inaugurated this new era where capital gained hegemony in Britain and other European societies. Large movements of

---

[3] In its most recent forms, capital migration includes digital circulations through the networks of "global assemblages" (Sassen 2006).

populations were created by the cyclical and revolutionizing tendencies of capitalist development that attracted some working populations to centers of production and hurled other working populations into migrant currents. Statistics demonstrate these dynamics of migration. During the British period of hegemony, the total number of Irish, British, and German immigrants arriving in the United States per decade rose from fewer than a 100,000 in the 1820s to over 1.7 million in the 1870s (US DHS 2006: Table 2). In 1846–1875, when the industrial transformation solidified in Britain and other European areas, over nine million Europeans emigrated abroad, the majority for the United States (Hobsbawn 1979).

6.1 Discussion of Findings

This section summarizes and compares the findings from the Dutch, British, and US periods of hegemony for the four perspectives used in the book's analytical framework of class relations, technological development, the economic cycle, and the state. The period of Florentine dominance in the wool trade in western Europe during the thirteenth and fourteenth centuries is not included in the discussion because Florentine capitalist development in that period was still in a nascent stage and the levels of labor migration involved were considerably smaller than in the three periods of hegemony that followed.

6.1.1 Class Relations

The perspective of class relations introduced in Chap. 1 proposed that workers would migrate to areas where worker struggles have improved working conditions. The migration of workers from the southern Netherlands to the industrial centers in Holland, the migration of Irish workers to manufacturing cities in Britain, the migration of Blacks from the southern United States to large industrial centers in the northern regions of the country—all represented the movement of labor to areas where worker struggles had led to improvements in work conditions, especially in the form of higher wages. Yet, as I demonstrated in my analysis, the migrations did not always result in the migrants benefiting directly from the struggles of organized workers. Even as early as the Dutch period of hegemony, work structures were segmented and, except for skilled labor, migrants often settled in the jobs of the inferior sector. Improvements in working conditions achieved by workers in the upper levels of the work structure thus did not necessarily transfer to the jobs in which immigrants worked.

This situation limited the employers' ability to use immigrant labor as a means to oppose the advances of native workers. Craftworkers in the textile centers of Holland blocked capitalist entrepreneurs in their industry from using migrant labor by not accepting immigrants into their guilds, English factory owners were not able to massively displace native workers with cheaper Irish workers, and with some exceptions management in the monopoly corporate sector in the United States usually could not turn away higher wage suburban labor for the cheaper minority workers of the inner-city.[4]

But the employers' limitations to substitute immigrant labor for native organized labor were not absolute. In Holland, entrepreneurs started new industries (trafieken) with immigrants fleeing the war-torn southern Netherlands. These new capitalistic enterprises did not fall under the supervision of organized craftworkers, but under the control of employers. During the Industrial Revolution in England, owners used mechanization to replace skilled male workers with rural migrants, particularly women and children. Moreover, in some cases employers placed foreign workers in workforces with native workers. For example, Catholic foreign workers were used aboard Dutch fishing vessels in the 1600 s, Irish immigrants were hired in Boston-area textile factories in the 1800s, and bracero workers were used in US farms in the mid-1900s. It should be pointed out, however, that in these cases the native workforces into which immigrant labor was introduced were generally composed of unorganized labor, with the exception of some women in the Boston-area textile mills that belonged to the militant Factory Girls Association. Thus, while employers could use immigrant labor in workforces that included native unorganized workers, they could not do the same with facility in workforces of organized workers.

6.1.2 Technological Development

According to the perspective of technological development, a relationship exists between the level of production technology and migrant labor: the introduction of mechanization to deskill production will attract migrant labor to fill the jobs in the new non-skilled division of labor of factory work. Moreover, the deskilling of production will bring about an out-migration of skilled labor that is displaced by the new factory system. The first association was found in the Dutch and British periods of hegemony. For example, in the central fishing industry of the Dutch, the large fleets of "factory ships" divided work into processes of catching, curing, and barreling of fish, and the ships operated heavily with seasonal migrants from the northern hinterland of Holland. In industrial England, rural migrants, especially women and children, filled operative positions in the new factory system. However, the new jobs of machine operatives produced by the factory system were filled mainly by native workers. It was mainly in the Scottish Lowlands that Irish immigrants worked in factories as machine operatives.

By the period of US hegemony, the relationship between the deskilling of craftwork and the use of migrant labor no longer existed. The deskilling of craftwork

---

[4] A notable exception of the US case was the use of undocumented immigrant workers to replace US workers during a restructuring of the automobile-parts manufacturing industry in Los Angeles, California, in the 1980s (Morales 1983).

had been mostly completed in US manufacturing. Further technological development in the form of automation did not result in new operative positions. Automation, attended mainly by technicians and system analysts, led to an absolute displacement of labor in the enterprises where it was introduced.

In the Dutch period of hegemony, technological development did not involve large-scale mechanization that simplified craftwork. The Dutch industrialization proceeded mainly along the lines of increasing the size of the working population and using lifting and transporting devices to alleviate the strenuous work of craftworkers, such as in shipbuilding. Thus, the purpose of technological development was not so much to deskill craftwork but to increase its productivity.

By contrast, in the British period of hegemony the factory system of deskilled production caused some out-migration of skilled workers. Some of the displaced skilled workers migrated to the United States to continue their artisan trades. But on the whole, the emigration of skilled workers to resume craftwork in other countries did not emerge as a principal pattern of migration. That is to say, the thousands of artisans that were displaced by mechanization did not develop a regular pattern of emigrating to the United States or other semiperipheral or peripheral areas to practice their trades.

There were several reasons for the lack of a major pattern of artisan emigration from Britain. Firstly, in a relatively short time, the machines and accompanying detailed divisions of labor that simplified craftwork in England were introduced in the industrialization settings of the United States and of other areas of the world-system. Indeed, because of the conditions of labor scarcity, mechanization was introduced in the United States at a fast pace. Secondly, some of the skilled workers displaced in the Industrial Revolution in Britain worked in the building trades and mining, which were industries that native workers abroad entered in substantial numbers. Thirdly, some of the displaced British skilled workers adopted a new craft trade that had not been deskilled, e.g., silk cloth production. Finally, rather than face unemployment, many displaced craftworkers entered the waged labor forces of the new factory system.

6.1.3 The Economic Cycle

The propositions regarding the economic cycle and migration used in the analysis of the book were that economic upturns attract migrant workers and that economic downturns can cause the out-migration of migrant workers. Migration in the setting of Dutch hegemony illustrated the proposition that areas experiencing an economic upturn will attract migrant labor from rural and foreign areas. As I described, the industrial centers of Holland (e.g., Amsterdam, Leiden, and Haarlem) contained substantial numbers of migrant and immigrant workers during the rise of Dutch hegemony. These workers included the propertyless waged workers who wandered from town to town, small farmers who migrated seasonally, and craft and unskilled workers from the southern Netherlands and from other parts of Europe. The patterns of labor movement into industrializing Holland also included the importation of child workers who were obtained from orphanages in the northern Netherlands and other countries.

The industrial development in Holland demonstrated another association between an economic upturn and labor in-migration. This association was that labor in-migration could precede and substantially contribute to an economic upturn. As I described, refugees from the war-torn southern Netherlands became the labor supply in the northern Netherlands for the redevelopment of industries from the southern Netherlands that had been destroyed in the battles with the Spanish forces of Philip II. No doubt, capitalist entrepreneurs who fled Antwerp and transferred their investment funds to the Bank of Amsterdam served as a catalysis for the establishment of the new industries in the northern Netherlands.

Labor in-migration during an economic upturn may also be promoted by employers who see migrant labor as an opportunity to increase the labor supply in order to stop or slow down wage increases. In the industrialization of England, this appeared to be one of the reasons for the development of Poor Law migration in the 1830s. According to Redford (1968), in the mid-1830s factory owners in northern England and in the West Riding saw in the rural unemployed of southeastern and southern England the opportunity to combat rising wages and trade unionism that accompanied the mid-1830s' economic upturn. By paying Poor Law migrants only about two-thirds of the wages paid to other factory workers, employers were able to lower labor costs.[5] With the curtailment of child labor under the Factory Act of 1833, factory owners no doubt perceived Poor Law migrants as a significant resource.

But the strategy of using immigrant workers to combat labor advances during an economic upturn had limitations. Labor segmentation in the work structure prevented English factory owners from introducing massive numbers of Irish immigrant workers in their enterprises. With the segmentation of work, it was principally small employers, including small farmers, who benefited from the use of Irish immigrant workers. By the beginning of US hegemony in the mid-1940s, the use of immigrant labor to counter labor advances in the manufacturing industrial sector of the country was an obsolete strategy. Capital-labor accords reached in the earlier part of the century (particularly in the 1930s) provided collective bargaining to settle workplace disputes between capital and organized labor in the manufacturing sector. Thus, corporate management could not turn to the cheaper labor power of non-union minority workers, including immigrants, who were concentrated in the central cities of the metropolitan settings of monopoly capital. To be sure, there was a way to circumvent this limitation. Corporate managers could contract with firms that hired minority workers and undocumented migrants to do service-maintenance work in the facilities of the corporations.[6]

---

[5] As Redford (1968, p. 115) describes, mill workers anticipated the low-wage plans that employers had for Poor Law migrants and in many cases "refused to instruct the new-comers.".

[6] By the end of the twentieth century and the beginning of the twenty-first century, the use of immigrant labor from Mexico, Central America, and other world regions became an employment pattern

Agribusiness was one sector of monopoly capital that could and did use foreign workers to check the advances of labor. Agribusiness used braceros and undocumented Mexican workers to combat the threat of native labor advances. From 1942 to 1964, a period that contained most of the upswing of the long wave that followed the Great Depression, US agribusiness used Mexican foreign workers as "shock troops" in harvest operations in the Midwest, the Southwest, and in Arkansas. Yet, given that big commercial growers had regularly used immigrant workers in their fields, it is difficult to argue that the use of bracero and undocumented workers was a response to labor advances in an economic upturn.

The proposed relationship between economic decline and the out-migration of foreign workers was found in the analysis only in the US period of hegemony. Two conditions, I believe, explain why this relationship may not have been significant in the Dutch and British periods of hegemony. One condition was segmentation in the labor structure. As I have described, immigrant workers in the United Provinces and in Britain were not incorporated into the workforces of craftworkers during the hegemonic periods of the two countries. Thus, generally speaking, immigrants were not perceived as direct job rivals by higher-status native workers, although they may have been viewed with scorn for ethnic differences. In England, for the most part, in times of economic decline, native workers battled factory owners and government policies, not immigrant workers.

The second condition had to do with the consumption of social welfare resources. If in times of economic hardship foreign workers and their families turned to public relief measures for survival, the public might have perceived this as an unnecessary burden on their already strained society. A simple solution to this problem would be to expel the foreign workers. As mentioned in the Dutch chapter, using monies from the sale of confiscated properties of the Roman Catholic Church, government officials in Holland developed public relief programs for the poor. But it is doubtful that these benefited unemployed immigrants; more likely the welfare services were for the local poor. Confinement in workhouses and sentencing to galley slavery were measures used to handle the wandering unemployed Dutch workers. Workhouses were also a means to deal with unemployment in Britain during its industrialization. While some measures of poor relief existed at the parish level for local indigents, there was no social welfare program to support poor immigrants.

In the United States, however, social welfare programs for general poor relief had been developed by the early twentieth century. The belief that public relief costs could be substantially reduced motivated many public-welfare administrators to participate in the massive deportations of Mexican immigrants during the years of the Great Depression. While European immigrants in the East Coast of the country were viewed as worthy of social welfare support, Mexican immigrants

---

in many food-processing companies in the southern Unites States, as well as in other regions processing beef. To some extent, these new immigrant employment patterns resulted from the new destinations of Mexican and other immigrants who were attracted to new immigrant settlements by employment opportunities (Zúñiga and Hernández-León 2006; Marrow 2011).

6.1 Discussion of Findings

in the Southwest of the country were not viewed in a similar manner (Fox 2012). The belief that hundreds of thousands of jobs could be recovered for US workers prompted US federal officials to initiate the repatriation of Mexicans. Operation Wetback in 1954 was a similar campaign to deport undocumented Mexican migrants. But the economic setting was not an economic downturn. The increasing visibility of undocumented Mexican workers (especially in urban areas) probably added to bureaucratic pressures to deport Mexican migrants. Racist and nativistic sentiments also figured in the public support for the deportation campaign.

6.1.4 The State

As the bodies of regional authority, states have been concerned with migration throughout the history of the capitalist world-system. From the medieval prelude through the US period of hegemony, with some exceptions states have dealt with patterns of labor migration in one form or another and have done so especially to promote economic development and the accumulation of wealth.[7] As described in Chap. 2, as early as 1271 King Henry III of England decreed that foreign cloth workers, males and females, were welcomed in his realm and would be free from taxation for five years. In 1331, Edward III issued a special permission for Flemish cloth workers to migrate to England. Once in England, the Flemish immigrant workers were exempted from having to pay a loom-tax and from having to join the guilds of native workers. But in the medieval era, the actions taken by town governments in Europe probably had a greater aggregate impact on the migration of workers for economic growth. In the woolen production areas in Flanders and in England, for example, town governments passed laws that gave freedom to runaway serfs who were able to evade capture by their former lords and remained in the towns for a year and a day. This sanctuary policy helped provide workers for town employers.

In the Dutch period of hegemony, town governments in Holland offered inducements to attract Flemish cloth workers who fled the Spanish reign of terror in the southern Netherlands. Dutch town governments also attempted to attract Flemish workers that had migrated to England. Since the Dutch West India and East India trading companies were quasi-governmental bodies of the United Provinces, the actions of these two companies that affected the movement of labor also represented a relation of the Dutch state to labor migration. The largest part of this effect concerned forced labor migration. The two quasi-governmental companies transferred slaves from Africa to trading stations in the Indian Ocean and to plantations in the East Indies and the West Indies. In the Atlantic slave trade alone, the Dutch

---

[7] Japan was a notable exception as it kept foreign workers out in the 1960s-1970s partly out of concern that these workers could affect the supposedly ethnic homogeneity of the Japanese people (Yamanaka 1993).

accounted for an estimated 500,000 slave transfers in the seventeenth and eighteenth centuries (Curtin 1969). Slave transfers thus were a major migration effect of the Dutch state, even if the effect was carried out through quasi-governmental agencies.

It was in the period of British hegemony that British and US state actions to facilitate labor migration were more discernable as interventions of the "capitalist state." That is, the British and US governments undertook measures to directly support capitalist employers and industries. Through the new Poor Law enacted in Britain in 1834, English factory owners worked with Parliament Commissioners to carry out the relocation of thousands of unemployed persons and their families from southern England to industrial centers in Lancashire and the West Riding. In the United States, big industrialists successfully lobbied Congress in the early 1860s for the passage of legislation to allow contract labor (but not Chinese workers) and establish an office of immigration to place immigrants in jobs (Silverman 2015), but not without opposition from labor groups who sought to restrict labor immigration.

By the post-World War II period of US hegemony, national governments formally assisted segments of capital to obtain labor power through the development of programs to import foreign workers, or in the US case to use undocumented migrant workers. In western Europe, a wide range of industries benefited from government-supported "guest worker" programs in the rebuilding of economies after World War II. In the United States, agribusiness was the primary benefactor of the government-sponsored bracero program, with the exception of railroad corporations that used braceros during World War II.[8] Given the low level of US enforcement at the US–Mexico border at the time, many businesses benefited informally from the large currents of undocumented migrant workers. The enactment of a federal measure in 1952 protected employers from fear of penalties for hiring undocumented workers.

US government action to support the creation of the bracero program in 1942 and then to end the program in 1964 reflects the changing nature of the state in the developmental phases of the capitalist world-system. In the early phase of medieval capitalism, absolute states exercised authority and power to support migration for economic development, but centuries later the emergence of liberal democracies introduced diverse interests into policy-making arenas. The diverse interests affecting foreign labor policies included the representation of sectors, e.g., organized labor and population-control movements, traditionally opposed to immigration. In the United States, almost invariably the biggest restrictions were against immigrants from peripheral regions of the world-system, including from peripheral areas of southern and eastern Europe.

---

[8] In the bracero agreement with Mexico, the US government was the designated manager of braceros, but agents of the American Farm Bureau played important roles in the actual operation of the bracero program.

The immigration restrictions of the National Origins Quota Act of 1924 had little to do with labor market economics, but a lot to do with perceptions that southern and eastern European immigrants, as well as Asians, were socially and culturally incompatible with US society (Higham 2008). While many employers remained attracted to immigrant labor, other nativist and racist interests prevailed in Congress and dramatically reduced immigration. With the exclusion of Asian countries, a country received a quota of 2% of the number of immigrants from the country present in the United States in 1890. The quotas favored countries from western and northern Europe, which had many immigrants in the United States in 1890, and disfavored countries from southern and eastern Europe, which had sent fewer immigrants to the United States.

In settings of liberal democracies, economic interests share or compete with other interests in attempts to influence the migration policies of the state. Yet, agribusiness seems to have maintained a privileged relation with the state in the allotment of temporary work visas. In 2018, over half a century after the end of the bracero program in 1964, US agriculture had a workforce of almost 300,000 imported temporary workers, and about 130,000 undocumented workers in the larger agricultural labor force of 876,000 workers (Passel and Cohn 2018; USDHS 2019: table 25). While the role of foreign-born labor from the periphery is much reduced in US agriculture, it still remains a significant resource, given the continuing dependence on manual laborers for many crop harvests and the diminishing attraction of agricultural work for US workers.

6.2 Labor Migration and Work Segmentation

Throughout the cases of Florentine dominance and periods of Dutch, British, and US hegemony, labor migration was associated with work segmentation. Capitalists used migrant labor to segment work and divide workers. Work segmentation was an historical strategy used by capitalist employers' in their struggles with craftworkers organized in guilds. In the artisan system of production, workers' guilds controlled all facets of production such as the rates of production, the sizes of workforces, and the wages paid to workers. While craftworkers saw work as a livelihood, capitalist employers saw work as a means to produce profit to accumulate capital and expand production. Work restrictions imposed by craft guilds thus limited the ability of capitalist employers to increase production by increasing the exploitation of labor.

By segmenting work through the development of new industries operating with labor forces of unskilled workers, emerging capitalist employers could circumvent the authority of guilds and organized work in a manner that enhanced production and profit. This class strategy enabled employers to increase work productivity, increase the length of the workday, increase the sizes of their workforces, and maintain tight control of workers' wages (Marx 1967). The success of the strategy depended on developing workforces with unskilled workers who were not members of guilds. Labor migration helped to form these unskilled labor forces needed by capitalist employers to segment work.

As described in Chap. 2, thirteenth-century Florence was an exception of the need to use unskilled migrant labor to restructure artisan woolen production to a capitalist mode of production. Merchant-capitalists in Florence used political struggles in the commune and the support of a French king to subordinate woolen craftworkers in most of the woolen industries in the city-state. Nonetheless, Florentine merchant-capitalists also sought migrant workers, voluntary or forced, to expand their workforces.

Capitalist entrepreneurs used a host of migrant categories to segment work across the eras of capitalism presented in the four previous chapters. Rural migrants were the most common category used for this purpose across the history of capitalist production: from runaway serfs in medieval capitalism, to the grauw in mercantile capitalism, to rural women migrants in industrial capitalism, to braceros in the advanced stage of US capitalism.[9] The conditions that made rural migrants the most common category for segmenting work were that rural areas usually had the poorest and most desperate workers and the most populous working populations. A second category had to do with religious ethnic difference. Seventeenth-century Dutch shipping companies hired Catholic workers to divide their contentious ship crews of Protestant workers to make them easier to control, and Dutch capitalist entrepreneurs hired Catholic refugees from the southern Netherlands to organize the new trafieken industries, which operated outside guild controls. Dutch employers also turned to children, including orphans from other European countries, to carry out production in the least-skilled segments of work.

In industrial capitalism, migrant women and children were important sources of labor in the restructuring of production from craftwork to capitalistic industries. It was during the introduction of steam-powered machinery and detailed divisions of labor in factories that women and children were especially used to reinforce the industrial labor supply. The reluctance of British workers to enter capitalist factories, and their militancy against these factories, during the rise of industrialism elevated the significance of the lowly valued Irish migrant workers as an alternative industrial labor supply in some British areas.

While US growers in the era of US hegemony cited labor scarcity for their request for temporary Mexican braceros, the militancy of farmworker organizing in the 1930s must have also played into the growers' request for temporary Mexican workers. The bracero program segmented farm work, especially in the corporate farm sector, reducing the sector's vulnerability to unionization of its workforces. Braceros could not join unions and thus presented a barrier to unionization in the farms where they worked. Apart from the financial gains it gave farmers, the

---

[9] While not all braceros were from rural areas of Mexico, rural migrants constituted a large part of the bracero program's workforces.

6.2 Labor Migration and Work Segmentation

bracero program also gave cotton growers time to transition to mechanical cotton harvesting to completely replace manual cotton pickers.

In the general economy, the growing number of undocumented migrants in the United States enabled employers to create conditions of segmented work in various industries. In agriculture, manufacturing, and service industries, undocumented labor provided the advantages to employers of paying low wages, paying in cash and thus not paying Social Security taxes, and having workforces less resistant to poor working conditions (Piore 1979). Before the Immigration Reform and Control of Act of 1986 prohibited the hiring of unauthorized workers, corporations in the formal economy also drew some of these advantages from undocumented labor. Undocumented men and women migrants also filled many jobs in the informal economies of immigrant neighborhoods. These low-paying jobs such as ethnic restaurant workers and street vendors helped to maintain the low-cost, social reproduction of undocumented labor.

The greatest segmentation of work affected by migration, however, occurred in the expansion of the capitalist world-system in peripheral regions. Early Dutch planners of commercial expansion into the East Indies and West Indies desired to introduce Dutch workers in the colonized areas to create workforces, but the plans soon changed for coerced forms of indigenous and transported slave labor. Before the Dutch arrived in the West Indies in the seventeenth century, Spanish colonizers in New Spain and in South America used systems of force labor tributes (*encomiendas* and *repartimientos*) to organize work in the mines, agricultural lands, and in construction projects in the conquered lands. Some Spanish crown officials viewed these forced labor systems as temporary transitions from previous indigenous systems of work to a European system of wage work (Poole 1963).[10] But the coercive features of the colonial labor systems in Latin America lasted until the eighteenth and nineteenth centuries.

The Spanish, Dutch, and other European colonizers deepened the segmentation of work in the Caribbean and Latin American peripheral regions with the introduction of African slaves beginning in the sixteenth century. European colonizers used African slaves to supplement indigenous labor, or to replace it as it declined due to the harshness of colonization and contagious European diseases introduced by the colonizers. For European colonizers, Africa was a vast labor reserve, a labor supply of people who under bondage had both exchange-value as commodities to buy and sell and use-value as laborers to work in harsh and dangerous conditions without compensation. Women slaves presented the additional economic

---

[10] The repartimiento system required that the Spanish colonizers, including Catholic clergy, to pay wages to indigenous workers, but most did not, and when the indigenous were paid they received only a small fraction of the wages due. Indeed, it was the indigenous workers who sometimes paid the Spaniards to be exempted from forced labor. According to archives of the findings of the Third Mexican Council of Catholic bishops, which met in the province of Mexico from January to November in 1585, the Spaniards, including Catholic priests and bishops, treated indigenous people as "slaves" (Poole 1963). As late as the 1860s, Spaniards sold Mayan slaves to work in sugarcane fields in Cuba (Elassar 2020).

value for European colonizers of being the means to biologically reproduce the slave population (Donato and Gabaccia 2015).

With regional variations, the whole capitalist world-system became an organization of segmented work. Waged labor in core and semiperipheral regions, and conditions of slavery and tribute labor in many peripheral areas, characterized the early stages of the world-system. This segmented beginning matches present global inequalities. In the early twenty-first century, more than 500 years after the initial peripheralization by European powers in the sixteenth century, many peripheral regions, e.g., in Asia, Africa, the Middle East, and Latin America, still fall substantially behind the social and economic conditions in core countries.[11] Research has not yet answered the question how much of this social inequality can be attributed to the historical processes of peripheralization, but it must be substantial.[12] For centuries, capitalist penetration in the periphery prioritized exploitation over concerns for the social development of the region.

6.3 After US Hegemony

The decline of US hegemony in the late 1960s saw a dynamic rise of migration in the world-system. New global configurations of capital, new regional pressures, civil wars, etc.—all drove the continuation of migration patterns in the world-system and added some new patterns after the end of US hegemony. In the United States, the undocumented Mexican immigration that grew with the implementation of the bracero program expanded in the 1970s and into the early twenty-first century. Moreover, family migration, often in stepwise fashion, emerged as a major form of undocumented Mexican migration (Garip 2017). Beginning in the 1980s, thousands of Central American migrants fleeing social unrest and economic decline in their home countries added to the migrant streams entering the United States, mostly without visas through the southwest border (Rodriguez 1987; Menjívar 2006). By the 2000–2014 period, the total size of the undocumented migrant population in the United States was estimated to be 12.1 million (USDHS 2017). Mexicans and Central Americans comprised about two-thirds of the undocumented

---

[11] One indicator of inequality in the world system is the infant mortality rate of how many infants die in the first year of birth per 1000 live births. This rate is sensitive to nutritional, health, and other qualities of life. Overall, in 2020 the infant mortality rate of less-developed countries was 8.5 times higher than in the more developed countries, and in the least-developed countries it was 12.2 times higher than in the developed countries (Population Reference Bureau 2020).

[12] The human loss alone of peripheralization presented incalculable destruction. The many millions of African workers forcefully taken from Africa to the Americas in the slave trade, the many millions of indigenous people who perished in just the first century of European colonization in the Americas, the slaughter and forced resettlements of indigenous populations in the East Indies, etc.—all represented immeasurable losses to their cultures and to humankind in general. Peripheralization constituted a destructive force so great that it changed the course of human development in the periphery.

population, and migrants from many countries in the periphery of the world-system comprised most of the remaining one third.

A host of world-system linkages between core societies and semiperipheral and peripheral countries undergirded flows of authorized and undocumented migrants to the United States, Europe, and other developed regions. The "bridges" that channeled the migrations were created by longstanding relationships of colonialism, investments, interventions, and trade between the core and the periphery (Sassen 1992). Migrants from former colonies or trading areas, or from areas of intervention, added to the immigrant populations in the three former hegemonic states by the late twentieth century. These immigrant groups include Surinamese and Indonesians in the Netherlands; Indians, Pakistanis, and Bangladeshis in Britain; and Mexicans, Central Americans, and Vietnamese in the United States (Moch 2003; USDHS 2019).

The era of post-US hegemony also brought greater openings of international borders for capital and labor migration in Western Europe and for capital in the Canada-United States-Mexico region. In Europe, the formation of the European Union (EU) in 1993 increased the intra-regional migration that had begun under the European Economic Community (EEC) established by treaty in 1957. The EEC integrated member countries into a single economic market to facilitate the movement of capital, goods, services, and peoples (Geddes 2008).

European developments in the 1990s demonstrated a movement to facilitate migration among core states. In 1993, the establishment of the EU created European citizenship and gave citizens of member countries the right to live and work in the other member countries (Caviedes 2016). In 2015, 19.9 million persons born in the EU had migrated to another EU country (Connor 2017). This number of internal migrants constituted about 4% of the EU population. EU countries that received more than a million migrants from another EU country were Germany (5.3 million), Britain (2.9 million), France (2.3 million); Spain (2.0 million), and Italy (1.9 million). The countries that sent more than a million migrants to other EU countries were Poland (3.5 million), Romania (3.0 million), Germany (1.8 million), Italy (1.4 million), Britain (1.2 million), and Portugal (1.2 million) (Connor 2017). The demographic proportions of these statistics varied considerably. Poland, for example, sent 9.2% of its 38.0 million population to other EU countries in 2015, while Romania, with only 52.4% the size of Poland's population, sent 15.1% of its population to other EU countries (Eurostat 2015).

In 1994, the North American Free Trade Agreement (NAFTA) established by Canada, Mexico, and the United States opened the borders of the three countries for the movement of capital but not for the movement of labor. With manufacturing hourly compensation only one-tenth of what US manufacturing workers received, Mexico became a low-wage manufacturing region for US and Canadian companies.[13] Mexico also became attractive for Chinese and other Asian manufacturers who wanted to produce closer to the US market. A trickle of Mexican capital entered the United States into retail, construction, and mining businesses. To accommodate NAFTA capital in Mexican agriculture, the Mexican government changed Article 27 of the Mexican Constitution to enable communal peasants to sell or lease their ejidos or enter into joint ventures with investors, such as multinational food corporations. The change threatened to dispossess many ejido peasants who lived at the margins of survival (Nuijten 2003).[14] In 2017, NAFTA annual trade reached US$1.1 trillion (Global Affairs Canada 2020).

The among the most dramatic migrations of capital and labor that developed after the era of US hegemony concerned the migration of foreign capital to China and the internal migration of peasants to Chinese cities and towns in the late twentieth and early twenty-first centuries. Famine, poverty, and a wide gap between rural and urban living conditions drove almost 300 million peasants to migrate to cities and towns. Much of the migration was illegal, given Chinese laws to control internal movement to urban areas. There is no other single migration event to compare it with in human history, especially given that much of the migration occurred in three decades. The heightened mobility of manufacturing capital in the world-system, the state- and private-supported system of urban development, and the great abundance of rural, low-wage labor in China's population of 1.4 billion people have been at the base of the migration (Theurillat 2017).[15]

Soon after taking power, the Communist government in China sought to prevent a "blind flow" of rural migration to urban areas by setting migration restrictions between 1953 and 1956 and strengthening the *hukou* system of registration in 1958 (Davin 1999). In 1990, the Chinese census counted 34.1 million internal migrants, with rural migrants accounting for 62%. Cities received 62% of the internal migrants, and 60% of these were rural migrants (Davin 1999).

After the Chinese government began economic reforms in the late 1970s, and after joining the World Trade Organization in 2001, China became a major attraction for foreign capital. By 2021, foreign direct annual investment in China reached $181 billion, making the Chinese economy the second-largest world market for foreign investment (Statista 2022). The sharp growth of foreign-owned manufacturing in China further stimulated rural–urban migration to industrial centers, creating an ideal labor force of low-wage workers for foreign manufacturers in China that

---

[13] In 2022, average hourly wages averaged $25.08 in US manufacturing, and $3.10 in Mexican manufacturing (Trading Economics 2022a, b).

[14] The beginning of the Zapatista armed revolt by peasants in southern Mexico on January 1, 1994, was timed to coincide with the first day of NAFTA as an expression of opposition to the capitalist treaty (Barry 1995).

[15] World Bank statistics estimate the 2021 rural population of China of 529,465,517 to be 37% of the total Chinese population of 1.4 billion (World Bank 2022). Many rural families live in poverty, which motivates migration to urban areas to look for wage work and remit monetary support to families back home (Wu, Zhang, and Webster 2015).

6.3 After US Hegemony

mass-produced commodities (e.g., clothing, computers, cellular phones, etc.) for a global consumer market.

The number of rural migrants in China grew to 291 million men and women in 2019, creating an enormous labor supply for manufacturing, construction, and service industries in urban areas (China Labour Bulletin 2020). In just one of its manufacturing centers, "Foxconn City," in suburban Shenzhen, the Foxconn Technology Group from Taiwan employed 300,000 mostly rural migrant workers to produce electronic devices for major companies across world regions (Yang 2015). Through its internal migration, China developed into the largest manufacturing power in the world (Morrison 2019), becoming a workshop of the world economy in the early twenty-first century, as the United Provinces, Britain, and the United States had done in earlier eras.

Given its meteoric rise as a major economic power, China is viewed by some analysts as the new hegemon, or soon to become one, in the world economy (Tonon 2021). China has the second largest economy in the world after the United States. Its "One Belt, One Road" initiative of infrastructural development and financial expansion in Asian and other world regions seems geared to significantly increase China's economic world power, giving the country formidable political clout (Yu 2016).

During 2012–2021, China substantially outpaced GDP growth in the United States. China's GDP growth rate averaged 8.3% per year during the 10-year period, while the US rate averaged 3.4% (Megatrends 2022). In 2012, the Chinese GDP of $8,532.23 billion was 52% of the US GDP, but by 2021, the Chinese GDP of $17,734.06 billion was 77% of the US GDP. By 2010, China reached upper-middle income status, according to the gross national income per capita (GNI) classification of the World Bank. The country's per capita GNI stood at $8,690 in 2017, and rose to $11,890 in 2021, which was only about $1,300 below the classification of high-income status (World Bank 2021).[16] The arrival of the COVID-19 pandemic, however, slowed China's economic development, as did problems in the country's rapid-paced real-estate construction industry, which was based heavily on financial debt.

There are several reasons, however, why China may not attain hegemony in the world-system. The Dutch, British, and US rise to hegemony demonstrated that the rise to global dominance involves aggressive foreign military interventions. In contrast to the Dutch, British, and US cases of hegemonic aggression, China has not developed a tradition of foreign military involvement in regions far from the Chinese mainland. During their periods of hegemony, the Dutch, British, and the United States attacked and invaded regions in Latin America, Southeast Asia, and the Middle East to implement political and economic policies. It is difficult to imagine the People's Liberation Army carrying out similar aggressions in areas

---

[16] By comparison the US per capita GNI stood at $70,430 in 2021. Given that the GNI per capital is roughly a country's final income in a year divided by the size of its population, the very large size of the Chinese population, which is 4.25 times the size of the US population, tends to lower the Chinese GNI per capita.

far-flung from China. While the US naval ships regularly patrols the South China Sea, there are no similar patrols by the Chinese military in the Caribbean or Gulf of Mexico, or in the waters off the East Coast or West Coast of the United States.

Hegemony is also about seizing and controlling territories in regions far from the hegemonic state. China has not demonstrated any interest or initiative in planting its national flag in far-off territories, as was done by the three former hegemonic powers. Where it has demonstrated interests in extending its territorial control has been in areas close to its national borders such as Taiwan, Tibet, the South China Sea, and small areas on the border with India.

Perhaps the most important reason why China may not rise to hegemonic status is that the cycles of hegemony are likely over. That is, the hegemonic status of the Dutch, British, and the United States was historically specific eras in which great disparities in political and economic power among countries in the world-system enabled a single county to gain dominance. But these disparities no longer exist at the levels they once did, making it impossible for a single country to attain hegemony in the present era. Military power has become too diffused worldwide for any one country to gain political control of the world-system. Nine countries have nuclear weapons, and several other countries share in the nuclear arsenal. Rather than rule by a single country, the capitalist world-system has seen the emergence of geo-political blocs, or zones of political and economic allies, as a new mode of control in the world-system. This does not mean that China cannot dominate certain economic spheres of the world-system, but that it is unlikely to achieve the level of global dominance that the Dutch, British, and United States attained in their periods of hegemony.

6.4 Future Migration in the World-System

Refugees, asylum-seekers, and other displaced persons constituted categories of migrants that grew after the era of US hegemony ended. By 2021, the population of displaced persons numbered 89.5 million worldwide (UNHCR 2020).[17] Similar to economic migrants, many refugees and asylum-seekers have been the products of world-system developments (Zolberg, Suhrke, and Aguayo 1989). Populations have been forced to flee in peripheral regions where violence and conflict surged as political groups struggled to hold or gain power. In some of these areas, the struggles began mainly after Western powers exited their colonial territories, leaving local groups to fight it out for control of the areas after the end of colonial rule. In other peripheral settings, people were forced to flee after criminal groups took over communities by sparing no form of violence to bring residents into submission. Both settings of violence and conflict are related to conditions of structural inequality that frame relations between and within regions in the world-system.

---

[17] Worldwide in 2021, the millions of displaced persons included 27.1 million international refugees, 53.2 million internally displaced people, and 4.6 million asylum-seekers (UNHCR 2020).

6.4 Future Migration in the World-System

In the twenty-first century, caravans of Central American asylum-seekers headed to the United States and torrents of Middle Eastern and African refugees headed to Europe have experienced opposition, similar to the opposition faced by migrants in earlier eras. Some asylum-seekers and refugees found the security and refuge they sought, but many others did not.[18] The United States has reacted to Central American asylum-seekers through a number of harsh measures that include raising the requirements for asylum, separating children from migrant parents who seek asylum, sealing off the country's southwest border, and sending migrants back to countries they traversed in their journey. EU efforts to deter the refugee inflow have included offering large sums of money to security forces and militias in Libya to disrupt smuggling networks and detain migrants who attempt to embark for Europe, and by patrolling the Mediterranean to turn back refugees (Albahari 2015; Hooper 2017).[19]

Aging in populations of core countries of the world-system will reduce the impetus for internal migration (Cooke 2018). Three conditions, however, suggest that migration will continue at high levels between world regions of unequal development. One condition is the need of capital to constantly secure new markets and human resources for growth. Capitalist development has been a powerful force for stimulating migration between and within regions, and there is no indication that this will abate in the foreseeable future. A second condition is the population growth in the periphery. This growth is expected to account for most of the 2-billion increase in the world population by 2050 (United Nations 2019). Continuing restrictions in the quality of life, political and social instability, impending negative effects of climate change on food production, etc.—all can be expected to pressure many people, especially the most vulnerable, in the growing populations of the periphery to view migration as a survival strategy, as has already been seen in the early twenty-first century.[20]

The third condition is the stratification of the world-system of core, peripheral, and semiperipheral regions. As long as world populations are divided by these categories without expectation that core powers will invest in the periphery for the sake of development, and not for the sake of profit, the economic gap between prosperous regions and poor regions will continue to stimulate the migration of people seeking survival and social mobility.

---

[18] Notable exceptions include Germany. In 2019, Germany received 165,938 applications for refugee status, and granted refugee status and subsidiary protection to 64,472 persons from the Middle East, Africa, and eastern Europe, and rejected 54,034 applications, with the remaining applications in pending status (The Federal Office for Migration and Refugees 2020). Children accounted for about half of the refugee applications.

[19] Some of the militia leaders paid by the EU "outsource" migrants to other groups for exploitation (Michael, Hinnant, and Brito 20,190).

[20] At the time of this writing, the arrival of thousands of desperate and poor Haitians and Central Americans at the US southwestern border to seek asylum illustrates the flight from economic misery and social turmoil in the periphery (NBC News 2021). The US Border Patrol reported a record 2.5 million encounters in fiscal year 2022 with persons without visas to enter the United States mainly at the country's southwest border (US CBP 2022).

Taken together these three conditions raise the possibility that the capitalist world-economy may yet see its most dynamic phase of migration, especially in emigrant flows from the periphery. What gives the periphery the greatest propensity for migration is that it has the highest concentration of the most mobile age cohorts and the highest levels of population growth and economic need, with increasing devastative effects of climate change. The present large-scale migrations of refugees, asylum-seekers, and economic migrants from countries in the Middle East, Africa, Latin America, and other peripheral regions to core and semiperipheral states represent the historical tendency of world capitalism and its political framework to generate and maintain social inequality in regions of the world, propelling the migration of dispossessed populations for survival.

Some may argue that automation and offshore production will reduce the need for foreign labor in core states, but the advance of labor-having technology and the movement of manufacturing abroad has occurred with more immigration in core states, rather than less, including the immigration of peoples seeking protection from violence. Historically, capital has converted economic transformations into new opportunities for capital accumulation that stimulate migration. The sectoral transformation from industrial production to the service economy in the late twentieth century produced a major opportunity structure for migrant workers to locate employment in a variety of service jobs (Browning and Singelmann 1978). As long as capital and labor maintain a dialectical relationship, it is logical to expect that capital will continue to seek opportunities to use migrant labor to gain advantages for capital accumulation.

References

Albahari, Maurizio. 2015. *Crimes of Peace: Mediterranean Migrations at the World's Deadliest Border*. Philadelphia: University of Pennsylvania Press.

Barry, Tom. 1995. *Zapata's Revenge: Free Trade and the Farm Crisis in Mexico*. Boston: South End Press.

Browning, Harley L., and Joachim Singelmann. 1978. The Transformation of the U.S. Labor Force: The Interaction of Industry and Occupation. *Politics and Society* 8 (3–4): 489–501.

Caviedes, Alexander. 2016. The Wayward Path Toward Convergence in European Immigration Policy. In *Migration in an Era of Restriction and Recession: Sending and Receiving Nations in a Changing Global Environment*, ed. David L. Leal and Nestor Rodríguez, 57–74. Switzerland: Springer International Publishing.

China Labour Bulletin. 2020. Migrant workers and their children. Hong Kong, May 11. Accessed August 2, 2020. https://clb.org.hk/content/migrant-workers-and-their-children.

Connor, Phillip. 2017. After Brexit, an uncertain fate for UK's nearly 3 million EU-born migrants. Pew Research Center. Accessed August 2, 2020. https://www.pewresearch.org/fact-tank/2017/06/19/after-brexit-an-uncertain-fate-for-uks-nearly-3-million-migrants-from-eu/.

Cooke, Thomas. 2018. United States: Cohort Effects on the Long-Term Decline in Migration Rates. In *Internal Migration in the Developed World: Are We Becoming Less Mobile?*, ed. Tony Champion, Thomas Cooke, and Ian Shuttleworth, 103–121. London: Routledge.

Curtin, Philip D. 1969. *The Atlantic Slave Trade: A Census*. Madison: University of Wisconsin Press.

Davin, Delia. 1999. *Internal Migration in Contemporary China*. New York: Saint Martin's Press.

Donato, Katherine M., and Donna Gabaccia. 2015. *Gender and International Migration*. New York: Russell Sage Foundation.

Elassar, Alaa. 2020. Mexican archaeologists identify the first Mayan slave ship to have been discovered. CNN, September 19. Accessed September 26, 2020. https://www.cnn.com/2020/09/19/americas/mexico-mayan-slave-ship-trnd/index.html.

Eurostat. 2015. EU population up to 508.2 million at 1 January 2015. Accessed September 10, 2022. https://ec.europa.eu/eurostat/documents/2995521/6903510/3-10072015-AP-EN.pdf/d2bfb01f-6ac5-4775-8a7e-7b104c1146d0#:~:text=On%201%20January%202015%2C%20the,million%20on%201%20January%202014.

Fox, Cybelle. 2012. *Three Worlds of Relief: Race, Immigration, and the American Welfare State, from the Progressive Era to the New Deal*. Princeton: Princeton University Press.

Garip, Filiz. 2017. *On the Move: Changing Mechanisms of Mexico-U.S. Migration*. Princeton: Princeton University Press.

Geddes, Andrew. 2008. *Immigration and European integration: Towards fortress Europe*. Manchester: Manchester University Press.

Giddens, Anthony. 1979. *Central Problems in Social Theory: Action, Structure and Contradiction in Social Analysis*. Berkeley: University of California Press.

Global Affairs Canada. 2020. A New Canada-United States-Mexico Agreement. Government of Canada, Trade Negotiation—North American Division. Ottawa, Ontario. Accessed August 1, 2020. https://www.international.gc.ca/trade-commerce/trade-agreements-accords-commerciaux/agr-acc/cusma-aceum/index.aspx?lang=eng.

Higham, John. 2008. *Strangers in the Land: Patterns of American Nativism, 1860–1925*. New Burnswick: Rutgers University Press.

Hobsbawn, E.J. 1979. *The Age of Capital: 1848–1875*. New York: New American Library.

Hooper, Kate. 2017. European Leaders Pursue Migration Deals with North African Countries, Sparking Concerns about Human Costs. Migration Policy Institute. Washington, D.C. Accessed August 4, 2020. https://www.migrationpolicy.org/article/top-10-2017-issue-3-european-leaders-pursue-migration-deals-north-african-countries.

Macrotrends. 2022. "US/China GDP 1960-2022. Accessed August 30. https://www.macrotrends.net/countries/USA/united-states/gdp-gross-domestic-product

Marrow, Helen B. 2011. *New Destination Dreaming: Immigration, Race, and Legal Status in the Rural American South*. Stanford: Stanford University Press.

Marx, Karl. 1967. *Capital*, vol. I. New York: International Publishers.

Menjívar, Cecilia. 2006. Liminal Legality: Salvadoran and Guatemalan Immigrants' Lives in the United States. *American Journal of Sociology* 111 (4): 999–1037.

Moch, Leslie Page. 2003. *Moving Europeans: Migration in Western Europe since 1650*. Bloomington: Indiana University Press.

Morales, Rebecca. 1983. Transitional Labor: Undocumented Workers in the Los Angeles Automobile Industry. *International Migration Review* 17: 570–596.

NBC News. 2021.More than 10,000 migrants packed under Texas bridge, number still rising. Accessed September 17, https://www.nbcnews.com/politics/immigration/more-10-000-migrants-packed-under-texas-bridge-number-still-n1279423.

Nuijten, Monique. 2003. Family Property and the Limits of Intervention: The Article 27 Reforms and the PROCEDE Programme in Mexico. *Development and Change* 34 (3): 475–497.

Passel, Jeffrey S., and D'Vera Cohn. 2018. *U.S. Unauthorized Immigrant Total Dips to Lowest Level in a Decade*. Pew Research Center. Washington, D.C. Accessed July 28, 2020. https://www.pewresearch.org/hispanic/wp-content/uploads/sites/5/2019/03/Pew-Research-Center_2018-11-27_U-S-Unauthorized-Immigrants-Total-Dips_Updated-2019-06-25.pdf.

Piore, Michael. 1979. *Birds of Passage: Migrant Labor and Industrial Societies*. Cambridge: Cambridge University Press.

Poole, Stafford. 1963. The Church and the Repartimientos in the Light of the Third Mexican Council, 1585. *The Americas* 20 (1): 3–35.

Population Reference Bureau. 2020. *2020 World Population Data Sheet*. Washington, D.C.

Ravenstein, E.G. 1885. The Laws of Migration. *Journal of the Statistical Society,* XLVIII, Part II (June): 167–235.

Redford, Arthur. 1968. *Labor Migration in England, 1800–1850.* New York: Augustus M. Kelly Publishers.

Rodriguez, Nestor. 1987. Undocumented Central Americans in Houston: Diverse Populations. *International Migration Review* 21 (1): 4–25.

Sassen, Saskia. 1992. Why Migration? *NACLA Report on the Americas XXVI* 1: 14–19.

Sassen, Saskia. 2006. *Territory, Authority, Rights: From Medieval to Global Assemblages.* Princeton: Princeton University Press.

Silverman, Jason H. 2015. *Lincoln and the Immigrant.* Carbondale, IL: Southern Illinois University Press.

Statista. 2022. Annual inflow of foreign direct investment (FDI) to China from 2011 to 2021. Accessed September 25, 2022. https://www.statista.com/statistics/1016973/china-foreign-direct-investment-inflows/#:~:text=In%202021%2C%20the%20value%20of,compared%20to%20the%20previous%20year.

Theurillat, Thierry. 2017. Financing Urban Growth in China: A Case Study of Qujing, a Medium-Sized City in Yunnan Province. *China Perspectives* 1: 57–68.

The Federal Office for Migration and Refugees. 2020. Overview of Statistical Practice. Asylum Information Database, Germany. Accessed August 4, 2020. https://www.asylumineurope.org/reports/country/germany/statistics.

Trading Economics. 2022a. United States Average Hourly Wages in Manufacturing. Accessed September 25, 2022a. https://tradingeconomics.com/united-states/wages-in-manufacturing.

Trading Economics. 2022b. Mexico Average Hourly Wages in Manufacturing. Accessed September 25, 2022b. https://tradingeconomics.com/mexico/wages-in-manufacturing.

Tonon, Andrea. 2021. Is China the world's next global hegemon? Roar News, April 14. Accessed July 2, 2022. http://roarnews.co.uk/2021/is-china-the-worlds-next-global-hegemon/.

United Nations. 2019. Population Facts. Population Division of the United Nations, Department of Economic and Social Affairs. Population Fact No. 2019/6. New York/Geneva. Accessed August 5, 2020. https://www.un.org/en/development/desa/population/publications/pdf/popfacts/PopFacts_2019-6.pdf.

US Department of Homeland Security (DHS). 2006. *2005 Yearbook of Immigration Statistics.* Washington, D.C. Accessed March 16, 2021. https://www.dhs.gov/sites/default/files/publications/Yearbook_Immigration_Statistics_2005.pdf.

US Department of Homeland Security (DHS). 2017. *Estimates of the Unauthorized Immigrant Population Residing in the United States: January 2014.* Washington, D.C. Accessed July 31, 2020. https://www.dhs.gov/sites/default/files/publications/Unauthorized%20Immigrant%20Population%20Estimates%20in%20the%20US%20January%202014_1.pdf.

US Department of Homeland Security (DHS). 2019. *2018 Yearbook of Immigration Statistics.* Washington, D.C. Accessed September 24, 2021. https://www.dhs.gov/immigration-statistics/yearbook/2018.

World Bank. 2021. GNI per capita, Atlas Method (current US$)-China. Accessed August 30, 2022. https://data.worldbank.org/indicator/NY.GNP.PCAP.CD?locations=CN.

World Bank. 2022. Rural Population—China. Accessed September 25, 2022. https://data.worldbank.org/indicator/SP.RUR.TOTL?locations=CN.

Wu, Fulong, Fangzhu Zhang, and Chris Webster, eds. 2015. *Rural Migrants in Urban China: Enclaves and Transient Urbanism.* New York: Routledge.

Yamanaka, Keiko. 1993. New Immigration Foreign Policy and Unskilled Foreign Workers in Japan. *Pacific Affairs* 66 (1): 72–90.

Yang, Daniel You-Ren. 2015. A tale of Foxconn City: urban village, migrant workers and alienated urbanism. In *Rural Migrants in Urban China: Enclaves and transient urbanism,* ed. Fulong Wu, Fangzhu Zhang, and Chris Webster, 147–163. New York: Routledge.

Yu, Hong. 2016. Motivation behind China's 'One Belt, One Road' Initiatives and Establishment of the Asian Infrastructure Investment Bank. *Journal of Contemporary China* 26 (105): 353–368.

Zolberg, Aristide R., Astri Suhrke, and Sergio Aguayo. 1989. *Escape from Violence: Conflict and the Refugee Crisis in the Developing World*. Oxford: Oxford University Press.

Zúñiga, Víctor., and Rubén Hernández-León. 2006. *New Destinations: Mexican Immigration in the United States*. New York: Russell Sage Foundation.